An Introduc  ılish

Edinburgh Textbooks on the English Language

TITLES IN THE SERIES INCLUDE

An Introduction to English Syntax
Jim Miller

An Introduction to English Phonology
April McMahon

An Introduction to English Morphology: Words and Their Structure
Andrew Carstairs-McCarthy

An Introduction to International Varieties of English
Laurie Bauer

An Introduction to Middle English
Jeremy Smith and Simon Horobin

An Introduction to Old English
Richard Hogg

An Introduction to Early Modern English
Terttu Nevalainen

An Introduction to English Semantics and Pragmatics
Patrick Griffiths

An Introduction to English Sociolinguistics
Graeme Trousdale

An Introduction to Late Modern English
Ingrid Tieken-Boon van Ostade

An Introduction to Regional Englishes: Dialect Variation in England
Joan Beal

An Introduction to English Phonetics
Richard Ogden

An Introduction to
Late Modern English

Ingrid Tieken-Boon van Ostade

Edinburgh University Press

© Ingrid Tieken-Boon van Ostade, 2009

Edinburgh University Press Ltd
22 George Square, Edinburgh

Typeset in 10.5/12 Janson
by Servis Filmsetting Ltd, Stockport, Cheshire, and
printed and bound in Great Britain by
CPI Antony Rowe, Chippenham and Eastbourne

A CIP record for this book is available from the British Library

ISBN 978 0 7486 2597 0 (hardback)
ISBN 978 0 7486 2598 7 (paperback)

Contents

Abbreviations

BNC	British National Corpus
c.	circa
cf.	compare
CHEL	*Cambridge History of the English Language*
CONCE	Corpus of Nineteenth-Century English
ECCO	*Eighteenth Century Collections Online*
EModE	Early Modern English (1500–1700)
fl.	floruit, 'flourished'
HSL/SHL	*Historical Sociolinguistics* and *Sociohistorical Linguistics*
LModE	Late Modern English (1700–1900)
MS	manuscript
NRA	National Register of Archives
ODNB	*Oxford Dictionary of National Biography* (online edition)
OED	*Oxford English Dictionary* (online edition)
PDE	Present-Day English
PRO	Public Record Office
RP	Received Pronunciation
s.v.	sub verbo (= see)
WL	women's language

To readers

With the release in 2005 of the film based on Jane Austen's *Pride and Prejudice* (1813) and the BBC mini-series *Sense and Sensibility* (1811) launched in the Spring of 2008 there is currently considerable interest in Jane Austen and her time. This is also clear from publications like *The Jane Austen Cook Book* (Black and Le Faye 2002) and *Jane Austen's Guide to Good Manners* (Ross and Webb 2006), and the number of times her name comes up during the BBC Radio 4 talk show Woman's Hour. Interest is not confined to Jane Austen, as the publication of *The Short Life & Long Times of Mrs. Beeton* (Hughes 2005), the author of the popular *Mrs Beeton's Book of Household Management* (1859–61), demonstrates. General interest may be considerable, but how much do we know about these authors' language? Mrs Beeton is said to have had a Cockney accent, but how do we know? And was it true? Did people really speak like the characters in Beryl Bainbridge's historical novel *According to Queeney* (2001)? Film adaptations of books like Tillyard's *Aristocrats* (1994; BBC mini-series 1999) do similarly. The politeness marker *please*, which occurs in both, was, however, not yet used in Queeney's time, but even if it had been, members of the aristocracy did not use it. Bainbridge was criticised for her linguistic anachronisms, such as that a new dress was 'too loud' (Mullan 2001): this usage was current only about a century later. Bainbridge is not a historical linguist, so it seems unfair to blame her for what she was not really in a position to know.

This book is meant for readers who want to discover how people in the Georgian, Regency and Victorian periods spoke and wrote. Late Modern English (LModE, 1700–1900) is currently receiving a lot of scholarly attention. While Görlach (2001, 1999a), in his overviews of eighteenth- and nineteenth-century English, still complained of a lack of empirical data for these periods, the present century has already shown a considerable increase of publications on this important period of English. Our current knowledge of LModE is therefore in a state of flux, expanding almost daily.

In what follows I will draw on recent research to update earlier accounts of LModE, such as Görlach's books, but I will also draw upon studies from the 1970s on the language of Austen, Dickens and Thackeray. This Introduction aims to show how existing resources – primary texts, background literature, empirical studies, electronic databases – can be used to learn more about the period, its people and their language. In my approach to LModE, I will focus on the people of the age and their language, and my account will draw upon insights from sociolinguistics. The LModE period is still largely underresearched, but this need hardly be a drawback: I have seen many original papers from students which deal with new material, producing important new insights into the language and its speakers. Examples are a third-year paper written by Rianne Snoek, analysing taboo words in the Old Bailey records, an MA paper by John Gruson on the language of Sir Joseph Banks, and a BA thesis by Carlene Tromp on wills as a source for reconstructing a social network; their research is discussed in Chapter 7, where I deal with text types like depositions, letters and wills. Further research was also done for this Introduction by myself.

Apart from pronunciation, and after a general outline of the period, this Introduction deals with spelling and lexis – showing in particular how use can be made of the *Oxford English Dictionary* (*OED*) to gain insight into a person's lexicon and into important sociocultural and technological developments of the period; it will deal with grammar and the relationship between LModE grammars and usage, with the importance of social networks, with their own linguistic norms, and their influence on the language of individuals and on the language generally, and finally with a selected number of text types. The purpose of this final chapter is to suggest further research on these and other text types, many of which are easily accessible through recently published digital resources. Each chapter is followed by suggestions for further reading and research questions.

This Introduction to LModE was written in the context of my research project 'The Codifiers and the English Language', funded by the Netherlands Organisation for Scientific Research. In writing this book I have profited from suggestions by my fellow project members, and from comments made by Joan Beal. I also want to acknowledge the comments and suggestions from the students from the English Department of the University of Leiden with whom I explored the potential of this book during the second semester of the academic year 2006–7. I particularly enjoyed reading their final essays for this course.

1 English in the Late Modern period

1.1 Introduction

The eighteenth and nineteenth centuries have been characterised as the 'Age of Prose' (Gordon 1966: 133), the 'great age of the personal letter' (Anderson and Ehrenpreis 1966: 269) and 'the golden age of letter writing' (Arnaud 1998: 125). At the same time, it is traditionally assumed that little of linguistic interest happened during the period (Rydén [1984] 1998: 223). With the rise of new genres of writing, however, such as the novel, the cookery book and the newspaper, as well as the increasing numbers of private letters that were produced, it seems unlikely that the language was not affected as a result. Throughout much of the eighteenth century, the language of Joseph Addison (1672–1719), as found in *The Tatler* (1709–11) and *The Spectator* (1711–12), formed a model of correctness for people in his immediate social circle (Wright 1994) but also well beyond. Even the language of James Boswell (1740–95) is in some respects still more similar to that of Addison than to that of his admired Dr Johnson (1709–84), whose biography he published in 1791. Later in the century, Johnson's periodical *The Rambler*, published between 1750 and 1752, became a source of influence on people like the novelist Fanny Burney (1752–1840), who in her early years 'formed the nucleus of "a bookish little coterie" that met every week to read current works like the *Ramblers*' (Hemlow 1958: 8). I will discuss in Chapter 6 how Johnson's influence on her writing was not always considered very favourably.

Not only the language of important periodicals but also that of individual people served as models to people from the period. 'Saving every farthing [he had] been able to scrape together since Christmas last' (Austin 1991: 77), William Clift (1775–1849), in his attempt to educate himself, bought the novels of Fielding, Goldsmith, Smollett, Sterne and Swift. When he wrote this to his sister in 1793, Clift had been in London for about a year, having left his native Bodmin in Cornwall to take up an apprenticeship with the famous surgeon John Hunter (1728–93). His self-imposed educational programme proved successful, for he soon lost all traces of his local dialect (Austin 1994). Though his master served as an important linguistic model to him, his reading of the popular novelists of the period must have had its effect on his language as well.

1.2 Language and social aspirations

The case of William Clift is exemplary of much that went on during the LModE period: coming from a working-class provincial background, William Clift moved to London to become an apprentice, educated himself and adapted his language in the process. And his social ambitions proved successful, for he married someone with a slightly higher social status – his wife Caroline Harriet Pope was described by one of William's sisters as a 'fine Lady' (Austin 1983: 2) – and was able to educate both his children, a boy and a girl. His daughter Caroline Amelia's marriage to Richard Owen (1804–92), who is described in the *Oxford Dictionary of National Biography* (*ODNB*) as a 'comparative anatomist and palaeontologist' and who received a knighthood in 1884, marks the success of Clift's social aspirations. But throughout his life William Clift continued to keep in touch with his poorer relatives by letter, and the large number of letters from the Clift family that have survived not only allow us to study the changes his own language underwent after his move to London but also the language of his sister Elizabeth (1757–1818), who did not have the same opportunities as her brother, and who worked as a servant in the provinces for much of her life.

The Clift family correspondence (Austin 1991) shows that letter writers at the time were not necessarily members of the better-educated middle classes. Letter writing became an important means of communication to all people alike, largely as a result of the developments of the postal system. With the establishment of the Penny Post throughout Britain in 1840, postage became cheaper and was now paid for by the writer instead of the receiver. The result was phenomenal: while according to Mugglestone (2006: 276) 'some 75 million letters were sent in 1839', they had increased to 347 million ten years later. Just before the widespread introduction of the Penny Post, the average person in England and Wales received about four letters a year (Bailey 1996: 17), which rose to about eight times as many in 1871, and doubled further at the end of the century. The effects on the language were significant: more people wrote than ever before, either themselves or, as with minimally schooled writers, through the hands of others who had had slightly more education. Letter-writing manuals, such as *The Complete*

Letter Writer (Anon., 2nd edn 1756), had been appearing in increasing numbers since the mid-eighteenth century, and they gained in popularity during the nineteenth, both in England and in the United States. Such guidebooks were particularly useful to less educated people like the Clifts, who benefitted from the sample letters – 'on all Occasions, in a polite, easy, and proper Manner' – included in the book. In 1756, the book offered 'some necessary *Orthographical Directions*', but in 1800 it included an English grammar as well; this is shown by a comparison of the title pages of both editions as they may be studied through the electronic database *Eighteenth Century Collections Online* (ECCO). The manual also provided 'Instructions how to address Persons of all Ranks' (1756) – indispensible to its target audience.

An example of a category of books that similarly catered for the socially ambitious is Hannah Glasse's *Art of Cookery, Made Plain and Easy* (1747), which offered the aspiring middle classes the means to entertain in style. The book ran through many editions, and was not merely one of the most successful cookery books published during the eighteenth century, but 'one of the most successful books full stop' (Hughes 2005: 206). Not very original itself, it was also one of the sources for Mrs Beeton's *Book of Household Management*. That in both cases the copying went unacknowledged was not unusual at the time: this is how grammars and dictionaries were compiled as well.

1.3 Linguistic guidance

Throughout the period, but particularly from the 1750s onwards, all kinds of manuals appeared for people with social aspirations, especially grammars and pronouncing dictionaries. Around this time we see the beginnings of what today is called the age of prescriptivism, the final stage in the standardisation process of the English language, which started in the fourteenth century. Linguistic prescriptivism saw its culmination in the nineteenth century. It had been preceded by the codification of the rules of the language into grammars and dictionaries, and well-known examples of such works are Dr Johnson's *Dictionary of the English Language* (1755) and Robert Lowth's *Short Introduction to English Grammar* (1762), both of which were extremely popular in their own time and beyond. By taking a normative view of language and by being available to whoever could afford them, these works taught readers that social advancement through language was in principle within reach of everyone and could be obtained with the help of the proper guidance. Lowth's grammar had originally been composed to provide his son Thomas Henry, though already born into the middle classes, with every opportunity of further social improvement, and when it was published the book became available to all those with similar ambitions. In showing that grammatical errors were made by even the greatest authors, Lowth (1710–87) demonstrated that grammatical correctness could be attained if only the rules of correct usage were adopted. Johnson's dictionary and Lowth's grammar were both published by Robert Dodsley (1704–64), who knew exactly what the public wanted and what would sell well. People were evidently keen on rising in society and on acquiring the new linguistic norms that went with it, so they could take part in what was known as 'polite society' at the time (Fitzmaurice 1998). The grammars of the period increasingly included women among their readership, while the period also saw the birth of grammars for very young children, such as those by John Ash (1724–79) and William Ward (1708/9–72) published in 1760 and 1765, as well as by a new class of female teacher grammarians (Cajka 2008). In the absence of teacher training colleges – with education not even being compulsory to begin with – or of any other kind of formal preparation for prospective teachers, women formed a new and important target group. Around the end of the eighteenth century, mothers received specific guidance in teaching grammar to their children at home in the form of Lady Ellenor Fenn's popular *The Mother's Grammar* (1798) as well as her book called *The Friend of Mothers; Designed to Assist them in their Attempts to Instil the Rudiments of Language* published a year later (Navest 2008).

A Grammar of the English Language (1818) by William Cobbett (1763–1835) had likewise originated as a grammar for his children, but unlike Lowth's grammar it was aimed at the working classes. Cobbett wished to teach these people to write proper grammar, for, according to Aarts (1994: 322), 'petitions addressed to Parliament, advocating universal suffrage [= the right to vote], were often rejected in those days because of the vulgar language in which they were written'. Possibly due to its high price – 2s. 6d., later increased to 3s. – Cobbett's readers consisted of members of the lower middle classes instead (Aarts 1994: 323). The eighteenth century witnessed an enormous growth in the publication of grammars, which led to a veritable explosion during the following century. Michael (1997) writes that the nineteenth century was a period characterised by a 'hyperactive production of English grammars', but that nevertheless no new insights were reached in the process: the grammars of the period 'were repetitive; many were merely commercial ventures, scholastically naïve' (Michael 1991: 11).

In its focus on linguistic mistakes, Lowth's grammar is the ancestor of the usage guide. The first of these was published in 1770 by Robert Baker, and the genre increased in popularity during the nineteenth century. Today, many people regularly consult Fowler's *Modern English Usage* (1926, 3rd edn 1996) if they need guidance on a usage question. Works listing grammatical errors were especially popular during the nineteenth century, and a typical example is Walton Burgess's *Five Hundred Mistakes of Daily Occurrence in Speaking, Pronouncing, and Writing the English Language, Corrected* (1856). The items, according to the author, are 'grouped miscellaneously, *without classification*' (Burgess 1856: iv), and the first page typically lists the following: that it is impossible to say that one would be *enjoying* bad health, that it is *corporal* not *corporeal punishment*, that *notable* for *careful* as in *She is a notable woman* is obsolete, that *advertisement* is to be pronounced with the stress on *vert*, not *ise*, that *up* in *rose up* is superfluous and that *set* in *set down* is wrong as '*setting* is said of the sun in the west, but cannot be properly applied to a person taking a seat' (Burgess 1856: 19). I will show in Chapter 2, however, that the latter problem is not so much a matter of lexis as suggested here but of variable pronunciation among different groups of speakers. In its lack of any kind of ordering principle, Burgess's book is strongly reminiscent of Baker (1770), and both are part of the tradition that gave rise of Fowler's *Modern English Usage*. Burgess's *Five Hundred Mistakes* was published in New York, which puts an interesting perspective on the advice on the pronunciation of *advertisement* in the light of British vs. American usage today.

The first pronouncing dictionary was published by James Buchanan (fl. 1753–73) in 1757, and, as in the case of Lowth's grammar and *The Complete Letter Writer*, it offered its readers directions on how to 'speak, read, and write English with Propriety and Accuracy'. In 1780 Thomas Sheridan (c. 1719–88), father of the well-known playwright, published *A General Dictionary of the English Language*, likewise a pronouncing dictionary. Its 'main Object', he wrote on the title page, was 'to establish a plain and permanent STANDARD of PRONUNCIATION', but its critical reception showed that, as an Irishman, he was not considered to be an authority on English pronunciation. Though the evidence presented is not always easy to interpret, these dictionaries offer invaluable information on how people spoke in those days. By attempting to provide a pronunciation standard that was available to everyone, Sheridan's aim had been to do away with class differences and to provide equal opportunities for all. The effect was, however, the opposite, and during the nineteenth century accent developed into an important means of signalling social class membership (Mugglestone 2003). This becomes evident from the way in which literary authors from the period drew upon social and regional accents in order to present their characters, caricaturing them in the process.

A similar effect is found with grammar. As a result of the emphasis on correctness in usage, especially during the nineteenth century, people were more than ever before aware of the need to conform to the norm of correctness, which had been laid down in practical grammars of English in the course of the period. Many of the grammatical rules and strictures that were imposed upon speakers, however, were 'contradicted by the everyday experience of the children to whom they were taught' (Michael 1991: 11). There was therefore a large gap between the imposed linguistic model and actual usage, and this phenomenon was exploited by novelists like Charles Dickens (1812–70) and William Makepeace Thackeray (1811–63). At the same time, it has been widely assumed that the prescriptive grammarians had an enormous influence on shaping the English language into what it is today. Though the grammarians indisputably had an effect on the language, their influence has been overrated, since many complaints today about incorrect usage refer to the same features as those that were criticised in eighteenth-century grammars. This evident lack of effect is only now beginning to draw the attention of scholars.

1.4 Language and education

During much of the LModE period, formal education, for those who could afford it, continued to be mostly the prerogative of boys, who would receive a thorough grounding in the classical languages. Education became compulsory in Britain only after 1870, and literacy rates, for men and women alike, rose significantly as a result. Previously, teaching had primarily been the responsibility of parents, and had predominantly a moral purpose, teaching people to read the Bible and the Book of Common Prayer. Universities mainly trained young men for the clergy. The first college to offer a university education for women was Girton College, founded in Cambridge in 1869, but it would only be possible for women to take a university degree some ten years later (Raftery 1997). This does not imply that women had no means to be educated, and in her study of Dr Johnson's women Clarke (2000: 17) notes that there were plenty of women 'with a love of knowledge and an ability to think'. The women she deals with include the poet Anna Williams (1706–83), the classicist Elizabeth Carter (1717–1806), Hester Thrale (1741–1821), founder of the Streatham Circle, a group of writers, actors and painters who regulary got together at her house in Streatham, and the bluestocking writers Elizabeth Montagu (1718–1800) and Hannah More (1745–1833). The first grammar of Old English was, moreover, written by a woman, Elizabeth Elstob (1683–1756).

In a number of cases, women themselves took the initiative to be educated; others were stimulated to do so by fathers, brothers or friends of the family. An early example is Lady Mary Wortley Montagu (c.1689–1762), who secretly taught herself Latin at the age of thirteen, so that, according to one contemporary, after only two years 'she [had] learned the language as well as most men' (Halsband 1956: 7). A woman whose skill at Greek surpassed that of her brother was Sarah Fielding (1710–68) (Tieken-Boon van Ostade 2000a); she even produced an English translation of Xenophon's *Memoirs of Socrates* (1762), which remained the standard edition of the text until the early twentieth century. Sarah Fielding had been taught Greek by Arthur Collier (1707–77), a friend since their school days in Salisbury. Collier later also taught Latin to Hester Thrale who, in turn, taught her own children Latin. She proudly boasted in her diary that her daughter Queeney (1764–1857) was able to tell the difference between a noun and an adjective at the age of four and a half (Hyde 1977: 34). But learning Latin was not generally considered suitable for women, for in 1781 Fanny Burney's father, disapproved of Dr Johnson's offer to teach his daughter Latin, considering a skill in this language as 'too Masculine for Misses' (Troide et al. 1988–, Vol. III: 452n). The fear was widespread that women who were too highly educated might miss out on the marriage market, and Fanny Burney was already nearly thirty. (She did marry eventually, at the age of forty-one, the French émigré Alexandre D'Arblay.) George Eliot (1819–80) was very up to date with recent philological developments in Germany, as appears from the way she depicts one of her characters in *Middlemarch* (1872):

> 'I merely mean,' said Will in an offhand way, 'that the Germans have taken the lead in historical inquiries, and they laugh at results which are got by groping about in woods with a pocket-compass while they have made good roads.' (Bailey 1996: 15)

Though she had never had much higher formal schooling, like many other women of the age Marian Evans, as her real name was, had found the means to educate herself well all the same.

English was not a subject in the school curriculum during most of the LModE period, except for the so-called dissenting academies, which were attended by children from English families who did not belong to the established Church. An example of such an academy was Warrington Academy, where Joseph Priestley (1733–1804), the author of another important eighteenth-century grammar, was a teacher. English, according to Bailey (1996: 10–12), developed into a university subject as a result of the Scottish Enlightenment, due to which 'rhetoric and belles lettres became focal subjects in higher-education not only in Scotland but also in colonial American colleges'. In England, an important influence on the establishment of English as a school subject was that of Thomas Sheridan's 'Attic Evenings'. These were series of lectures organised by Sheridan as a kind of literary entertainment for the general public. Primarily, however, the lectures served as instruction on how to read and recite prose and poetry (Benzie 1972: Chapter 4). Such lectures continued to be extremely popular during the nineteenth century. For the purpose of these readings, collections of so-called 'elegant extracts' began to appear, consisting of texts by the best authors of the day. These collections are the ancestor of the modern literary anthology. By the end of the LModE period, there were English departments in universities all over the English-speaking world, though the study of English was organised very differently from today: modelled on the example of the study of the classical languages, it was typically philological in nature (Bailey 1996: 12).

In the United States, literacy spread more rapidly in the course of the nineteenth century than in Britain (Bailey 1996: 64). By the end of the century, being literate was considered an important condition for those who wished to advance in society. Literacy tests were devised, which people had to pass if they wanted to obtain American citizenship (1996: 13). In England, by the mid-nineteenth century, examinations were set for those who wished to be employed in government jobs. The examination included questions on etymology, grammar and history of English, and many self-help guides were published to cater for a new demand here. The outstanding success in America (though also in England and elsewhere) of Lindley Murray's *English Grammar* (1795) is due to the presence in New England of great multitudes of readers, and to the rise of many private academies there for people who wished to educate themselves (Tieken-Boon van Ostade 1996a: 15). Bailey (1996: 62) writes that in America by the mid-1850s, 'commercial schools and business colleges were established, not only in urban centers but in isolated villages as well (many of them served by itinerant teachers)'.

1.5 Literacy: reading and writing

One of the results of the widespread increase in literacy during the period was that written English grew explosively, and not only in the form of letters (Bailey 1996: 63). There was an increasing demand for novels, journals, magazines and newspapers. Novels largely had a female readership, while they also enabled women to develop a source of income, though not at first a highly respected one. James Harris (1709–80), author of the philosophical grammar *Hermes* (1750), successfully lured his friend Sarah Fielding away from novel writing to academic publishing, while George Eliot and the Brontë sisters, Charlotte (1816–55), Emily (1818–48) and Anne (1820–49), still had to employ male pseudonyms to avoid censure. Whether they also adopted a male style of writing is a subject worth investigating. Women increasingly wrote for journals and magazines, and one example was Elizabeth Carter, who published her poetry in Edward Cave's *The Gentleman's Magazine* (Clarke 2000: 32), and who was one of the very small number of women invited to write for Johnson's periodical *The Rambler.* Another is Mary Wollstonecraft (1759–97), who earned a meagre income by writing for Joseph Johnson's *Analytical Review.* Hack writing was not merely an option open to men like Samuel Johnson in his early career as a writer.

Magazines began to flourish, particularly during the nineteenth century. This was largely due to the fact that middle-class women had more time for reading. Isabella Beeton (1836–65) and her husband Sam (1831–77) profited from this interest by publishing *The Englishwoman's Domestic Magazine*, which ran from 1852 to 1877, at only 1d or 2d an issue. As with the newly introduced Penny Post, this guaranteed mass readership. According to Hughes (2005: 162), *The Englishwoman's Domestic Magazine* is a direct ancestor of the magazine today, and it similarly catered for the entire family. However, it did more than create a readership: by setting up essay competitions and inviting readers to write to the editors on love matters, it 'encouraged its readers to think of themselves as writers too' (Hughes 2005: 173). In this innovative approach, the Beetons' *Magazine* contributed towards increased literacy skills among the middle classes.

Newspapers saw the light of day in England during the first decades of the eighteenth century. While at first they were printed in small numbers, with news still largely being passed around orally in the streets or read out to a collected audience, they eventually had increasing numbers of readers. Newspapers continued to be expensive due to the so-called stamp duty, but when this tax was lifted in 1855 they came within reach of more and more readers (Bailey 1996: 26). Görlach (1999a: 146) describes the effect of this: 'It made news available to unprecedented numbers of readers including the lesser-educated, for whom it became the preferred or exclusive reading matter.' He also notes that for this new medium, particularly since the 1830s, 'new combinations of text, headline and illustration had to be developed'. Bailey (1996: 53) describes how the *New York Sun* developed a special grammar for headlines, which later spread to England. Newspapers can be considered as a new text type, with its own linguistic characteristics.

1.6 A dynamic period

The LModE period was a dynamic period in all respects, even linguistically. It saw the beginnings as well as the major effects of the Industrial Revolution, which led to new technological developments and consequently to a large increase in travel, on a national as well as an international scale. 'People were on the move like never before,' Hughes (2005: 25) writes. This in turn led to an increase in communication, aided considerably by cheap postal rates. Letters were an important vehicle for keeping in touch with faraway relatives and business relations. They are therefore a major source of information on the immediate effects on the English language of the many changes during this period.

Throughout the LModE period there was a lot of geographical mobility, with people at first being drawn primarily to London as the centre of culture and polite society and later, due to the development of new industrial centres, to other towns as well, especially in the north of England. Mugglestone (2006: 274) notes that 'Manchester almost quadrupled in size between 1801 and 1871, Birmingham expanded by 73 per cent, and Leeds by 99 per cent'. The new economic opportunities led to considerable social mobility, too, and the potter Josiah Wedgwood (1730–95) is an example of this. People also travelled back and forth between England and the United States, such as Dickens, who visited America twice, first in 1842 and the second time between 1867 and 1868, while voyages of discovery, like those by Captain James Cook (1728–79) between 1763 and his death on Hawaii in 1779, brought people within reach of different cultures and their languages. The grammarian and scientist Joseph Priestley left England for America for good, a few years after the Birmingham riots in July 1791 when his house, library and laboratory were destroyed.

Examples of socially mobile families are the Burneys and the Beetons. Charles Burney (1726–1814), whose father had been a dancer, musician and portrait painter, obtained a doctorate in music from the University of Oxford, and gave music lessons to children from most of the important London families of the time. He saw his social aspirations rewarded when his daughter Fanny was given a position at court as Queen Charlotte's second keeper of the robes. Though this position brought her the considerable annual salary of £200 with a personal footman and a maid,[1] Fanny was not happy there, and asked to resign after a period of five years. Isabella Mayson, later Beeton, came from a family of tradesmen: her father was a cloth merchant and her mother's family had been servants who became small-scale business people. By marrying Sam, she herself moved up into the middle classes, for whom they catered by their publications, the *Book of Household Management* to begin with but also the fashion magazines they brought out. The latter allowed them to take yearly trips to Paris, to consult fashion designers as well as to go clothes shopping, and take holidays in Ireland and Germany (Hughes 2005). It is only to be expected that the language of such people adapted itself to their new social and economic circumstances. If they wished to be integrated into the new communities they had joined, they would have to adjust to new linguistic norms. At the same time, moving into new social networks also involved cutting ties with relatives and former friends, and giving up modes of speech that would have made them conspicuously different if they didn't. From a sociolinguistic perspective, such people are of great interest, as due to their social and geographical mobility they served as bridges between different groups of speakers along which linguistic change might travel, particularly if this kind of mobility occurred on a large scale.

1.7 Concluding remarks

Despite the fact, therefore, that LModE comes at the latter end of the standardisation process, and despite the influence of prescriptivism which flourished during the nineteenth century, the language of the period is not a uniform variety – far from it. Bailey (1996: 80–1) mentions '"native" versus "foreign" sounds, archaic versus innovative styles, rural versus urban dialects, central varieties (i.e., the emergent London "standard") versus peripheral ones (e.g., those of Scotland, Ireland, and the overseas communities), higher versus lower social class'. To these might be added, as we are learning increasingly, differences between male and female speakers. During the nineteenth century, English was developing into a world language, as a result of which distinct national varieties – Canadian, South African, New Zealand – came into being (Beal 2004).

Linguistically speaking, the LModE period was far from stable. Chapter 2 deals with the pronunciation of the period, variable as it will be shown to be, and with the attempts at providing speakers with a pronunciation standard. In Chapter 3, the most standardised level of the language, spelling, will be discussed, and it will be demonstrated that, while there were in the eighteenth century still two recognised systems of English spelling, a public and a private one, by the end of the period the two had coalesced. Chapter 4 will explore how new developments in science, culture and technology left their mark on the English lexicon, which can be traced, even at the level of individual speakers, in the most important record of the English language, the *OED*. The *OED* originated during the LModE period, and, at least before the current major revision process, it can be regarded as very much a product of its age. Traces of this are evident in the results that searches with this research tool produce. Chapter 5 discusses how different grammatical norms operated in society and what the relationship is between the norm of correctness formulated by the grammarians and enforced upon the language user by the prescriptivists, and actual usage. In Chapter 6, I will look at language from the perspective of an important sociolinguistic research model, social network analysis. This model allows us to understand why, contrary to the fear that linguistic varieties would disappear due to the impact of the new media and increased communication processes, this did not happen, and also why the language of women is often closer to the standard than that of men. Chapter 7 will provide an overview of a selected number of LModE text types. This chapter in particular is meant to stimulate further research on the kinds of texts discussed.

The material dealt with here is, of course, no more than the proverbial tip of the iceberg. Much research still needs to be done, and no matter how small the scale of research projects that will be undertaken, the results will provide greater insight into the language of the period as a whole. An important resource for this will be electronically available databases, especially ECCO. This database includes about twenty-six million pages from about 150,000 books published in the eighteenth century, original titles as well as reprints and later editions, and it allows full-text searches. ECCO is accessible through library subscription only, but more and more university libraries are acquiring access to it. For the nineteenth century, an increasing number of books become available through Google Book Search, and many of these also allow textual searches. Another important database with LModE texts is Project Gutenberg. Links to the relevant websites will be provided at the end of this book (see Weblinks).

Further reading

To acquire a 'feel' for the period, including its language, the novels by writers like Tobias Smollett (1721–71), Fanny Burney, Jane Austen (1775–1817), Mrs Gaskell (1810–65), Charlotte Brontë's biographer, Dickens, Thackeray, George Eliot and Thomas Hardy (1840–1928) will provide an excellent starting point, as do films and mini-series available on DVD. A good documentary, published on DVD, is *A Midwife's Tale* (1997), on the early New England midwife Martha Ballard (1735–1812) who kept a diary for twenty-seven years. The documentary deals with the significance of this diary as a textual resource in illuminating detail (see Chapters 2 and 7 for a discussion of its language). There are many historical studies on the people of the age and their social circumstances, some examples of which for the eighteenth century are Tillyard (1994) and Vickery (1998). Picard (2000) provides an excellent idea of what it must have been like to live in London during the age of Johnson, as she does in her book *Victorian London* (2006). Biographies of well-known as well as less well-known writers are of course invaluable sources of information, too. On women and education during the LModE period, see for instance Raftery (1997).

For general linguistic introductions to the period, see especially Bailey (1996: 1–68), Beal (2004: 1–13), Görlach (2001: 1–74) and Görlach (1999a: 1–43), Phillipps (1984: 4–127), Tieken-Boon van Ostade (2006) and Mugglestone (2006). The standard work of reference for the history of the English language is the *Cambridge History of the English Language* (*CHEL*), particularly Volumes III, 1476–1776, and IV, 1776–1997. General introductions to the period may be found in Vol. III, Chapter 1 (Lass 1999a) and in Volume IV, Chapter 1 (Romaine 1998).

Research questions

1. Look up Smollett, Burney, Austen, Mrs Gaskell, Dickens, Thackeray, Eliot and Hardy in the *ODNB*, and consider the question of how the amount of schooling they received would have influenced their language.
2. Look up *The Complete Letter Writer* (Anon., 2nd edn 1756) in ECCO (Search type: Title; Year of Publication: 1756). Using 'eTable of Contents', select one sample letter and isolate its opening and closing forms. Compare these with a letter from a similar (or different) category. How did children address their parents, parents their children and so on? How formulaic and how formal are the forms used?
3. Look up Hannah Glasse's *The Art of Cookery, Made Plain and Easy* in ECCO (Search type: Author). Sort the results by 'Publication Date Ascending'. What was the date of the first edition? Compare the title pages of the first and last editions of the book (note that the Dublin editions were pirated editions, that is, not sanctioned by the author). Why would the one edition be anonymous and the other no longer so? How popular was the book at the time?
4. Hannah Glasse's *The Art of Cookery, Made Plain and Easy* contains a list of subscribers (see 'eTable of Contents'), which was how books

like this could be financed. What does the list tell us about Hannah Glasse's readership?

5. What was the price of Hannah Glasse's cookbook? See the title page. Would this have been a lot of money in those days? Check the appendix 'Cost of Living, Currency and Prices' in Picard (2000). To what extent were grammars and dictionaries affordable at the time? Johnson's dictionary cost £4.10.0. What about Priestley's grammar? (Do an Advanced Search in ECCO: Author = Priestley, Title = grammar, Front Matter = price.) How much would a second-hand copy of Lowth's grammar have cost at the time William Clift first arrived in London? Look for John Binns's book catalogues in ECCO (Advanced search: Author = Binns; Title = catalogue; Full Text = Lowth). What was the book's condition?

6. What kind of usage problems did Robert Baker discuss in his *Reflections on the English Language* (1770)? See 'eTable of Contents'. (What was the price of the book?) Select one or two items and compare them with their treatment in Walton Burgess's *Five Hundred Mistakes* (1856) and Henry Fowler's *Modern English Usage* (3rd edn 1996 [1926]). (Burgess is available through Google Book Search and Fowler can be found in any library.) How do their systems of classification differ?

7. Look up Elizabeth Elstob's grammar of Old English in ECCO. When was it first published? How aware was she of the importance of her publication? See the title page. Elstob did not publish the grammar anonymously. For the sake of comparison, look at what Ann Fisher did (or, indeed, Hannah Glasse). Searching ECCO for Elstob not as an Author but through a Full Text search, you will find that she also published other books. Which ones?

8. Look up Lady Mary Wortley Montagu or Sarah Fielding in the *ODNB*. What was their 'profession' in life? Check ECCO for their publications.

9. Arthur Collier taught Greek to Sarah Fielding and Latin to Hester Thrale, yet he never got an entry in the *ODNB*. But he is mentioned in the *ODNB*, and he can be found through Quick Search: Full Text search for Arthur Collier. What are his life and death dates? Who else did he teach Latin and Greek to apart from Sarah Fielding and Hester Thrale? Comment on this person's characterisation in the *ODNB* as a 'beauty' in the light of her biography.

10. Grammar, during the LModE period, was taught through rote learning, and the result of memorising grammatical rules, particularly those in Murray (1795), is evident in many novels from the period (e.g. Eliot, Dickens, Thackeray, Melville and Joyce; see

Tieken-Boon van Ostade 1996a: 18). Study the praxis in Murray's grammar (1795: 142–5) to discover how this may have happened.

Note

1. According to Picard (2000), who provides an appendix with indications of the value of particular sums of money around the 1750s, this sum is equivalent to 'Boswell's annual allowance from his father, to live in London'.

2 Evidence of pronunciation

2.1 Introduction

In her biography of Isabella Beeton, Hughes suggests that Mrs Beeton had a Cockney accent, or at least that she did not speak like a lady (2005: 31–2). The book she is best known for, *Mrs Beeton's Book of Household Management* (1859–61), is both a cookery book and a manual for nineteenth-century middle-class housewives. It was phenomenally popular, and continues to be reprinted today. Hughes took her evidence from a biography of Mrs Beeton, which records a first visit to Isabella's sisters Bessie and Esther by one of their great-nieces in the 1920s, when Isabella had long been dead. The young visitor was comically surprised to hear her great-aunts drop their aitches and say *ain't* instead of *isn't* – features she associated with Cockney speech. Such first-hand evidence, though from a casual observer, is of great significance to anyone trying to discover how people spoke in the days before the availability of electronic recording devices. The question is, though, whether the information on her sisters' accent also applied to Mrs Beeton, who had moved up in society and out into the London suburbs in the course of her short life as a result of her professional activities (see Chapter 1). Such mobility, as I will show in Chapter 6, cannot have left her accent unaffected.

Nor are we often certain about how to interpret such first-hand evidence. What, for instance, should we make of the comment, recorded by Betsy Sheridan (1758–1837), the sister of the playwright Richard Sheridan (1751–1816), in a letter of 1784 to her sister in Dublin, that a friend had accused her 'of having some brogue which [her] Father would by no means allow' (Lefanu 1960: 23). The word 'brogue' as the *OED* defines it could refer to pronunciation but also to grammar, as in the case of the Irish bishop Edward Synge (1691–1762) who rebuked his daughter Alicia (1733–1807) for having used 'a fine piece of Brogue-English as ever I met with' in a letter to him (Legg 1996: 198–9). The sentence in question, (1) below, is a typical feature of Irish English (Bliss 1979: 294).

(1) Have you heard any thing of B.C. since you *are* [British English 'have been'] in the Country.

In Betsy's case we can be fairly sure that the comment referred to her pronunciation, as her father had published an English pronouncing dictionary a few years before (Chapter 1). But what feature provoked the comment we will never know. Possibly it was the typically Irish pronunciation of what is known as the PRICE diphthong,[1] for which Fanny Burney had mocked Richard Sheridan in her diary:

(2) I assure you I took it quite *koind* in him [Sheridan] to give me this advice. (1779, Troide et al. 1988–, Vol. III: 232)

The evidence in (2) informs us of the salience of the feature commented upon, as well as of Fanny Burney's linguistic awareness, but it doesn't tell us much about Sheridan's pronunciation otherwise.

According to Görlach (1999a: 53), the first recordings of spontaneous speech date only from 1890. What other resources are available to us to reconstruct how people spoke during the LModE period? Actual speech is recorded in the proceedings of the Old Bailey of London, and the database containing these proceedings makes accessible the accounts of '197,745 criminal trials held at London's central criminal court' between 1674 and 1913 (Old Bailey Online). As criminals are very often members of the lower social orders, this is material that allows unique access to the language of ordinary people, men, women and children, who may not even have been able to read and write and who would not have left behind any trace of their language otherwise. But the transcripts were made by clerks, not linguists, and the purpose of the records was to preserve the contents of the proceedings, not the pronunciation of the speakers. Diarists like Fanny Burney also reproduced actual dialogues, and she was quite good at it according to contemporary comments, but again the dialogues are not phonemic transcripts, nor were the records made on the spot as in the case of the Old Bailey trials, and we only find occasional information on pronunciation as in example (2). Verse, at first sight, would seem to be a more promising source, and as an example we might consider Lady Mary Wortley Montagu's poem 'The Lover: A Ballad' (1747) (Weblinks). From the rhyme words employed, we can conclude that *breast* rhymed with *press't*, but also *along* with *young*, *buy* with *joy*, *find* with *joined* (and *mine* with *design*), *bow* (meaning 'bend') with *low* and *coquette* with *wit*. But how are we to interpret this evidence? Did *joined* indeed sound like *mind*, that is, pronounced with the PRICE diphthong, or was the diphthong in *find*, *mine* and *design* pronounced like the one in *joined*? Given Fanny Burney's comment in (2) this seems unlikely, for it would have made Lady Mary Wortley Montagu sound like an Irishwoman, which she wasn't. To what extent were the vowels in *along* and *young* indeed similar? Was *coquette* pronounced with the BET or the BIT vowel, as in the case of *wit*? And what about *bow/low*, or do we have to do with a case of eye rhyme here?

One important though not easy to interpret source of information that will help answer these questions consists of contemporary documents that deal with pronunciation, such as Thomas Sheridan's pronouncing dictionary. The second half of the eighteenth century saw an increasing interest in pronunciation, which was due to significant changes in society, particularly of what Jones (2006: 117) calls 'the rise of a monied, non-aristocratic middle class'. Jones notes that there was 'clearly a desire for improvement and betterment in native language use and description' (2006: 118). What was needed were guidebooks and pronunciation manuals, as well as methods by which pronunciation could be effectively described and means to introduce pronunciation models to the general public. As we will see in Chapter 5, the same phenomenon can be identified for grammar, though for the nineteenth century Jones notes a shift in focus away from pronunciation and towards grammar and vocabulary (2006: 273); as already explained, prescriptivism in the field of grammar was particularly strong during this period.

The language commentators, as Jones calls them, can be called relatively professional, and they became increasingly so during the LModE period. But they were not the only writers with an interest in pronunciation: there are many novelists throughout the period who showed an interest in representing the non-standard pronunciation of their lower-class characters. Blake (1981: 110), for instance, refers to Goldsmith's *She Stoops to Conquer* (1773), which features a servant called Diggory 'who says *yeating* "eating", *ould* "old" but *bauld* "bold", *canna* "cannot" and *wauns* "wounds" . . . and the other servants say *pleace* "place", *sartain* "certain" and *I'se* "I shall"'. Dickens is perhaps most famous for the representation of non-standard speech in his novels, particularly that of Cockney, as in the language of Sam Weller in the *Pickwick Papers* (1836). Thus, Weller

confuses *v* and *w* . . . as in *vith* . . . [and] *wery*. The assimilation of *rs* to *ss* as in *'oss* and *nuss* 'nurse' is common, as is the omission of the final *g* in the group *ng* such as *shillin'*. Omission of vowels in unaccented syllables occurs commonly as in *reg'lar*, and the consonants *t* and *d* are likewise omitted in certain consonantal groups as in *mas'rs* 'masters'. There are in addition various spellings which indicate Cockney pronunciation such as *biled* 'boiled'. (Blake 1981: 157–8)

Dickens had quite a reputation among his contemporaries for his ear for the niceties of actual speech, because he was a journalist and knew how to use shorthand (Bailey 1996: 68). His *Pickwick Papers* shows 'an unusual attention to spoken English', as Bailey puts it, but we should realise that he primarily made use of the features of non-standard English for humorous purposes and that he caricatured many of his characters through their language. As evidence of actual speech Dickens's representation of his characters' pronunciation should therefore be handled with care. He was, after all, a novelist, not a sociolinguist. For all that, it would be of interest to compare the novelists' renderings of the pronunciation of their non-standard characters with the information provided in the linguistic studies and handbooks of the period.

A final source of information is the evidence of pronunciation in the letters of what what Fairman (2003) calls 'minimally schooled' writers. Such writers are people who could barely write because they had had only a minimum of formal education (compare Section 1.4). Though the information is not always easy to interpret, such letters, but also other documents, like diaries, might contain important information on pronunciation. One letter from 1814, for instance, signed by a man called Luke Bratt but not actually written by him, suggests that the writer (and presumably, the author as well) did not pronounce /r/ in post-vocalic context:

(3) she is So very weack that She dose every things as She lasse as i am **foust** for to Have som Body every night for to sett oup ~~wif~~ oud kar. (Fairman 2003: 268)

The same letter shows the word 'little' spelled as *Lettell*, suggesting that the word was pronounced with the BET rather then the BIT vowel, as in present-day standard English (compare the rhymes *coquette*/*wit* referred to above). Sources like these are of great value, but their linguistic significance is only just beginning to be explored.

2.2 The language commentators

For his study of eighteenth- and nineteenth-century pronunciation, Jones analysed a variety of primary sources – spelling books, grammars, pronouncing dictionaries, inventories of speech errors, critical studies, dialect treatises and the like – produced in England and elsewhere. For the eighteenth century, most of these are available through ECCO. Many of the nineteenth-century books analysed by Jones will increasingly become accessible – and searchable – through Google Book Search. One grammar is, however, strikingly absent from Jones's study: Lowth's *Short Introduction to English Grammar* (1762), which, as explained in Chapter 1, was an important guidebook for those wanting to improve themselves and to gain access to the linguistic norms of polite society. Lowth's grammar, however, barely deals with pronunciation, which suggests that around the 1760s the road to propriety in language still led through grammar, not pronunciation. Cobbett's grammar, published more than fifty years later in 1818, barely deals with pronunciation either, perhaps because he had been influenced by Lowth (though believing his own grammar to be superior), or because his grammar primarily focussed on the written language (Aarts 1994).

Interest in pronunciation grew significantly within the next few decades, as is evident from the publication of Sheridan's pronouncing dictionary in 1780. Though not the first of its kind, Sheridan's dictionary is part of a systematic attempt to try and disseminate what he considered the 'best dialect', hoping it would 'displace all other "inferior" forms of speech' (Mugglestone 2003: 15). Sheridan's aim was to standardise English pronunciation by 'creating a uniform, and non-localized, variety of pronunciation which was to be used throughout the entire country' (Mugglestone 2003: 17). To this end, he organised lectures on elocution, and advertisements for them have come down to us. One of these, dated Oxford, 16 May 1759, suggests a severely restricted audience, as the announcement was addressed to gentlemen who were able to afford as much as a guinea for a course (Mugglestone 2003: 18), a considerable sum of money at the time.[2] Sheridan's pronouncing dictionary was followed by that of John Walker (1732–1807) in 1791, which proved so popular that over one hundred editions and reprints appeared, continuing well into the nineteenth century. According to Beal, Walker's *Critical Pronouncing Dictionary* 'is a valuable source of information . . . on what was considered prestigious pronunciation in late eighteenth-century England' (2004: 132). A century later, Walker had developed into a household name, so that Dickens, according to Mugglestone, 'could allude to Walker's dictionary (without further elaboration being necessary) in *Dombey and Son*, specifying this as part of the preferred reading of the highly erudite Miss Blimber' (2003: 35), one of the characters in the novel. Eventually, however, the notion of a single uniform pronunciation that would promote equality proved a mere utopian vision (Mugglestone 2003: 42). Accent continued to be a marker of social group membership, partly because, as will be discussed in Chapter 6, different linguistic norms serve an important social function, and partly because those without money or the amount of literacy needed to be able to consult pronouncing dictionaries lacked access to the proposed norm (compare Chapter 1, Research Question 5). Accent in fact became very much a class matter, as the birth of Received Pronunciation (RP) at the end of the LModE period has proved to show, and this was the very opposite of what Sheridan had hoped to achieve. In retrospect, Sheridan's attempts can be called naive 'in the face of social reality in the late eighteenth and nineteenth centuries' (Mugglestone 2003: 43).

For all that, pronouncing dictionaries are invaluable as sources of information on the pronunciation of the period. On the basis of his analysis Jones (2006: 350) notes a number of phonological changes that took place during the LModE period. To begin with, the Great Vowel Shift, by which all long vowels moved up in their position in the vowel diagram while the high vowels /i:/ and /u:/ diphthongised into the PRICE and MOUTH vowels, had largely completed itself, with the exception of regional and socio-economic varieties of the language. Further, we see the split between the BIT/BEAT vowels as well as that between the vowels in FOOT and STRUT. As innovations Jones mentions the diphthongisation of the SAY and GO vowels in London usage and the split between BATH/TRAP and POOL/PULL words. As far as consonantal changes are concerned he notes widespread 'fricativization of voiced and voiceless obstruents in *ion* environments, much by way of syllable-initial [h]-loss, as well as [loss of] [hw]/[w] alteration in WHICH/WITCH words' (2006: 350).

The BIT/BEAT split, according to the evidence in Peter Walkden Fogg's *Elementa Anglicana* (1792–96), which Jones says contains 'a fascinating section on regional pronunciation variants' (2006: 128), was first found in the language of dialect speakers (Jones 2006: 176). Jones here refers to Fogg's 'Scheme or scale of sounds' (1792: 8), a kind of lexical set avant-la-lettre in which he presents the 'thirty-six primitive [i.e. basic] sounds' of the English language (1792: 7; see Figure 2.1 overleaf). This scheme suggests that different vowels are used to pronounce words like *feel* and *pity*. The example of *pity* with [ɪ] for both vowels suggests that 'happY-tensing', the phenomenon in modern British and American English by which the final vowel of words like *happy*, *pretty* and indeed *pity* are pronounced with 'a tensed, close high [i] value' (Jones 2006: 67), did not occur in the variety Fogg described or had not been noticed by him.[3]

Fogg's scheme also provides evidence for the FOOT/STRUT split (*woo* and *bud*) as well as for that between BATH and TRAP (*father* and *man*), but not for the distinction between the POOL/PULL vowels. A clear

A SCHEME or SCALE of SOUNDS*.

1. au in laud.	13. oi in foil.	25. s in *so*.
2. o in not.	14. yoo in *use*.	26. zh in fu*si*on.
3. a in father.	15. ou in noun.	27. sh in *shy*.
4. a in man.	16. b in *by*.	28. g in *go*.
5. ai in pain.	17. p in *pay*.	29. k in *key*.
6. e in men.	18. v in *vain*.	30. l in *lo*.
7. ee in feel.	19. f in *foe*.	31. r in *ray*.
8. y or i in pity.	20. d in *due*.	32. m in *me*.
9. oa in doat.	21. t in *tea*.	33. n in *no*.
10. oo or w in *woo*.	22. dh in *thy*.	34. ng in fong.
11. u in bud.	23. th in *thin*.	35. nk in *ink*.
12. auee in find.	24. z in *zeal*.	36. h in *ho*.

Figure 2.1 Fogg's inventory of the basic sounds in English (1792–96, Vol. I: 9; ECCO).

description of the latter distinction is not found until the nineteenth century, for which Jones refers to Smart (1810, 1836) and Cooley (1861), who make a 'three-way contrast for the high labial exemplified through a *pool, book, but* contrast' (Jones 2006: 321). Fogg's scheme suggests that fricativisation of the consonant preceding *ion*, as in *fusion*, was current practice, and that diphthongisation as a result of the Great Vowel Shift had not yet fully reached its completion: it reads 'ou in no*u*n' but, however it is to be interpreted, 'auee in f*i*nd'. With *soil* being pronounced with *oi*, it seems unlikely according to his scheme that by this time, that is, some fifty years later, the words *find* and *joined* in the poem by Lady Mary Wortley Montagu would have been complete rhymes.

Fogg was a schoolteacher from Lancashire (Jones 2006: 176), so the question arises as to which linguistic variety he described here. As a Northerner he would have been aware of the existence of a different pronunciation in London, but according to Jones (2006: 135), 'he was unimpressed by the pronunciation models presented by the Court, Pulpit and Stage' – the most prestigious forms of speech in the Metropolis; instead of this, he preferred the pronunciation 'of that middle class of men who unite the advantages of learning, good sense, and access to polite company' (1796: 165). As according to Jones by the nineteenth century the FOOT/STRUT split, also noted by Fogg in his scheme, was observed in London (2006: 320), it seems likely that Fogg's scheme reflects metropolitan usage, and particularly that of the educated members of polite society. This would also explain his interest in regional pronunciation already referred to (see his 'Dissertation VII, On pronunciation', 1792–96, Vol. II: 164–9).

From Fogg's scheme it doesn't become clear whether the words *father* and *man* were pronounced with the BATH or the TRAP vowel: it only indicates that the vowel in *father* is long and that in *man* short. Though Jones (2006: 185) writes that a BATH/TRAP split was noted by commentators from 1750 onwards, what exactly was believed to be the difference between the two is not clear. To Fogg, it appears to have been a matter of length, not vowel quality, and this is similarly maintained by Batchelor (1809) who argues 'that the vowel sounds in the pairs *mat, pan* versus *bard, task* "are justly considered by modern grammarians to differ only in length"' (Jones 2006: 310). But Jones also refers to A. J. Ellis (1814–90), whose five-volume book called *On Early English Pronunciation* (1869–89) he calls 'an unsurpassed masterpiece of philological data, . . . indispensable for information on period data, the direction of phonological change, sociolinguistic and regional distribution' (2006: 274). With respect to the BATH/TRAP vowels Ellis notes that usage correlates with age and gender. Jones cites Henry Sweet (1845–1912), who had recorded the speech of a twenty-year-old girl from London in which *ask* was pronounced with the BATH vowel and *add* with the one in TRAP (2006: 317). This evidence suggests that we have to do with a change from below here, initiated by members from the lower social classes, and also that women might be leading this particular change. As I will show in Chapter 6, this would not be at all unlikely, for many sociolinguistic studies, modern as well as historical ones, have shown that women are often ahead of linguistic change.

Fogg's scheme includes the letter *h*, pronounced as in *ho*. In his Chapter 4, 'Of the Consonants', he notes that '*H* when single is the only and uniform mark of the *thirty-sixth* sound; but it is silent in *heir,* air; *honest,* onist; *honour,* onur; *hospital,* ospitul; *hostler,* oslur; *hour* (twelfth part of a day) our; *humble,* umbl; *humour,* yoomur' (1792–96, Vol. I: 35). Fogg merely gives a few examples of words in which syllable initial /h/ is not pronounced, but he does not provide any rules as to when to pronounce and when not to pronounce /h/. According to Beal (2004: 159), /h/-dropping became socially stigmatised during the second half of the eighteenth century, along with its hypercorrecting counterpart, /h/-insertion. Beal refers to the radical Thomas Spence (1750–1814) who in 1814 'gave "a *Horange*" as an example of a vulgarism that could be corrected by teaching the poor to spell' (2004: 159). The first language commentator who discovered the problem of /h/-dropping was Thomas Sheridan, who suggested a simple 'method of curing this', which was to 'read over frequently all the words beginning with the letter *H* and those beginning with *Wh* in the dictionary, and push them out with the full force of the breath, 'till an habit is obtained of aspirating strongly' (Mugglestone 2003: 34). Sheridan wrote this in 1762, and the dictionary he was obviously referring to was the one by Johnson, published in 1755. In his own dictionary, published twenty-five years later, he remarked in the prefatory 'Rhetorical Grammar' (1780: 16) that *h* was 'no mark of any articulate sound, but is a mere sign of aspiration, or effort of the breath', and that 'all words beginning with that letter are to be preceded by an effort of the breath', providing the same list of exceptions as Fogg would do later. What would be simpler than memorising the exceptions?

But that is precisely the reason why /h/-dropping developed into the shibboleth it still is today: both the rule for the pronunciation of *h*, including the exceptions listed by Sheridan and Fogg, and the means suggested by Sheridan to overcome the problem require access to the educational system in order to acquire the ability to read and subsequently, if at all possible, access to dictionaries and pronunciation guides. Until education became compulsory in 1870, soon after which also the teaching of English became obligatory in the British Isles, acquiring literacy was restricted to those whose parents could afford to send them to school. Bailey (1996: 8) writes that 'one estimate suggested that as many as 40 percent of the people in England and Wales were illiterate in the 1840s, with slightly lower figures for Scotland and considerably higher ones in Ireland'. The exceptions to the rule of *h*-pronunciation, *heir, honest, honour, hospital, hostler, hour, humble* and *humour*, are all loan words, originally derived from French, which, as those with some education would have known, lacked initial /h/. To the rest of the population, the set of exceptions, if indeed they were aware of them, would seem no more than a random collection of words, and this resulted in an almost natural tendency to hypercorrect and say *horange*, with social stigmatisation as a result. Consequently, in 1881, Alfred Leach in his book called *The Letter H. Past, Present and Future*, divided speakers into 'good' and 'bad' ones on the basis of whether their accents were /h/-full or /h/-less (Mugglestone 2003: 47). Particularly to the socially mobile, according to Görlach (1999a: 58), /h/ presented a problem, and many linguistic jokes arose that made fun of the phenomenon. One joke is cited by Fogg (1792–96, Vol. II: 161) in a footnote: 'In some periodical print, a few days ago, I met with a bon mot of Mr. Hill, who, hearing its claim to be a letter denied, observed, "Then I shall be ILL all my life".'

Sheridan's advice on how to acquire /h/ in the proper places also included the pronunciation of /wh/. By the end of the eighteenth century, Jones writes, the alternation between /hw/ and /w/ 'was markedly sociolinguistically salient in many parts of Britain as a sign of both social status and gender' (2006: 109). He cites an interesting list compiled by John Owen in 1732: *hoop/whoop, wails/Wales/whales, weal/wheel/wheal, wey/whey, wen/when, wat/what, while/wile, whoes/woes, Wight/white/weight, wist/whist* and *woe/who* (2006: 110). I have already commented on the fact that the vowel in *Wight* and *white* had not yet fully reached its present position in the vowel diagram, but the question arises as to whether *who* was indeed pronounced like *woe*. Jones repeatedly stresses that the information provided by many commentators, and particularly lists like these, are hard to interpret. Sheridan's advice on the pronunciation of *h*, in any case, suggests, that fifty years after Owen's book was published, variation in usage still occurred.

Fogg's list doesn't offer any guidance on whether or not to pronounce post-vocalic /r/. The evidence presented in example (3) in Section 2.1 suggests that by the early nineteenth century /r/-loss was a fact among the lower orders, at least in the area where the writer in question origi-nated from. The phenomenon as such is much older, for Dobson (1968: 966) cites evidence of it from dictionaries published in the final quarter of the seventeenth century. At first the development was lexically based, as may be illustrated by Dobson's examples *burst, curse, horse* and *harsh*. Dobson also shows that at the time /r/-loss, as in *wusted* 'worsted', a type of woollen yarn, was considered 'barbarous' (1968: 722), and this continued to be the case in Dickens's time, as the representation of Sam Weller's speech ('*oss* and *nuss*) referred to in Section 2.1 indicates. Jones (2006: 260) notes that /r/-loss continues to be lexically driven, and Fogg (1792) listed only a small number words without /r/, such as *roquelaure* (defined by Sheridan in his dictionary as 'a cloak for men') and, indeed, *worsted*. That Sheridan, who originated from Ireland where /r/-loss didn't occur (Bailey 1996: 98), similarly transcribed these words without a post-vocalic <r> confirms the lexical status of the development. The example from Fairman's minimally schooled writers, however, shows that by the early nineteenth century /r/-loss was becoming more widespread, and also that the development was evidently a change from below. American usage was divided, Bailey notes: 'only New England, southern New York and the coastal South (from Baltimore to New Orleans) took part in the general weakening of noninitial *r*' (1996: 105). With the loss of post-vocalic /r/, intrusive /r/ made its appearance, and Bailey notes as first evidence of this the representation of speech by the novelist Tobias Smollett: 'your aydear is' and 'the windore opened' (1996: 103). I will discuss the nature of the evidence of speech represen-tation by writers of fiction in Section 2.3. Though still generally used today, this use of linking /r/ was already stigmatised at the end of the eighteenth century (Jones 2006: 262–3).

To conclude this section, is it possible on the basis of the evidence from the language commentators to decide whether the rhyming pairs in Lady Mary Wortley Montagu's ballad 'The Lover' (1747), *along/young*, *buy/joy*, *find/joined*, *bow/low* and *coquette/wit* did indeed constitute full rhymes? I've already answered this question for *find/joined*. As for *along/ young*, by the end of the eighteenth century the second word would be pronounced with the STRUT vowel, which according to Jones (2006: 204) was a novelty in Fogg's eyes. The stressed vowel in *along*, which today would be pronounced with the LOT vowel, had undergone lengthening in the course of the period, so that it had merged with the THOUGHT vowel, certainly by the 1850s when Londoners pronounced *cross* as *craws* (Jones 2006: 319). This pronunciation, according to Beal (2004: 142), was stigmatised, and associated with lower-class Cockney speakers. All this suggests that in Lady Mary's poem the words *along* and *young* formed no more than an eye rhyme.

Due to its spelling, the case of *buy* seems more complicated than it actually is. Deriving from Old English *byc an*, the vowel would have been subject to unrounding at the end of the period after which, as /iː/, it became subject to the Great Vowel Shift. The pair *buy/joy* is therefore similar to *find/joined*. How about the pair *bow/low*? Jones (2006: 234) writes that 'examples of what appear to be LOW/HOW mergers are quite common in the contemporary records', and that Walker rhymed *prow* with *now* but Sheridan with *go*. It is, however, unlikely that *low* would have been pronounced with the HOW vowel: the anonymous *Vocabulary of such Words in the English Language as are of Dubious or Unsettled Accentuation* (1797) only discusses the divided opinions as to the pronunciation of the word *low* in the sense of 'to bellow'. If *bow* were to be pronounced with the LOW vowel, we would have a perfect rhyme but if it was pronounced with the HOW vowel, as it is today, *bow/low* would represent an instance of eye rhyme. Which of the two it was we will never know. As for the final pair of rhyme words, *coquette/wit*, both Sheridan (1780) and Walker (1791) note that *coquette* is pronounced with the DRESS vowel and *wit* with the BIT vowel. Jones (2006: 298) discusses the pronunciation of words such as *again*, *instead* and *trivet* with what was possibly the BIT vowel in the second syllables as instances of stigmatised usage, but not until the early nineteenth century. Conversely, he notes that around the same time words like *grid*, *sits* and *width* were pronounced 'vulgarly' with the DRESS vowel. Either, therefore, the words in Lady Mary's poem did not rhyme, or they might be taken as evidence that at the time the words could be pronounced with a vowel that was neither that of BIT nor that of DRESS but of something in between. Whatever it was, a century later, to pronounce *coquette* with the BIT vowel would very likely have been considered unacceptable.

2.3 The novelists

As already discussed, Dickens is primarily remembered for the use of Cockney in his novels. Thackeray, too, according to Phillipps (1978: 106), 'enjoyed finding ways of representing both affected and substandard [i.e. non-standard] pronunciation', and he used pronunciation as a sure way of '"placing" a person socially'. Features he adopted were the use of the lisp and the inability to pronounce r^4 to depict the 'fashionable man-about-town' and he adopted hypercorrect features such as the insertion of /h/, intrusive /r/ (see Section 2.2) and the use of /ŋ/ for /n/ as in *foring* 'foreign' to ridicule people with aspirations to gentility. The appendix in Brook's *Language of Dickens* (1970) contains an elaborate list of the non-standard features of pronunciation Dickens used in his novels, sixty-two items altogether (1970: 223–38). An interesting example of the representation of a number of these features may be found in (4), from Dickens's *Sketches by Boz* (1836):

(4) the celebrated Mr. Sluffen, of Adam-and-Eve-court, whose authority not the most malignant of our opponents can call in question, expressed himself in a manner following: 'That now he'd cotcht the **cheerman's** hi, he **vished** he might be jolly **vell** blessed, if he **worn't** a **goin'** to have his innings, **vich** he **vould** say these here **obserwashuns**—that how some **mischeevus** coves as know'd **nuffin** about the **consarn**, had tried to **sit** people **agin** the mas'r **swips**, and take the shine out o' their bis'nes, and the bread out o' the traps o' their preshus kids, by a **makin'** o' this here remark, as **chimblies** could be as **vell svept** by 'sheenery as by boys; and that the **makin'** use o' boys for that there purpuss **vos** barbareous; **vereas**, he **'ad** been a chummy—he begged the **cheerman's parding** for **usin'** such a **wulgar hexpression**—more nor thirty year—he might say he'd been born in a **chimbley**—and he know'd uncommon **vell** as 'sheenery vos **vus** nor o' no use: and as to **kerhewelty** to the boys, everybody in the **chimbley** line know'd as **vell** as he did, that they liked the climbin' better nor **nuffin** as **vos**.'

Though Dickens used these dialectal representations for humorous effect, some of these features may well have been accurate renderings of the way the lower classes spoke; others, however, were not.

The phenomenon of /h/-loss as in *appiness* and *usband* and its hypercorrect counterpart /h/-insertion as in *hexpression* in (4) have already been discussed (Section 2.2). Thomas Batchelor, in *An Orthoëpical Analysis of the English Language* (1809), regarded the feature as an error typically found in the dialect spoken by 'the peasantry of Bedfordshire' (Jones 2006: 344), and so /h/-loss was not necessarily characteristic of Dickens's Cockney-speaking characters alone. The same applies to what Brook calls the confusion of /w/ for /v/ as in *obserwashuns* 'observations' and *wulgar* in (4), and, though less common, the reverse, as in *vos, vich, vished* and *vould*. According to Brook, /w/-/v/ substitution is 'often thought of as one of the most important characteristics of the London dialect' (1980: 223), adding that this is quite possibly due to the popularity of the novels by Dickens. Brook quotes A. J. Ellis saying that the phenomenon was common in other dialects, too.

Another typical feature of Dickens's non-standard speakers is the use of /f/ for /θ/ and /v/ for /ð/, as in *nuffin* in example (4). Wyld (1936) believed it to be characteristic of the 'low type of Cockney English'. The phenomenon is known as TH-fronting, and Beal (2004: 198) finds evidence of it in the speech of lower-class London speakers already at the end of the eighteenth century. Like a number of other features from London speech it is now characteristic of Estuary English, 'an accent originally based . . . around the Thames Estuary, but said to be spreading throughout the south-east of England' (Beal 2004: 197). More features from (4) worth discussing are *cheerman, worn't, goin', mischeevus, consarn, sit*'set', *agin, swips* 'sweeps', *chimblies* and *parding*, all of which were stigmatised at the time. The spelling *cheerman* 'chairman' suggest a raised vowel, which W. H. Savage, in his *Vulgarities and Improprieties of the English Language* (1833), disapproved of (see Jones 2006: 302). *Goin'* and *parding* are instances of related tendencies, the first of the use of *in* for *ing* in syllable-final position, which Walker (1791) had already observed with 'our best speakers', and the second of hypercorrect replacement of final unstressed syllables by *ing* (compare Thackeray's *foring*). Along with hypercorrect usage of /h/, this feature, often mistakenly referred to as the dropping of the *g*, is typically found in nineteenth-century non-standard fictional speech (Mugglestone 2003: 129–31). *Mischeevus* suggests the kind of criticism levelled by Batchelor at Walker and Lindley Murray (1745–1826), who would have promoted the pronunciation of long /iː/ in unaccented syllables (Jones 2006: 295–6). In the first edition of his grammar, however, Murray notes that the word is pronounced with a 'short *i*' (1795: 8). Dickens's spelling thus suggests non-standard pronunciation. *Sit* and *agin* are listed by Savage as 'vulgarisms' (Jones 2006: 298), while *swips* suggests shortening of the BEAT vowel. Despite evidence for a BIT/BEAT split, Dickens's spelling here suggests that among Cockney speakers this split was not categorical. The spelling *consarn* indicates a vulgar pronunciation, though a few decades earlier usage was somewhat more divided than this example suggests. Walker (1795: 129) notes that 'the vulgar always, and even polite people sometimes, pronounce this word [i.e. *servant*] as if spelled *sar-vint*' (Jones 2006: 242). The question of how vowels were to be pronounced in pre-/r/ contexts received a lot of socio-phonetic comment, and according to the author of *A Vocabulary of Such Words in the English Language as are of Dubious or Unsettled Pronunciation* (1797), 'everywhere sees the pre-[r] lowering/centering as non-prestigious' (Jones 2006: 243), as in *consarn, sarvint*, as well as *warmin* 'vermin' and *arnest* mentioned by Brook (1970: 232–3). If *worn't* in example (4) is supposed to render 'weren't', it would be an instance of the same phenomenon. If it is intended to render 'wasn't', as it seems to do in example (5), *r* is used not so much to indicate pronunciation of this consonant, which was in the process of disappearing in post-vocalic position in many dialects including that of London (see also Section 2.2 above), as to signal non-standard pronunciation of the word generally.

(5) 'Why he said, sir, – leastways so Mr. Bouncer reported, – that it **worn't** by no means a bad idea, and that p'rhaps Mr. Bouncer'd find it done in six months' time, when he come back again from the country. (Cuthbert Bede, *The Adventures of Mr. Verdant Green*, 1853; Hodson and Millward 2007)

The same applies to *vus* 'for us' and *kerhewelty* 'cruelty' in (4) and *p'haps* in (5). As for *chimbley* in example (4), this is likewise an instance of stigmatised usage: the *OED* marks it as 'also *dial.* and *vulgar*' (s.v. *chimney*, n.). A full-text search in the *OED* produced six examples, ranging from 1798–1955, so the spelling already had some currency before it was used by Dickens.

One of the features of Estuary English as well as of other regional accents today is glottalisation of /t/, as in *butter* and *water* (Beal 2004: 165). I have not come across any evidence of it in the studies of the language in the novels by Dickens or Thackeray, who, I believe, would certainly have made use of this stigmatised feature for the language of their lower-class characters. Bailey (1996: 76–7) finds a first reference to it in the 1860s in the work of Alexander Bell, but in Scotland only. By the early 1880s, the feature was observed with London schoolchildren, and not just for /t/, and a decade later in New York City, also in the language of schoolchildren. Bailey further notes that the absence of the phenomenon in Australian English 'suggests that it arose after the massive deportations of poor people from the British cities in the first half of the [nineteenth] century' (Bailey 1996: 79). So if glottalisation of /t/ (and possibly of other stops as well) came to be a feature of non-standard London English during the second half of the nineteenth century, this would have been too late for Dickens and Thackeray to be able to make use of it.

The nineteenth century, according to Blake (1981: 160), 'was the great age for recording dialect words and phrases', and as the examples of Dickens and Thackeray have shown, this interest is particularly evident in the novelists of the period. Another well-known example is Emily Brontë, in whose novel *Wuthering Heights* (1847) dialect plays a major role. Other examples are Maria Edgeworth and Walter Scott, who both 'made innovative attempts in serious fiction to render dialogue in "authentic" colloquial styles' (Bailey 1996: 68). While Blake's study of the use of non-standard language in English literature is largely confined to authors belonging to the literary canon, Hodson and Millward (2007) provide an overview of the use of dialect in novels by minor Victorian writers. An example from their database has already been provided in (5). The database shows how authors use dialect to characterise the speech of dif-ferent kinds of non-standard English fictional characters – for example, a Cockney speaker, a Cornish villager, an American miner, an Australian bushranger, a footman, a groom, a 'labouring husband', a 'country wife' and many others. The dialect features include /h/-dropping (*'avin, umble, 'oss*), hypercorrect /h/-insertion (*hain't, haingel, hask*), 'g-dropping' (*makin', movin'*) and the pronunciation of [ŋg] for syllable-final [ŋ] which accord-ing to Jones (2006: 347) had already been commented on negatively in the early nineteenth century, the unrounding of the CHOICE diphthong (*j'ined, appintment*), the lowering of the central vowel before /r/ (*sarve, sartain*) and many other stigmatised features dealt with in this section and much besides. Often, however, Hodson and Millward note, dialectal features are marked inconsistently, while they occasionally serve for comic effect, as with the use of *guitar* for 'catarrh'. Sometimes, the intended dialect is not specified, while the features employed by the author in question are those traditionally used to render Cockney speech. It should therefore be reckoned with that dialect representation in LModE novels, even by the better-known authors, need not be naturalistic, and that it merely repre-sents a writer's perception of what a certain dialect sounded like.

2.4 Minimally schooled writers

A different source of information on how people spoke, and especially on non-standard speech, is the language of writers who had received only a minimal amount of schooling. Letters by such people provide valuable information, as their limited abilities to spell according to the rules of standard English show frequent interference from the spoken language. Fairman's recent research into the letters of these writers and their language is of very great importance to our ability to understand the nature of the evidence. Example (3) in Section 2.1 already served to indicate what kind of evidence we can expect to find in such letters: the spellings *lasse* 'lays', *foust* 'forced', *sett* 'sit' and *oup* 'up' suggest that the writer's accent was characterised by absence of the modern FACE diphthong, that it was non-rhotic (/r/-less in post-vocalic contexts), that the DRESS vowel had a closer variant and that there was no FOOT/STRUT contrast. Furthermore, the erasure ~~wif~~, possibly intended to produce 'with her' with the author changing his mind halfway through the sentence, indicates TH-fronting. The letter in question is held in the Centre for Kentish Studies, Maidstone, and Fairman 'occasionally came across *Feverstone* for *Featherstone* in parish registers in mid-Kent' (2003: 271), so this would be early evidence for the presence of a feature that is characteristic of present-day Kentish. The evidence, however, is not always easy to interpret. According to Fairman, it is not clear whether the spellings *Leater* 'letter', *Bead* 'bed' and *leat* 'let' in the letter are evidence of pronunciation with the FLEECE vowel in these words or possibly with a diphthong, or if it was because the writer 'remembered *head, leather, instead*' (2003: 270). Perhaps, however, the spellings suggest a longer, more open vowel in the dialect in question, close to the one in Middle English (though not in words like the above, which all have short vowels) which in the course of the operation of the Great Vowel Shift merged with the FLEECE vowel. Jones (2006: 178), for instance, notes that in his study he came across language commentators who 'were able to distinguish between the vowel sounds in items like *beet* and *beat*'.

A somewhat better-schooled writer was the Cornish writer Elizabeth Clift, the eldest of the Clift family children already discussed (see Chapter 1). Her letters suggest that her schooling had taken her to the stage of learning to spell monosyllables and occasional polysyllabic words such as *Expectation* (on the teaching of spelling, see Chapter 3). See for instance the passage in (6):

(6) I once more take my pen to **writ** you a few lines wich I **hop** will find you in Good health as like **wis** is my Brother Tho[s] and to let you know that I am **livin** in Plymouth I Came here to Christmass I should have **wrot** to you as soon as I Came hear if things had answard my Expectation but far from it Every thing seemd to be a gainst me but I **hop** it is all for the best. (1799?; Austin 1991: 173)

As I have already mentioned, the Clifts originated from Bodmin in Cornwall, and Elizabeth's letter suggests that their accent was characterised by an undiphthongised, short vowel in *hope* and *wrote*. The diphthongisation of the GOAT vowel appears to have occurred around the time when Elizabeth was writing, though according to Jones (2006: 303) 'diphthongal forms were only firmly established in prestige speech by the middle of the nineteenth century'. William, her younger brother who had moved to London, consistently used the spellings *hope* and *wrote* in his letters. This was either because he had learned to spell better (which was certainly the case) or because he had soon caught on to the more prestigious London pronunciation (which does not seem unlikely either, given his linguistic developments after he moved to the capital). Elizabeth's spelling of *writ* and *wis* likewise suggests short undiphthongised PRICE vowels in these words (William always used *write*), and *livin* that her dialect was characterised by 'g-dropping'.

Apart from letters by relatively unschooled writers, diaries supply important information, too. A fascinating example of such a diary is the one kept by Martha Ballard (1735–1812), an early New England midwife who in the course of her career delivered some eight hundred babies. Martha Ballard originally kept a diary in order to have a financial record of her earnings as a midwife and general healer. The diary starts when Martha was fifty, and it continues for twenty-seven years. The entries are very short at the beginning, but they grow longer over the years. Martha came from a family which was fast improving itself and which thus seems typical of early New England society, which had at the time 'the most extraordinarily concentrated book-buying and reading public in the whole country' (Charvat 1959: 30). Her mother had been unable to write, but her uncle and two of her brothers-in-law became physicians, and her own brother was a librarian who later became a minister. As a midwife, Martha travelled widely within her community (Kiełkiewicz-Janowiak 2002: 105–6), and as a healer she must have occupied a fairly central position within her social network. This makes her a potentially interesting figure from the perspective of the concept of social network analysis (see Chapter 6). The diary is available online (see Weblinks), and the search facilities allow searches for spelling variants.

The website reads that Martha often spelled words phonetically, and that her spelling informs us of local spelling habits. The example in (7), however, primarily illustrates that she did not use standard spelling in her diary:

(7) Clear and very pleas[t]. mr Ballard Sumoned to Coart. I have Done hous work, gathered in y[e] last Beens in my **gardin**, Scolt my pickeles &C. got Some apples in. mr Ballard Came f[m] Coart & went to Son Lambds. I Sent them a q[t] Plumbs. they are wel. my **Dagt** Sent me Some Sugar. (7 October 1806)

But the word *Dagt* for 'daughter' in (7) is of interest, as it occurs in the diary in various different spellings:

(8) daughter daut daug^t daugl daught^s daug daugh^{tr} daug^{tr} dauters dater da^t dat^r dt^r dafter dafters daft^r daft.

The <f> spellings in (8) provide important information on what must have been the local pronunciation of the word, and so does *dater*, which is also used by Dickens to represent non-standard pronunciation in his novels (Brook 1970: 232). Jones (2006: 219) refers to Walker's condemnation of this pronunciation as an instance of the kind of 'corrupt pronunciation' that was in use 'amongst the vulgar' (1791: 27). Searching for *garden* in the diary indicates that her preferred spelling was the non-standard spelling variant *gardin*, as in (7), with 535 instances out of 555. She therefore almost certainly pronounced the unstressed vowel with a slightly raised variant. In contrast to Dickens's characters, she does not appear to have pronounced the vowel in stressed syllables with the closer BIT vowel, as the word *again* (150 instances) is never spelled differently. Her variant spellings of *lecture*, e.g. *Lecter* (23 instances) as in (9) below – though we also find *lectur* (6) and the more standard *lecture* (39) – suggests that obstruent affricativisation was either not a characteristic of her dialect or that her dialect still alternated between fricativised and non-fricativised variants.

(9) Clear. mrs Weston here. Shee went to mr Bisbes after^n. mr Ballard & Hannah went to **Lecter**. mr How performd. I gatherd parsnip & pepper Grass Seed. (13 August 1790)

The spellings *feater, wentur* 'adventure' and *creetur* in Dickens (Brook 1970: 225) indicate that the absence of the feature became stigmatised in the course of the nineteenth century, which is confirmed by the items provided by Savage in his *Vulgarities and Improprieties of the English Language* (1833) (see Jones 2006: 334): *fixters, feeturs, venter, futur, literatoor, creetur, natur, fortin, texter, natteral, jester, minniture* and *lectur.*

2.5 Concluding remarks

Trying to find out exactly how people spoke during the LModE period is a well-nigh impossible job. There are various kinds of resources that might be studied for evidence, but as I've tried to demonstrate in this chapter studies by language commentators, novels, and letters and diaries by less well schooled writers should be treated with caution.

Jones also notes that many of the LModE scholars who wrote on pronunciation took a metropolitan perspective, often 'casting a baleful eye on the usage of the Scotch and other provincials' (2006: 350). We will therefore never know how someone like Lowth spoke, though we can be fairly certain that his accent was very different from that of the bishop of London today: to our ears he would have sounded like a speaker of a local dialect rather than like the educated member of the higher clergy that he was. We can also deduce from the lack of information in his grammar that around the 1760s accent was not yet considered to be a social marker. This would soon change, as is evident from Sheridan's attempts to promote a single accent in an effort to create equal opportunities for everyone. A single non-localised accent did develop but it had the opposite effect from what Sheridan had intended. The rise of a prestigious form of speech is evident in the course of the nineteenth century, as is clear from the remarks made by the language commentators as well as from the use of non-standard features by the novelists in the course of the LModE period. According to Blake (1981: 160), 'the interest in local speech was in part a reaction against the purity of the standard' that was advocated as the period wore on. The letters and diaries by less educated writers continue to show evidence of how people actually spoke, and by learning to interpret the evidence we will perhaps come as close to reconstructing the spoken language as we may ever hope to get.

Further reading

Many primary sources discussed in this chapter can be consulted online through ECCO for the eighteenth century and Google Book Search for the nineteenth. An important standard work of reference, referred to throughout this chapter, is Jones (2006). This book, moreover, contains a wealth of Scottish material, which would deserve separate exploration. For Irish English phonology until 1740, see Bliss (1979: 186–252). For further studies that deal with pronunciation in LModE, see Bailey (1996: 69–137), Beal (2004: 124–89), Görlach (2001: 85–97) and (1999a: 53–64), Mugglestone (2003) and Phillipps (1984: 128–42). On LModE phonology, see in particular *CHEL* Vol. III, Chapter 3 (Lass 1999b) and Vol. IV, Chapter 5 (McMahon 1998).

Research questions

1. Look up the rhyme words in the poem by Lady Mary Wortley Montagu discussed in this chapter – or the apparently anomalous rhyming pairs in any poem from the first half of the eighteenth

century – in Sheridan's *General Dictionary of the English Language* (1780) in ECCO. First check his 'Scheme of the alphabet' on page 9 for guidance on his transcription principles.

2. Another writer who made extensive use of dialect for the purpose of characterisation – though not from a humorous perspective – is Mark Twain (1835–1910). From Project Gutenberg, select one of his novels and identify the main dialectal features used. How does Twain render the pronunciation of non-standard (in his case, black) speakers? How consistent is he?

3. For Lowth, pronunciation does not seem to have been important as a means of improving one's position in society. To what extent was this true for other grammarians from the same decade? How much does Lowth say about pronunciation in his grammar? And what about Priestley (1761), Buchanan (1762) or any other grammar in ECCO?

4. Make a selection of words from Sheridan's dictionary (1780) and compare their pronunciation with those in Walker (1791). Any differences?

5. How does Fogg's scheme of sounds (1792–96, Vol. I: 8) differ from those in Sheridan's and Walker's dictionaries (ECCO)?

6. Fogg does not appear in the *ODNB* or in Wikipedia. Write an entry for him for Wikipedia, paying attention to his contribution to our current knowledge of LModE pronunciation.

7. Compare the treatment of the following words in the dictionaries by Sheridan (1780) and Walker (1791): *alabaster, band, basket, bastion, bath, bombastic, brass, calf, caster, castle, clasper, command, dance, demand, exasperate, fan, fantastic, fast, father, glass, grass, hat, lack, lass, masculine, mass, master, mastif, nasty, palm, pan, part, path, plant, rascal, slander, trap* (compare Jones 2006: 313–14) (ECCO).

8. What are the views on /h/-dropping in different pronouncing dictionaries? And what about /r/-insertion or /r/-loss? (ECCO, Google Books)

9. On the basis of the evidence from Martha Ballard's diary, would you say that her accent was /r/-full or /r/-less?

10. Identify the entry in Walker's dictionary alluded to by Miss Blimber in Dickens's *Dombey and Son*: 'If my recollection serves me,' said Miss Blimber... 'the word analysis as opposed to synthesis, is thus defined by Walker. "The resolution of an object, whether of the senses or of the intellect, into its first elements." As opposed to synthesis, you observe. Now you know what analysis is, Dombey.' What is your conclusion? (ECCO, Google Book Search)

Notes

1. To indicate pronunciation in this chapter, I will make use of what are known as 'lexical sets'. Using standard English pronunciation as a starting point, such sets, which were developed by Wells (1982), indicate how vowel sounds are pronounced.

2. According to Picard (2000), one guinea was equivalent to the weekly wages of a journeyman silversmith.

3. Beal (2004: 152) argues that happY-tensing is older than is usually assumed, as Walker already identified the phenomenon in his dictionary.

4. For this, Jones (2006: 343) cites *Everyday Blunders in Speaking* (1866) by Edmund Routledge, who regarded this feature as a 'common mistake', typical of London speakers. By way of a cure the author recommended repeating the sentence 'Round the rugged rocks the ragged rascals ran to see the rural races' twenty times a day.

3 Spelling systems

3.1 Introduction

If the standardisation process of a language involves 'the suppression of optional variability' of that language (Milroy and Milroy 1985a: 8), one would have to conclude that for English only spelling comes close to having a standard. In the mid-1970s, when his *History of English* came out, Scragg still noted only a few variants in British English spelling, i.e. *loth/loath*, *curtsy/curtsey*, *hiccup/hiccough*, and *biassed* and *focussed* with single or double <s>, observing that 'brevity is the keynote of present developments in English spelling' (1974: 86). At the time, popular newspapers indeed took what was evidently a more advanced stand in preferring the shorter *dulness* and *fulness* to the more conservative versions with double <l> used in the more serious papers. More than thirty years later, and now that we have at our disposal the tools that allow us to test claims like these, I checked the variants listed by Scragg against the evidence in the British National Corpus (BNC), an online database of around one hundred million words of spoken and written English, made up of material from different sources of British English from 'the latter part of the 20th century' (BNC website).[1] The result is not, however, as Scragg predicted, as with only three words, *hiccup* (96/14), *biased* (556/7) and *focused* (1822/212), the shorter form is indeed the more common of the two, while three of the longer forms have remained in more general use, i.e. *loath* (102/23), *dullness* (63/2) and *fullness* (236/4). Of two other words, *program/programme* and *catalog/catalogue*, Scragg observed that with the shorter forms being characteristic of American spelling, 'it is likely that publishers will be unable ultimately to resist the saving in paper, ink, and type-setting labour involved in the shortened forms'. Again, his prediction failed to come true: the BNC includes an overwhelming majority of the longer form *catalogue* (2427/18). The case of *program/programme* shows a development that was unlikely to have been foreseen by Scragg as he wrote before the computer age: since then, British usage has shown specialisation of the two forms, with the shorter word being reserved for computer programs and the longer for the word's remaining senses (see *OED*, s.v. *programme/program* n. 9b). American English only has the shorter form. Evidently, future developments in English spelling prove impossible to predict, even though spelling has been almost completely standardised.

Choice between the suffix *-ise/-ize*, still a familiar variable today, is said to be determined by a preference for British or American spelling. For a recent publication I was instructed by the stylesheet 'that in British English the "-ize" ending should be used in preference to "-ise" where both spellings are in use (e.g., "criticize", "recognize")' (Stylesheet for GlobE publications). The BNC, however, does not confirm this preference, as the following figures show: *generalise* and *characterise* were found in almost equal numbers in either spelling (*ise/ize*: 117/137 and 265/226) but *criticise*, *recognise* and *realise* were preferred to their counterparts in *-ize* at a rate of four to three or almost two to one. There are therefore factors at play today other than a straightforward preference for either the British or the American English spelling system, and prescriptive rules such as those found in stylesheets may represent only a minority practice. Fowler's *Modern English Usage* (3rd edn 1996 [1926]), a standard work of reference on usage questions like these, provides a list of verbs in which *-ise* is obligatory (for example, *advertise*, *comprise*, *revise*), noting that the *-ize* spelling is appropriate for words of Greek origin, such as *baptize* (now commonly spelled with <s>). The difficulty here is that few writers will be aware of the etymology of the words they use, and though according to Burchfield the use of *-ise* or *-ize* is largely optional except for American usage, which prescribes *-ize*, 'the matter remains delicately balanced but unresolved' (1996: 422). For Dr Johnson the situation would have been more clear-cut, and his dictionary presents *baptize* in what was to him its proper spelling.

Apart from *-ize*, the features usually associated with American spelling are *-or* as in *color* (BrE *colour*) and *-er* as in *center* (BrE *centre*), but there are more. My 1981 edition of the *Oxford Dictionary for Writers and Editors* also lists the following under 'US spellings':

- *e* for *ae* and *oe* (*esthete, eon, estrogen, fetus, toxemia*)
- *-ense* for *-ence* (*defense, license, offense, pretense*)
- *z* for soft s (*cozy, analyze*)
- omission of final *e* before a suffix beginning with a vowel (*milage, salable*) except after soft *c* and *g* (*manageable*)
- final *-l* followed by a suffix beginning with a vowel (*counselor, teetotaler, rivaled, traveling*; cf. *clarinetist*)

- final *-ogue* shortened to *-og* [see above] (*analog, catalog, epilog, pedagog*).

Checking these guidelines against the data in the BNC shows that most of them still apply today, though many of the American spellings listed here are also, if less frequently, attested in British English usage, the most frequent ones being *eon* (17/22), *fetus* (128/225) and *clarinetist* (4/19). In all other instances the American variant was either not attested (*esthete, salable, teetotaler, rivaled, epilog* and *pedagog*) or was found to be in a distinct minority (the remaining items). As, according to Scragg thirty-five years ago, 'books and periodicals published in the United States become increasingly familiar in Britain, American spellings are inevitably more difficult to detect' (1974: 86), it will be interesting to see what the distribution of these features will be like in twenty years' time. In the light of the existence of these two major spelling systems for the English language it is interesting to observe that Canadian English shows a mixture of both, with variation according to Crystal (1995: 340) being determined by geographical, occupational and social factors. Such a situation is actually typical of what we find during much of the LModE period, which is still characterised by a great deal of variation, with significant differences occurring between printed and privately written documents.

3.2 The eighteenth-century printers' spelling

According to Scragg, by the early eighteenth century the English spelling system had become stabilised (1974: 80). By this he means that there was by that time no longer a lot of spelling variation, but in saying this he refers to printed usage. Since the publication of his book, research has increasingly come to focus on letters, too, and these continue to show a different spelling system throughout the eighteenth century despite the standardised spelling of printed books. Only at the end of the century do we find indications that correct spelling, according to what was advocated by the printers, began to be a prerequisite for good writing, even in letters.

Görlach (2001: 79–81) notes a small number of spelling features that still call for comment in the eighteenth century: the use of long <s> (ſ), the use of the ligatures <œ> and <æ>, typically found in words adopted from the classical languages and which were still more common in those days than today (compare Section 3.1), variation between *-ick* and *-ic* in words like *music* and *comic*, between *-or* and *-our* in words like *color* and *authour*, between *-ise* and *-ize*, as already discussed, the use of final *-e* when no longer functional, and the use of clipped words such as *tho'*, *can't* and *ain't*, in which the apostrophe marks the omitted characters. In addition, Görlach notes the abolishment of the use of capitalisation for all nouns, which in the eighteenth century approached that of modern German, and the use of *'d* in past tenses and past participles of weak verbs, as in the subtitle of the *An Exposition of All the Books of the Old and New Testament* (London, 3rd edn 1721–1725):

> (1) ... WHEREIN/ The CHAPTERS are ſumm'd up in Contents; the Sacred Text inſerted at large, in Paragraphs, or Verſes; and each Paragraph, or Verſe, **reduc'd** to its proper Heads; the Senſe given, and largely illuſtrated,/ WITH/ Practical Remarks and Obſervations (ECCO).

Example (1) also illustrates the uses of long <s>, i.e. at the beginning and in the middle of words, as in *ſumm'd*, *inſerted*, *Verſes*, *Senſe* and *illuſtrated*, but never when a word begins with a capital (*Sacred*) or at the end of a word (*Remarks*). Long <s> is also used as the first <s> in the double <s> cluster in words like *idleness* and *business* in the following example, the title of a poem by William Wycherly (1706):

> (2) *Upon the **Idleneſs** of* **Busineſs**. *A* SATYR; *To one, who ſaid,* A Man ſhow'd his Senſe, Spirit, Induſtry, and Parts, by his Love of Buſineſs (ECCO).

Long <s> disppeared as a printing device towards the end of the eighteenth century, and its presence or absence is today used by antiquarians to date books that lack a publication date as dating from either before or after 1800.

Examples (1) and (2) also illustrate the use of extra initial capitals at the time, i.e. for all nouns and only for nouns (in (1), the words *The* and *Practical* were capitalised because they occur at the beginning of a new section). The use of extra initial capitals, according to Osselton ([1984] 1998), steadily increased during the first half of the eighteenth century to about 100 per cent around the 1750s after which this practice was drastically reduced and, fifty years later, abandoned completely. The reason for giving up the practice to capitalise all nouns was pressure from writers, who felt that they could no longer make use of capitals to emphasise individual words, as they had been accustomed to do before such idiosyncratic use of capitals was standardised by the printers. In eighteenth-century manuscripts, it is not always easy to distinguish between capitals and lower-case letters, and giving every noun its capital would have saved typesetters a lot of time. Opposition to the printers' system is found in many eighteenth-century spelling books (Osselton [1984] 1998: 38), and eventually the practice was abolished. Osselton similarly found an increase – followed by a decrease – in the use of *'d* in past tense and past participle forms of weak verbs in the course of the eighteenth century, though this feature never became as categorical as the use of capitals.

Scragg calls 'the loss of final <k> from <-ick>' in words like *music* and *comic* as well as the change of spellings like *phantasy* and *controul* 'minor developments' (1974: 80). For the eighteenth century we can check the preference for the variants of these words by using ECCO (full-text search). The results show that *controul* was found about four times as often as *control, phantasy* and *fantasy* equally often, and *music* nearly ten times and *comic* five times as often as their counterparts in *-ck*. Dr Johnson, in his *Dictionary of the English Language* (1755), opted for the spellings *control, fantasy* and *comick* and *musick*, so except for the *-ick* words he offers a spelling that is more advanced than actual usage suggests. The preference for *-ick* spellings is peculiar, as they were by that time already old fashioned (Osselton 1963: 272). There are other differences from modern spelling in the dictionary, especially in relation to *-or/our* words: Osselton (1963: 269) notes *inferiour, governour, horrour, splendour, errour, emperour* and *terrour*, and explains that Johnson preferred these forms on account of their etymology, with Latin derived words ending in *-or* and words with a French origin in *-our*. Comparing these words as they occur in different editions of the *Universal Etymological English Dictionary* by Johnson's predecessor Nathan Bailey (c. 1691–1742), published between 1721 and 1783, Osselton noted a steady decrease of the *-our* spellings. Clearly, the printers had a different interest at heart from that of keeping the etymological distinction alive.

Final *-e* when no longer functional, as in words like *confesse, despaire* and *finde* but also in inflected verbs like *comeing, giveing, haveing, takeing* and *writeing*, are no longer very common in printed books, as a search in ECCO demonstrates. The inflected verb forms continue to occur in private letters, as I will show below. As for the use of clipped forms, like *tho', thro'* and *'em*, these were still frequently found at the time, alongside weak forms such as *shan't, can't* and *mayn't*, though 'only in informal texts such as printed plays' (Görlach 2001: 80); again, these are likewise much more common in letters than in printed texts. Complaints in the first decades of the eighteenth century, like those of Addison in *The Spectator*, issue 135 (1711), against the custom to 'clog [our Language] with Consonants, as *mayn't, can't, sha'n't, wo'n't*, and the like, for *may not, can not, shall not, will not*, &c.' had evidently not been without effect.

3.3 A dual spelling system

It is often said that, with the publication of his dictionary, Johnson imposed a fixed spelling on the English language. As Baugh and Cable put it, the dictionary 'offered a spelling, fixed, even if sometimes badly, that could be accepted as standard' ([1951] 1993: 267). But as shown above, the spelling system as it emerged from the dictionary was not fixed in that it shows considerable differences from that of Present-Day English (PDE), as with forms like *musick* and *arithmetick*, which were no longer really current at the time, nor does it necessarily represent what Johnson would have preferred himself. By analysing Johnson's private letters, for instance, Osselton found spellings like *companiable, enervaiteing, Fryday, obviateing, occurences, peny, pouns, stiched, chappel, diner* and *dos* ('does') (1963: 274). Some of these may have been slips of the pen, as even today we often mistakenly write *occurences*, and it would be interesting to find out to what extent such deviant spellings correlate with Johnson's mood. When he was suffering from depression, he may not have been paying a lot of attention to correct spelling. Other spelling variants in his letters seem more systematic, and they occur with other writers as well. In the private writings of literary authors like Lady Mary Wortley Montagu, Laurence Sterne (1713–68), Sarah Fielding and Robert Lowth, all of them highly educated, we come across *easyer, prettyest, intirely, unworthyness, agreable, opportunitys, supplyed, every thing, birth day* and *untill* (Erisman 2003; Tieken-Boon van Ostade 1998), all of which deviate from the spelling system advocated by the printers. The spelling *untill*, for instance, does not occur in ECCO even once, nor does *unworthyness*. The spellings *sew, intirely* and *agreable* were common variants throughout much of the LModE period. While Lady Mary Wortley Montagu would have learned to spell during the final decade of the seventeenth century, Sterne, Sarah Fielding and Lowth were all contemporaries of Johnson's and learned to spell around the same time.

Spelling instruction, if spelling was taught at all, was mostly done at home in those days; grammar schools, according to Fairman (2006), only accepted pupils who were already able to spell. If spelling was taught from a book – which may or may not have been the case, for according to Fairman (2006: 63), we know next to nothing about private spelling teaching – the method employed was not usually aimed at the teaching of spelling as a system of rules. During much of the period, spelling books taught children words by their number of syllables, starting with two-letter combinations like *ab, eb, ib, ob, ub* and *ba, be, bi, bo, bu,* 'Easie Syllables' according to the anonymous *Spelling Book for Children* (1707: 4). The next stage consisted of words with one syllable (*age, are, ask, best, bind*), leading up to the stage where learners were taught to spell words with as many as six syllables (*abominations, abecedarian, communication, confectionaries, determination*), without so much as having been offered any spelling rules. The purpose of this particular book and many others like it was to teach children to read the catechism, and the first lesson following the word lists begins: 'Come ye Chil-dren, heark-en un-to me, I will teach you the Fear of the Lord' (1707: 5). The main aim of another spelling book from the period, John Urmston's *London Spelling-Book* published in 1710, was to teach children to divide words into syllables rather than actually how to spell, as it starts from *duty* in the list of words of two syllables to go on to *dutiful* in the list of three-syllable words without explaining that final <y> changes to <i> when it is no longer word final. This, indeed, was not a rule that any of the authors referred to above had learned to apply, so it is no wonder that writers like Lady Mary Wortley Montagu, Laurence Sterne, Sarah Fielding or Robert Lowth seem such poor spellers to us. The spelling of their published books was a different matter, for this was the responsibility of the printers, not the authors.

The spelling books discussed here taught English spelling as it occurred in printed books, so in effect they taught children to read – the catechism or, as in the case of *The London Spelling-Book*, the Lord's Prayer and the Creed – but not to write. As spelling was not systematically taught for this purpose, the result was an enormous divide between the spelling of printed texts and of private documents; this explains the kind of unexpected spellings found in the private letters of the authors discussed. Osselton ([1984] 1998) therefore believes that there was a dual spelling standard in the eighteenth century:

i. a public one, as it was set forth in [Johnson's] Dictionary; and this corresponds largely though not wholly to one set of conventions already established by the printers of the day

ii. a private one, as evidenced in [Johnson's] letters.

(Osselton [1984] 1998: 34)

Private spelling actually has a systematicity of its own, in that it is not characterised by rules like the one for <y> and <i> mentioned above as these rules were not formally taught as such. From this perspective, words like *easyer, obviateing, unworthyness, opportunitys* and *supplyed* are perfectly regular in their own right.

The private spelling system is attested throughout the eighteenth century. We still find it in the letters of Boswell, who was thirty years younger than Johnson, and Fairman (2006) shows that the situation with respect to the teaching of spelling was still very similar at the end of the century. But things were beginning to change, for at a certain point Boswell abandoned much of this private spelling system in his letters in favour of the printers' system (Tieken-Boon van Ostade 1996b). This happened around 1767, when he apparently adopted a more serious attitude to life in view of his future career as a lawyer. Both as a result of his 'new daily routine of studying, dictating, consulting and arguing in court' as well as 'writing answers to memorials' (Pottle 1966: 293) and because of his great admiration of Dr Johnson, he seems to have adopted the printers' spelling system, even in his private letters. As a result, we even see old-fashioned spellings such as *fabrick* making their appearance in Boswell's letters, as this was the variant advocated by Johnson in his *Dictionary* (Section 3.2). The same phenomenon is found in Mrs Thrale's letters to Johnson. As I will discuss in Section 6.4, she switched from *-ic* to *-ick* in an effort to accommodate to him. The influence of the printers' spelling on an author's private writing is also evident in the case of Lady Mary Wortley Montagu, whose letters show a changing preference for the spelling of *-ed* in weak verbs to *'d*. As discussed in Section 3.2, the printers would eventually abandon this usage. Another spelling we first find towards the end of her life is the present-day spelling *always*. None of her earlier spelling variants for this word, *allwaies*, *allways* and *alwaies*, were typical of eighteenth-century printed books (Erisman 2003).

Spelling was indeed one of the points on which the printer of Laurence Sterne's memoirs disagreed with the author's own practice. The memoirs had been written in 1767, a year before Sterne's death, and were published in 1775 by his daughter Lydia (Monkman 1985). While the manuscript shows evidence of spelling habits Sterne must have acquired in his early youth, such as *supplyed*, *orderd*, *Arch Bishop*, *small Pox*, *Mony* and *Designe*, these words and many others besides were all corrected in the printed version. The printer also removed all the extra initial capitals Sterne had used. Printers continued to be responsible for the spelling of printed documents, for Mugglestone (2006) quotes a certain Caleb Stower, the alleged author of *The Printer's Grammar* (1808), saying: 'Most Authors expect the Printer to spell, point, and digest their Copy, that it may be intelligible and significant to the Reader.' By this time, however, the use of the extra initial capitals in this sentence is suspicious, and a search in ECCO shows that this sentence, and possibly more of the book, was lifted directly, capitals and all, from a book with the same title by a man called John Smith (a pseudonym?) published in 1755. The book was reprinted in 1787, with a title page specifying that the book contains 'DIRECTIONS to AUTHORS, COMPILERS, &c. How to Prepare Copy, and to Correct their own Proofs. Chiefly collected from SMITH's edition'. Stower had clearly done the same.

3.4 Spelling as a social phenomenon

Because women, especially those in the social class to which Elizabeth Clift belonged, had fewer opportunities of gaining access to formal education, they also had less highly developed linguistic skills, including spelling. Earlier in the period this had also been true of more highly placed women, and Görlach (2001) reproduces an example of a letter written in 1705 by Lady Isabella Wentworth, which illustrates her poor spelling skills:

> My dearist dear and best of children, I am much rejoysed at your fyne present, I wish you may often have such and better, tell you ar as ritch as the Duke of Molberry whoe is billding the fynest hous at Woodstock that ever was seen. (Görlach 2001: 297)

By the middle of the eighteenth century, women's spelling had improved, and the case of Lady Mary Wortley Montagu shows that this could happen within an individual woman's writing career just as well as in the case of men like Boswell. During her years of exile in Italy, Lady Mary had been an avid reader, asking her daughter to supply her with copies of the latest novels, including Richardson's *Clarissa* (1748) (Halsband 1956). It is therefore not surprising to see that her writing was influenced by the spelling she found in these books.

In March 1755 Lowth praised his wife Molly for her 'exceedingly well wrote Letter'. This was the first letter he ever received from her, and his comment possibly refers to her spelling, too. I calculated that Sarah Fielding's spelling was no poorer than that of Lowth, despite the fact that she lacked the kind of formal education Lowth had received (Tieken-Boon van Ostade 1998: 465–6). Her only real problem, as she pointed out herself in a letter of 14 December 1757 to Samuel Richardson (c.1689–1761), lay in the correct use of capital letters and punctuation marks, though this problem, she noted, would 'I suppose . . . naturally be set right in the printing' (Battestin and Probyn 1993: 149). The use of extra initial capitals for all nouns, discussed in Section 3.2, had been a feature introduced by the printers against what had been common preference among individual authors, so she was right in leaving the responsibility for its correct use to them. And Richardson was of course a printer.

Fairman (2006: 62) notes that around 1820, of the twelve million inhabitants of England and Wales, only 7.8 per cent were literate enough to have their writings printed. An additional 28 per cent were able to write, a section of the population consisting of people who belonged to the lower orders, and he mentions 'artisans, shopkeepers, hawkers, lesser merchants, household servants and others'. Children from less well-to-do backgrounds rarely spent more than three to four years in school, which meant they would never get beyond the stage where they were taught to read – and presumably to write as well – monosyllabic words (Fairman 2006: 63–8). As English lexis is characterised by a split into native and learned words, with native words being primarily monosyllabic and loanwords mostly polysyllabic, this would result in the more formal registers remaining virtually inaccessible to those with only a bare amount of schooling. The nature of English spelling teaching thus had far-reaching consequences from the point of view of acquiring proper literacy skills. As far as the ability to write is concerned, the majority of the population, about 64 per cent by the year 1820 by Fairman's calculations, had to rely on others to communicate with the parish in order, for instance, to apply for financial assistance. The members of the Clift family had been extremely fortunate in this respect.

Görlach (2001: 80) comments on the spelling, 'even by educated writers' as he specifies, of the possessives *its*, *yours* and *theirs* with an apostrophe. However, *your's*, for instance in the superscriptions to private letters, was standard practice at the time: it was part, in other words, of the epistolary spelling system (Section 3.3). In such letters, we also find clipped forms like *tho'* and weak forms like *can't* and *don't*. My collection of Lowth's letters shows that *your's* is found in over 90 per cent of the instances, *don't* in 38 per cent and *can't* in 8 per cent, and not only in letters addressed to his wife, as the following quotation from a letter to his publisher shows:

(3) My Wife, **tho'** better than she has been, yet still continues very ill. – Believe me, Dear Sr./**Your's** most Affectionately/R. Lowth. (Lowth to Robert Dodsley, 1758; Tierney 1988: 346)

The full form *though* is never found in his letters. The spelling of *its* with or without an apostrophe, by which the verb form is distinguished from the possessive, is a notorious problem today, and to get them wrong is branded by Lynne Truss in *Eats Shoots and Leaves* as 'an unequivocal signal of illiteracy' (2003: 43). Though Lowth himself never wrote *it's*, one of his far from illiterate correspondents, William Warburton, the future bishop of Gloucester, did, as in:

(4) to give merit **it's** due, (1756, Warburton to Lowth)

It is not, therefore, as though educated writers should have known better as Görlach suggests.

The case of Boswell discussed in Section 3.3 shows that spelling and the need to spell correctly became a serious issue in the course of the eighteenth century, and this would continue to be the case as time went by. Correct spelling eventually became a feature of social distinction. A particularly poignant illustration of this may be found in the Clift family correspondence. Despite their lowly origins – their father had been a journeyman miller who tried to augment his income by cutting sticks and laying hedges (Austin 1991) – the six Clift brothers and sisters had all, somehow or other, learned to read and write sufficiently to be able to keep in touch by letter in their adult life. Of only the youngest, William, do we know that he went to school until he was about twelve, when his mother died and there was no longer any money to continue his education. The other children possibly learned to read and write at a so-called Writing School or from 'the lady of the local squire or the wife and daughters of the clergyman' (Austin 1994: 285), as was common practice among the poorer ranks (Fairman 2006). As discussed in Chapter 2, the eldest of the Clift children, Elizabeth, never got much beyond the stage of learning to spell words of one syllable, but due to the opportunities for social improvement offered to him William fared much better. Not only did he improve his literacy skills by buying and reading popular novels, he may also have benefitted directly from his apprenticeship with John Hunter, who made him write from dictation (Austin 1991: 15). In addition, William had to copy manuscripts in Hunter's collection, which similarly contributed to his developing writing skills, particularly as regards spelling. According to Austin, William took great care over the letters he wrote to his relatives, and she notes that 'he often drafted and corrected them, tightening wording and phrasing for the posted copy' (1991: 15). William also copied the letters he received from his brothers and sisters in coded form, in the process of which he corrected their spelling; perhaps he did so by way of exercising his own spelling, as he would leave matters of wording and grammar alone (Austin 1991: 16). It is almost painful to read his criticism of Elizabeth's spelling, when he told her in a letter of 9 January 1798 to 'learn to mend [her] Orthography or spell better' (Austin 1991: 169). He added, 'Now you surely do not understand the true definition and derivation of the words Lutheran, Calvinist, Methodist, &c, otherwise you could not spell them wrong', ending his letter with a piece of advice on how to fold letters properly. This criticism must have hit Elizabeth hard, for it is not until 1 July 1799 that we have another letter from her to William. By this time, the ability to spell correctly had clearly become a matter of social significance.

Fifty years later, the social significance of correct spelling is commented on by Dickens in his novel *Bleak House* (1852–53), as in the following passage in which Caddy comments upon the poor spelling of her lover (Brook 1970: 108):

> Caddy told me that her lover's education had been so neglected that it was not always easy to read his notes. She said if he were not so anxious about his spelling and took less pains to make it clear, he would do better; but he put so many unnecessary letters into short words that they sometimes quite lost their English appearance.
>
> 'He does it with the best intention,' observed Caddy, 'but it hasn't the effect he means, poor fellow!' Caddy then went on to reason, how could he be expected to be a scholar when he had passed his whole life in the dancing-school and had done nothing but teach and fag, fag and teach, morning, noon, and night!

3.5 The nineteenth century

By the end of the eighteenth century, there are signs that the situation with regard to the teaching of spelling began to improve. The grammar by Lindley Murray (1795) offers three pages of actual spelling rules. Having first observed that 'the orthography of the English language is attended with much uncertainty and perplexity', he adds that 'a considerable part of this inconvenience may be remedied, by attending to the general laws of formation' (1795: 17). This is indeed what had been lacking in earlier approaches to spelling teaching (Section 3.3). He subsequently provides ten spelling rules, which, when applied, enabled writers to produce spellings like *earlier, unworthiness, opportunities* and *supplied* correctly, as well as *fulness, skilful* and *blamable* (Murray 1795: 17–19). Even the spelling *obviating* might be arrived at, though there is no explicit rule that teaches the learner to elide final *-e* in verb forms ending in *-ing*. Murray's spelling rules do not deal with features like the choice between *-or* and *-our* or *-ic* and *-ick*: for these, the reader was evidently expected to consult a dictionary. The grammar was frequently reprinted far into the nineteenth century, in as many as about 1.5 to 2 million copies, so vast numbers of people, in one way or another, must have had access to his spelling rules. The rules are, however, given in smaller print, which means that they are intended for the more advanced learner only, as Murray's grammar was a graded grammar (Tieken-Boon van Ostade 1996a).

Throughout the nineteenth century, there continued to be a discrepancy between private and public spelling, for Mugglestone (2006: 279) notes that in diaries and letters spellings are attested like *trowsers, poney, gulph, novellist* and *untill*, none of which are in current use today. Mugglestone also notes different spelling preferences with regard to the word *cosy* between someone like Dorothy Wordsworth (1771–1855), who used *cozie*, and Dickens, who wrote *cosey*, and also that writers continued to vary between *-or* and *-our* spellings in ways that have nothing to do with present-day American or British spelling. Dickens preferred *harbor*, *arbor* and *parlor* because he felt that the *-our* spelling 'belong[ed] . . . to another sound – such as *hour* and *sour*' (1756; Mugglestone 2006: 280). It is interesting to see that Dickens had his own ideas about spelling. Spelling played an important role in his writing, for, as example (4) in Chapter 2 shows, it was his main vehicle for rendering his lower-class characters' speech (Brook 1980: 107).

Spelling in the nineteenth century had developed, according to Görlach (1999: 45), into 'one of the most important indicators of social acceptability'. As discussed in Section 3.1, the spelling system still allowed for only small numbers of variants. Whatever variation there was inevitably presented problems to dictionary makers, and Görlach refers to James Murray (1837–1915), chief editor of the *OED*, who wrote in his preface to the fist volume of the dictionary about the problems he encountered in having to choose between variants. Murray identified variable spellings, for instance, for words like *aerie* (variants: *aery, eyrie, eyry*) and words ending in *-able, -eer/-ier* and *-ise/-ize*. In having been forced to make a choice, he assured the reader, it had not been his intention to imply 'that the form actually chosen is intrinsically better than others which are appended to it' (1888: x; Görlach 1999: 44).

3.6 Webster's spelling reform

Dickens's idiosyncratic views on spelling discussed in Section 3.5 date from between his first and his second visits to America (see Section 1.6). It would be interesting to speculate about whether there is a connection between the two as, by this time, Noah Webster's (1758–1843) spelling reforms, which culminated in a distinct American English spelling system, had already been in print for several years. Webster's proposals, which in addition to the items listed in Section 3.1 included *music*, *blamable* and *connection*, had been made public in his *Elementary Spelling Book* (1829). These spellings actually reflect a compromise, for he would have preferred to be far more radical, with spellings like *hed, proov, flem*, *hiz, giv, def, ruf* and *wel* (Monaghan 1983: 120). Critical reception of his earlier proposals, however, had taught him to proceed more cautiously. His primary motivation for proposing a spelling reform, according to Monaghan, was nationalistic: 'he genuinely believed that time was ripe for America to separate herself from England linguistically, as well as politically' (1983: 116). Monaghan credits him with having 'single-handedly . . . introduced permanent spelling changes into the written language' (1983: 122), a memorable feat indeed. Many of his spellings represent a conscious preference for the variant that had not been selected by Johnson in his dictionary.

One of Webster's other motivations for proposing a reform of English spelling was that it would 'render the acquisition of the language easy both for natives and foreigners' (Monaghan 1983: 115). Teaching English spelling is indeed problematic, as appears from the website of the Spelling Society, founded in 1908 as the Simplified Spelling Society, where the problem is highlighted and proposals for improvement are published. As for teaching foreigners, in my own country, The Netherlands, English spelling is not normally taught in secondary education for reasons that are in my view unjustified, given the nature of the spelling system. In this respect, the situation does not appear to have improved much since the days before Murray.

3.7 Concluding remarks

Readers unfamiliar with LModE spelling often draw the wrong kind of conclusions on the basis of the variants they encounter, whether in printed books or in private documents like letters. On the one hand, they are often struck by how 'American' LModE spelling looks, while on the other they find it hard to accept that even highly educated writers might be such poor spellers. An important starting point, however, is to distinguish between the printers' spelling of the period, which was already largely but not completely standardised, and the spelling used by writers in personal documents, which had a systematicity of its own that is independent of what is found in printed books. Throughout much of the eighteenth century, spelling was primarily the responsibility of the printers, and the teaching of spelling was not generally done in school but − for those who were fortunate enough, that is − at home. What is more, in the teaching of spelling rules no attention was paid to word-formation principles which, following the printers' habits, dictated for instance that -*y* would change to -*ie*- or -*i*- when a plural or any other kind of suffix followed. There were spelling books whose authors expressed their discontent with the spelling system imposed by the printers, but also private writers such as the poet Walter Savage Landor (1775–1864), who complained in the second edition of his epic poem *Gebir* (1798; 1803) about 'the stubborness [sic] of the Press' which prescribed the spellings *therefore* and *wherefore*, *freest* and *freer*, and *proceed* and *exceed* but also *recede* (Tieken-Boon van Ostade 1998: 457). To the ordinary writer, such spellings might indeed seem completely arbitrary, and the presence of guidelines in Fowler's *Modern English Usage* on how to spell *proceed* and *precede* shows that this is still the case today (interestingly, according to the third edition of this book, the spelling *therefor* still exists, though it is restricted to legal use; no advice is offered on the spellings *freer* and *freest*). Even Dickens had opinions of his own on certain spellings, but it is doubtful whether he was able to convince his publishers of the rationale behind his views. Since the days of Johnson and Bailey, as Osselton (1963) has shown, the opinions of the printers had steadily become fixed in this respect, not only in Britain but also in America, as the existence today of these two independent spelling systems demonstrates.

Further reading

Scragg (1974), though published well over thirty years ago, is still in a lot of respects the most authoritative study of the history of English spelling available. On the standardisation of English spelling as well as on spelling reform, see Carney (1994: 467–88). On LModE spelling, see Görlach (2001: 75–85) and (1999a: 44–53). The latter book also deals with the question of spelling reform during the nineteenth century. LModE spelling and punctuation is dealt with in *CHEL*, though, interestingly, only in Vol. III (Salmon 1999). On the development of rules for extra initial capitals in LModE spelling books, see Osselton ([1985] 1998).

Research questions

1. Select three books from ECCO, one from the early eighteenth century, one from the middle and one from the end, and study the use of extra initial capitals, '*d*/*ed* in weak verbs and the use of *-or/- our* spellings. Also compare different editions of a particular book published over longer stretches of time.
2. Analyse the uses of <s> on Jane Austen's tombstone (Weblinks). What is the date of the tombstone?
3. On the website of the Spelling Society (Weblinks), two questions are presented to illustrate the complexities of PDE spelling:
   a. Why don't *comb, tomb* and *bomb* rime?
   b. Why do *they, say* and *weigh* rime?
   Try to answer these questions with the help of the information on the spelling history of these words in the *OED*.
4. Are any traces of American spelling detectable in:
   a. Martha Ballard's diary (Martha Ballard's Diary Online)?

    b. the novels by Mark Twain (Project Gutenberg)?

    c. Webster's *Elementary Spelling Book* (for the 1839 edition, see Google Book Search)?

5. Study the occurrence of short forms (such as *can't, don't, tho'*) in eighteenth-century printed books (ECCO).

6. How do nineteenth-century novelists make use of spelling to render dialect speech? (See, for example, Hodson and Millward 2007.)

7. The lexicographer James Murray had problems choosing between variants of spellings ending, for instance, in *-able* for derivatives of verbs ending in silent *-e*. How did he solve the problem for words like *blam(e)able, dat(e)able, giv(e)able, mak(e)able, rat(e)able, sal(e)able*? What is the status of the different variants in the *OED*?

8. Look up the American spelling variants discussed in Section 3.1 in Johnson's *Dictionary* (ECCO).

    a. Did you encounter any changes in different editions?

    b. Any differences with the *OED*?

9. The *OED*, which is largely a nineteenth-century dictionary, is currently in the process of being extensively revised. Starting with the letter M, revision has been completed down to . . . (check the *OED* website for the most recent situation; see also Chapter 4). Make a list of suggestions for:

    a. the remaining American spelling features discussed in Section 3.1.

    b. any spelling features that were still variable in the twentieth century according to Scragg.

    Use the BNC as a reference database for PDE spelling.

10. To what extent was Dickens able to exercise control over his private spelling preferences for the printed text of his novels? Check, for example, the texts of *A Christmas Carol* (1843) and *A Tale of Two Cities* (1859).

Note

1. Access to the full version of the BNC is restricted to library subscription. However, the website allows for simple searches, which produce a maximum of fifty randomly selected quotations.

4 Writers and the lexicon

4.1 Introduction

To illustrate the growth of the English lexicon since the introduction of the printing press in 1476 by Caxton, Görlach (2001: 146) provides a graph showing the arrival of new words in the English language at intervals of twenty years down to the early twentieth century. The graph is based on dictionaries like the *Chronological English Dictionary* (Finkenstaedt et al. 1970). It shows two major peaks, one for the second half of the sixteenth century to the first half of the seventeenth and the other for much of the nineteenth century. The first peak can be explained by the developments the English language was undergoing at the time. As part of the standardisation process, the language was in the middle of a stage referred to as 'elaboration of function' (Milroy and Milroy 1985a: 27), during which English was taking over from Latin as the language of scholarship. It was widely felt, however, that the lexicon was seriously unsuitable for such a task, and there were various conscious and unconscious efforts to enrich the language accordingly (Barber 1997: 53–70; Nevalainen and Tieken-Boon van Ostade 2006: 279–82; Nevalainen 2006: 45–57). The second peak in Görlach's graph reflects the results of the Industrial Revolution and other important cultural and social developments of the time, which produced many new words. Mugglestone, who characterises nineteenth-century English as showing 'idiomatic vigour' (2006: 301), notes that the words *industrialism* (1833), *industrialize* (1882) and, as its inevitable result, *urbanization* (1888) are all nineteenth-century innovations (Mugglestone 2006: 274).

Görlach's results may be compared with data obtained from the *OED Online*. Comprising some 18.5 million words of text,[1] the *OED* can be used as a huge database, an 'unparalleled resource', as Mugglestone puts it (2006: 297), not only for the study of nineteenth-century English but also for that of the entire LModE period. Accordingly, I have collected all new words for the first year of every decade between 1700 and 1900;

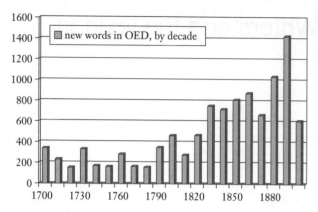

Figure 4.1 New words in the *OED*, selected for the first year of each decade (1700–1900).

to this end the *OED*'s Simple Search option 'first cited date' was used. The results can be found in Table 4.1.

At first sight, the figures confirm the data provided by Görlach: while not much seems to be going on during the eighteenth century, an increase becomes evident at the end of this century which continues throughout the nineteenth. The development shows a peak in the final decade, followed by a drastic drop for the year 1900. This drop also appears in Görlach's graph, and it continues in the early decades of the twentieth century; the same phenomenon is decribed in *Examining the OED* (Weblinks).

A closer look at the words that form the data for the graph in Figure 4.1, however, suggests that the above figures should be interpreted with care. (For illustration purposes, I will only discuss examples starting with *a* or *b*.) For some words the first quotation is a dictionary citation, for example, *adjudicate* (1700), which only reads '[See ADJUDICATING 1.] **1731** In BAILEY vol. II, whence in JOHNSON'; the noun *bludgeon* (1730) opens with a reference to Bailey's *Dictionarium Britannicum* of 1730; for the adjective *allegretto* (1740), we merely find a reference to Grassineau's *Musical Dictionary* of that year; for *anagnorisis* (1800), meaning 'recognition; the *dénouement* in a drama', the first illustration reads '*a*1800 BLAIR is cited in WEBSTER'; and *Achilles' tendon*, again, only reads '**1900** DORLAND *Med. Dict.* 674/2'. None of these words were therefore in general use at the time; *adjudicate* does not even have any actual illustrations. *Bludgeon* was not in general use until 1755, in a quotation from the *Gentleman's Magazine*; *allegretto* is only first attested in 1817 in an unfinished novel by Jane Austen; while *anagnorisis* does not have a proper quotation until

1833. For other words, no more than a single illustration is provided, which begs the question of whether they were ever part of the English language. Examples are *Bar* (1720) in the sense of 'baronet'; *amobrage* (1750), defined as 'the payment or proceeds of the Amober', a 'technical term in the Welsh Laws for the "maiden-fee" formerly payable to a lord on the marriage of a maid of his manor' (s.v. *amober*, 1727, with a single quotation only); *adamically* (1860), 'in an Adamical manner; nakedly'; *aculeation* (1870), 'the state of being sharpened or pointed'; *acheless* (1880), 'without ache or throb'; and *academicalism* (1890), 'Academical style (in a derogatory sense)'. The *OED* is under large-scale revision, and as this process started with the letter *M* and has at the point of writing this progressed to *ramvert*, it may take a while yet before the letters *A* and *B* are reached (see also Chapter 3, Research Question 9). (Current editorial policy, however, is that revisions of so-called 'high-priority words' are now also added elsewhere in the dictionary.)

For all that, it seems unlikely that later additions for the words discussed here (*Bar, amobrage, adamically, aculeation, acheless, academicalism*) will be found, as none occur in the BNC, which is more than five times the estimated size of the entire *OED*. While these words were thus apparently short-lived members of the English lexicon, others can be called 'nonce-words', words that are used only on specific occasions or in specific texts (*OED*, s.v. *nonce* C1b). One such example is the word *accommodableness* (1760), which is illustrated in the *OED* with: 'CATH. TALBOT *Ess.* iii. Wks. 1809, 83 Let me be allowed to make a new word, and let that word be accommodableness'. It is doubtful whether words like these should have been included in the *OED*. Interestingly, under the entry for *nonce*, sense C1b, the *OED* reads that *nonce-word* is 'one of a number of terms coined by James Murray especially for use in the *N.E.D.*', the original title of the dictionary (*New English Dictionary*). There may not be many words like these, but their presence inflates the data presented in Figure 4.1, as does that of the other words discussed here.

The lists of first words collected, however, also reflect recent developments at the time, such as:

- technical innovations (*air-tight* in 1728, with *airtightly* only in 1800; *bathroom*, 1780; *actinograph* in 1840, 'An instrument, invented by Sir J. Herschel in 1838, for recording the variations in the power of the solar rays')
- social and political developments, such as the abolition of slavery (the specific sense of *abolition* with reference to the slave trade dates from 1788 and the word *abolitionist* from 1790)

- and contact with other cultures due to increased travel and colonialism (*anarchic*, with a first quotation from Burke's *French Revolution* of 1790 referring to 'the barbarous anarchick despotism of Turkey'; Sanskrit *amrita*, first used in 1810 in the sense 'immortal, ambrosial' by the poet Robert Southey; *abattoir*, 1820, first recorded in 'M. STARKE *Trav. on Continent*'; *acclimatization*, 1830, 'The process of acclimatizing, or of being acclimatized, or habituated to a new climate'; *abalone*, 1850, a type of shell 'found clinging to the sides of rocks').

There are new words, such as *adrip* ('Oars adrip with silver foam', 1881) and *adream* ('I lie a-dream', 1854), that have a particular poetical ring about them, but neither of these stayed in the language for very long. The word *abattoir*, with sixty-six instances in the BNC, did become fully integrated into the English lexicon since its arrival in 1820, and the lists of firsts contain many other words that are now in everyday use: *amount* (1710), *athletically* (1750), *average* (1770), *adaptable* (1800), *accessibility* (1810), *anonymity* (1820). It is almost strange to realise that these words are only recent additions to the lexicon, and the word *bathroom*, discussed above, is another case in point.

4.2 The *OED* as a database

Görlach (2001: 145) attributes the difference in vocabulary growth between the eighteenth and nineteenth centuries to the possibility that the eighteenth century may not have been studied as thoroughly as the period after that. However, there seems to be a different explanation for this. Osselton, in his review of the second edition of the *OED* which was published, still in the form of a book, in 1989, notes a dual focus of the dictionary: an historical one and one that offers an inventory of words contemporary with the dictionary's editors. 'Editors of historical dictionaries,' Osselton (1993: 129) writes, 'are human: they find the language of their own age the most interesting (and certainly the best documented) and therefore tend to provide a cluster of quotations from their own time.' The eighteenth century, therefore, is not so much under-documented, as Görlach suggests, but rather the nineteenth century has been over-documented. This is confirmed by Mair (2006: 226), who calculated that the amount of text included in the *OED* for the eighteenth century is around three million words, whereas for the nineteenth century it is eight million words – almost three times as many – and for the twentieth century five million words. The smaller number of words for the twentieth century would agree with the dip in Figure 4.1 for the first year of the new decade of the twentieth century.

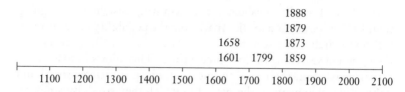

Figure 4.2. Date chart for *idyl* (sense 1) in the *OED*.

If the data in Figure 4.1 were to be normalised to eight million words, the resulting figure would look very different indeed.[2]

The *OED* is a magnificent instrument for the purpose of studying the language of the LModE period, particularly since it is available as an online database which allows full-text searches as well as searches by date of occurrence, such as those reported on here (Simple Search option).[3] These searches at the same time bring to light some of the major shortcomings of the *OED*, of which the most relevant one for our purposes is that frequency of information should be interpreted with care due to the fact that different amounts of material are included for the eighteenth and the nineteenth centuries. This makes comparisons hazardous to say the least. The *OED* contains another feature that should be consulted carefully, i.e. the 'Date chart', which lists the number of illustrations for each word or for different senses per century. The information may be misleading, as with the first sense of the word *idyl*, 'a short poem, descriptive of some picturesque scene or incident, chiefly in rustic life'. The date chart for this word, reproduced as Figure 4.2, suggests that the word was less common in the eighteenth century and that its frequency increased significantly in the century following.

In the light of the original intention of the *OED* editors to illustrate usage with one or at most two quotations per century, the imbalance in the number of illustrations may reflect no more than what Osselton (1993: 130) calls an understandable 'desire not to throw good material away'. In this light, the date chart offers more useful information for those involved in the revision process of the *OED* than for the everyday user of the dictionary: additional eighteenth-century examples must evidently be looked for. The absence of quotations for the twentieth century is due to the fact that the *OED* is primarily a nineteenth-century product: it was published between 1884 and 1928. Since then, two Supplements were produced, which were incorporated into the second edition of the dictionary (1989). The current revision process aims at making the *OED* fully up to date.

In what follows, I will show the potential of using the *OED* for doing research on LModE vocabulary and acquiring insight into ongoing linguistic processes as a result. Apart from the possibility of performing full-text searches and searches by 'first cited date', the *OED* also offers the option of searching by 'first cited author'. This allows us to focus on actual people and their lexicon, much of which illustrates social and cultural developments of the period in which they lived. By studying the language of the group of scientists who formed the so-called 'Lunar Society', it will, for instance, be possible to gain insight into developments in the language of science and technology. And as dictionary makers like Dr Johnson, Noah Webster and Sir James Murray were first and foremost language users, too, I will also discuss their use of vocabulary here.

4.3 First users in the *OED*

Searching the *OED* for 'first cited authors' would obviously only provide data for those LModE people who were literate enough 'to have a chance of being printed' (Fairman 2003: 265). Doing so nevertheless allows us to gain access to the language of actual people. I adopted this approach for Chapter 9 of *The Oxford History of English* (Mugglestone 2006), collecting information for the twenty or so people that formed the backbone of this chapter on eighteenth-century English. Not all people dealt with in the chapter occurred in the *OED* as first users of words but, interestingly, the majority did, and the results are the following: Samuel Richardson (245), Horace Walpole (214), Fanny Burney (160), Henry Fielding (108), Laurence Sterne (100), Samuel Johnson (72), John Gay (43), Lady Mary Wortley Montagu (35), Richard Sheridan (31), James Boswell (25), Benjamin Martin (18), Mrs Thrale (18), David Garrick (16), Robert Dodsley (8), Robert Lowth (8), Thomas Sheridan (8), Sarah Fielding (4) and Betsy Sheridan (4). The majority of these people, all five women and nine of the men, were writers; others, such as Martin (c.1705–82) and Lowth, were grammarians (though Martin was also a scientist), while Garrick (1717–79) was an actor and Dodsley a publisher. These figures may reflect no more than the interests of the voluntary readers who submitted quotations for the *OED*, as there was at the time no set reading programme for the collection of illustrations of words and their senses (Murray 1977; Schäfer 1980; Brewer 2007). This is why Shakespeare is the most frequently quoted author in the *OED*, with *Hamlet* being his most frequently cited play (*OED* website, 'Dictionary facts'). It should also be realised that the above authors may simply have done no more than record in their writings a word that was already in use in the spoken language, which seems to have been particularly the case with Fanny Burney and Jane Austen (see below). At the same time, both Richardson and Walpole (1717–97) are well known for their linguistic innovations (Keast 1957: 432; Beal 2004: 21), which is confirmed by the list, while it is interesting to see that Fanny Burney comes third. This reflects the results of the current revision programme of the *OED*, as in the first edition she was cited as a first user much less frequently. For the revised version of the *OED*, letters and journals were also used as evidence of usage, so Fanny Burney is now frequently cited, more so even than Jane Austen, and around 70 per cent of her first quoted instances are from her diaries and letters. Large parts of her journals are taken up by recorded conversations, which include the colloquial language of the time. Consequently, some of her quotations in the *OED* have a modern ring about them, and an example is the opening to the section called 'Mr Barlow's Proposal' in the *Norton Anthology of English Literature*, which reads:

(1) About 2 O'clock, while I was **dawdling** in the study, . . . we heard a **Rap** at the Door – & soon after, John came up, & said 'A gentleman is below, who asks for Miss Burney, – Mr. Barlow'. (1775; Troide et al. 1988–, Vol. II: 140)

Though the verb *to dawdle*, meaning 'to idle, waste time', was not new as such, Fanny Burney is quoted for 1768 as the first author to use this verb in a quasi-transitive sense while for the participial form *dawdling* two of the three illustrations are from Fanny Burney. The word *Rap* had already been in use for some time.

Most of the first usages in the list above reflect the nature of the author's interests, such as *Johnsonian* and *lexicographical*, which were first adopted by Boswell, Johnson's biographer (1791, when Boswell's *Life of Johnson* came out). Other examples are *geology* (1735) and *goniometer* (1766) for Martin who was first and foremost a scientist, *distichal* and *suffix* from Lowth's translation of *Isaiah* (1778) and *chanting* (1720) for the poet and playwright John Gay (1685–1732). There are many words that are now in common use, such as *dressing-gown* (Sheridan 1777), *heroism* (Lady Mary Wortley Montagu 1717), *lowbred* (Garrick 1757) and *ostensibly* (Walpole 1762). Vulgar or slang words were found to be much rarer: they are more frequently associated with the nineteenth century, as in the case of Thackeray, who made use of slang words to characterise upper-class speakers in his novels (see below). Foreign words are found with most of the authors, the result of their travels abroad. Examples are *accoucheur* (Sterne 1759), *casino* (Mrs Thrale 1789), *passé* (Fanny Burney 1775) and *poulard* (Fielding 1733). Richardson is the only exception: his list doesn't contain a single word to suggest an interest in foreign matters; and indeed, according to the *ODNB*, 'Richardson was one of the least travelled authors, who seldom ventured very far from London', that is, after he had moved there from Derbyshire as a child.

For the nineteenth century, I compiled a similar list, comprising authors most of whom, in one way or another, play a role in this book. The results are the following: Samuel Taylor Coleridge (638), Robert Southey (423), William Makepeace Thackeray (262), Charles Dickens (261), Percy Bysshe Shelley (151), Maria Edgeworth (108), Thomas Hardy (104), Elizabeth Gaskell (53), Jane Austen (51), Charlotte Brontë (47), George Eliot (31), Queen Victoria (13), Dorothy Wordsworth (12), Isabella Beeton (8), Emily Brontë (8), George Gissing (6), James Murray (5), William Wordsworth (4), Anne Brontë (3), Mary Shelley (3) and Lindley Murray (3). As above, the list, which consists of ten men and eleven women, includes mostly poets and novelists, but also an educationalist (Maria Edgeworth), a grammarian (Lindley Murray), a lexicographer (James Murray), the writer on household management and journalist Mrs Beeton, and Britain's longest reigning monarch, Queen Victoria (1819–1901). For reasons explained in Section 4.2, the figures are not quite comparable to those for the eighteenth century, but it is striking that the list is headed by the two major members of the Southey–Coleridge Circle, Coleridge (1772–1834) and Southey (1774–1843); possibly, they were read more by the *OED* volunteers because they stood out in the public eye due to their radical cultural and political ideas (Pratt and Denison 2000: 401–10). In this respect, it is striking that William Wordsworth (1770–1850), also a member of the Circle, occupies such a low position on the list. Possibly, this was because of the nature of his poetry, for Austin (1989: 16, 78) notes that the vocabulary of much of his verse is predominantly monosyllabic and characteristic of everyday usage, and she writes that 'amongst the forty-six most used words in *The Prelude* [1805] are *love* (used over one thousand times); *hope*; *pleasure*; *joy*; *fear*; *bliss*, and also *happy*' (Austin 1989: 86). None of these words were recent additions to the language. The first uses we do find in the *OED* for Wordsworth are *after-years*, *fieldward*, *monthling* and *pennied*, all of which are Anglo-Saxon in nature, though none survived into PDE.

Thackeray, according to Phillipps (1978: 129), was the first to use the word *loud* in the sense 'Vulgarly obtrusive, flashy':

(2) **1849** THACKERAY *Pendennis* xxxix, The shirts too 'loud' in pattern.

Phillipps describes him as having 'a keen eye for "what is what"' in society, which he attributes to the fact that he was a journalist. A similar social comment may be found in the word *snob*, which Thackeray was the first to use in the sense of 'one who meanly or vulgarly admires and seeks to imitate, or associate with, those of superior rank or wealth'. The illustration in the *OED* is from Thackeray's *Book of Snobs*, which was originally published in instalments in *Punch* during 1846–47, and which was subtitled 'by one of themselves'. It is indeed for the way in which he depicts – and criticises – mid-nineteenth-century society that novels like his *Vanity Fair* (1847–48) are appealing. Particularly striking in his list of firsts is the large French element in his lexicon, with words for food items, such as *bouillabaisse, écrevisse, entrecôte* and *Hollandaise* standing out in particular. *Hollandaise* refers to a type of sauce which was evidently not considered to be an elegant accompaniment in his day:

> (3) **1841** THACKERAY in *Fraser's Mag.* XXIII. 719/1 Turbot with lobster-sauce is too much; turbot *à la Hollandaise* vulgar.

Thackeray's interest in French culture and fashionable society was inspired by his visits to Paris while he studied mathematics and classics in Cambridge. French, according to Görlach (1999a: 108), enjoyed 'general prestige' at the time 'as the language of refinement' (see also Beal 2004: 26), and this is particularly evident in Thackeray's writings. In his published work, novels as well as journal articles, Thackeray was extremely knowledgable about current 'fashions in dress and items of adornment' (Phillipps 1978: 22), and in the list of first words we find fashionable French-derived words like *ceinture* and *ferronière*, a kind of head ornament, as in:

> (4) **1840** THACKERAY in *Fraser's Mag.* June 681/2 The sisters..with pink scarfs..and brass *ferronières*..were voted very charming.

According to Blake, 'Thackeray used slang in his novels to distinguish his characters', and it is the main instrument by which he 'is able to indulge in social comment and the ridiculing of affectation' (1981: 161–2). The following quotation from his novel *Pendennis* (1848–50) demonstrates that Thackeray had been responsible for coining the term *Oxbridge*:

> (5) **1849** THACKERAY *Pendennis* I. xxix. 286 'Rough and ready, your chum seems,' the Major said. 'Somewhat different from your dandy friends at **Oxbridge**.

Though he had left Cambridge without taking a degree, the university nevertheless features well in his novels. During his student days, he picked up enough university slang to be able to use it in his novels (Phillipps 1978: 72). One such word is *chum*, as in example (5), which may also be illustrated with a quotation from Southey from about twenty years earlier:

> (6) **1826** Southey *Vind. Eccles. Angl.* 502 The students were friends and **chums**, a word so nearly obsolete, that it may be proper, perhaps, to explain it, as meaning 'chamber-fellows'.

Chum, however, wasn't obsolete at all as Southey suggests here, and the *OED* cites a slightly older example by the writer Washington Irving (1783–1859), which confirms its status as a slang word with university students:

> (7) **1820** W. Irving *Sketch Bk.* II. 90 The parson had been a **chum** of his father's at Oxford.

Phillipps notes that there is much in Thackeray's novels in which he looks back to Jane Austen's time, and that his traditional use of vocabulary reflects this (1978: 43), but a search in the BNC suggests that this is not so for the word *chum*. In this context, it is striking that he occupies a much higher place in the list of first instances than Jane Austen. He is, moreover, quoted nearly three times as often in the *OED* (full text) as Jane Austen, though this may be due to the fact that in the first and second editions of the *OED* female novelists were generally underrepresented.[4]

Like Fanny Burney, Jane Austen has a reputation for representing the spoken language naturalistically in her novels, differentiating the language of her characters according to their age and social class (Phillipps 1970: 11–12). Evidence from her novels suggests, for instance, that the use of *please* as a courtesy marker, which first arose only in the course of the LModE period (Tieken-Boon van Ostade and Faya Cerqueiro 2007), originated in the language of servants, and that it subsequently spread upwards along the social scale. The following quotation is the first instance of *please* we found in the Chadwyck Healey Eighteenth-Century Fiction database:

> (8) **Please** Ma'am, Master wants to know why he be'nt to have his dinner (c.1805; Austen, *The Watsons*).

Jane Austen herself would have used older variants, such as *(be) please(d) to* or *if you please*, but the example suggests that she was familiar with servants using the form that has become the most generally used politeness marker in English. Other authors whose novels similarly contain relevant sociolinguistic material are Mary Brunton (1778–1818), Thomas Hardy and George Gissing (1857–1903).

Though Jane Austen is not quoted as often in the *OED* as would be expected in the light of her reputation, there are many first words to her name that are reminiscent of colloquial language: *coddle* 'to treat as an invalid in need of nourishing food and nursing' (1815); the noun *coze* 'a cosy, friendly talk' (1814); *itty* 'little . . . chiefly in reference to babies or small domestic animals' (1798); *to jib* 'of a horse or other animal in harness: to stop and refuse to go on' (1811); *midgety* or *nigetty* 'trifling or fussy' (1798); *raffish* 'disreputable, vulgar, low' (1801); *smarten* (1815); *sprawly* (1798); *steepish* (1814); and *tittupy* 'apt to tittup or tip up; unsteady, shaky' (1798). Not all of these were actual additions to the English language, but others, such as *to chaperon* (1796), *outsider* (1800), *spoilt* (1816), *sponge-cake* (1808) and *sympathizer* (1815), were. She was also the first to have recorded the words *baseball* and *door-bell*:

(9) *c*1815 JANE AUSTEN *Northang. Abb.* i. (1848) 3 It was not very wonderful that Catherine..should prefer cricket, **base ball**..to books

(10) *c*1815 JANE AUSTEN *Persuasion* (1833) II. ii. 330 Lady Russell could not hear the **door-bell**.

A *door-bell* must have been a new invention at the time, and so was the *bobbin-net* 'a kind of **machine**-made cotton net, originally imitating the lace made with bobbins on a pillow', one of the products of the Industrial Revolution:

(11) **1814** JANE AUSTEN *Let.* 22 Nov. (1952) 413 Mrs. Clement walks about in a new Black velvet Pelisse..& a white **Bobbin-net**-veil.

A large part of Jane Austen's list of first words are derivatives with the prefix *un-*, of which only *unmodernized* and *unpunctuality* gained any currency to the extent that they are still used today, as did *irrepressible*. We find the same phenomenon with earlier writers, for example, Richardson (17%), Fanny Burney (14%), Sterne and Walpole (10% each) (Tieken-Boon van Ostade 2006: 267). The prefix *un-* clearly was enormously productive at the time, as was the feminine suffix *-ess*, as in *artistess* (Walpole, 1773), *bankeress* (Thackeray, 1854) and *barristress* (anon. 1898).

If Jane Austen first recorded the *sponge-cake* in writing, and

Thackeray fashionable food items like *bouillabaisse* and the *entrocôte*, an important source of cooking terms in the *OED* was Mrs Beeton's *Book of Household Management* (1859–61). There are seven new words to her name all from this source, though some from a later edition of the book: *bifteck* (1861), *carotene* (1861), *croûte* (1906), *demi-glace* (1906), *marengo* (1861), *poacher* (1861) 'a vessel or pan for poaching eggs', and *sides to middle*, as in:

(12) **1861** Mrs. Beeton *Bk. Househ. Managem.* ii. 24 Sheets should be turned **'sides to middle'** before they are allowed to get very thin.

There are altogether 214 quotations in the *OED* from her work (full text). Mrs Beeton, however, was a journalist and as such not an original writer, for she plagiarised many earlier cookery books (Hughes 2005: 197–8, 206), including Hannah Glasse's *The Art of Cookery Made Plain and Easy* (1747). In retrospect it therefore only seems fitting that Hannah Glasse is quoted much more frequently as a source of quotations for the *OED*, so that we owe far more new words, mostly cookery terms, to her than to Mrs Beeton – for example, *bechamel* (1796), *blanquette* (1747), *currant jelly* (1747), *mint sauce* (1747), *mock turtle* (1767), *piccallilly* (1758) and *sauce-boat* (1747).

One of the people who occupies a very low place on the list of first usages by nineteenth-century writers is James Murray, the chief editor of the *OED* itself. The only words yielded by searching for him as first cited author are *anamorphose* (1876), *aphesis* (1880), *echoic* (1880), *pseudo-archaist* (1895) and *tailorless* (1876). However, as I discussed in Section 4.1, he was in the habit of coining terms for the *OED* himself, so there should be more words to his name, though perhaps not as first recorded instances. One such word is *arrival*, which is illustrated in the sense of 'one that arrives or has arrived' with:

(13) *Mod.* The new **arrival** is a little daughter.

As an illustration of a modern use of the indefinite article (sense 1c), the second edition of the *OED* also included

(14) *Mod.* . . . As fine **a** child as you will see.

Both quotations celebrate the fact that his wife had just given birth to a little girl (Murray 1977: 200–1). Without openly acknowledging this, the *OED* is thus also to some extent a private record of the Murray family.[5]

4.4 First usages by the 'Lunar Men'

Many of the new words in the *OED* from the LModE period reflect recent advances in technology, and some of the words already discussed in this respect are *air-tight, bathroom, actinograph, door-bell* and *bobbin-net*. To show the extent to which additions to the English lexicon can be attributed to individuals who were part of the developments in science and technology that contributed to the Industrial Revolution, I searched the *OED* for first occurrences linked to the names of the twelve men who formed the so-called 'Lunar Society'. The Lunar Men were a 'small informal bunch who ... [met] at each other's houses [in Birmingham] on the Monday nearest to the full moon, to have light to ride home (hence the name)' (Uglow 2002: xiii). Their names are Matthew Boulton (1728–1809), Erasmus Darwin (1731–1802), Thomas Day (1748–89), Richard Lovell Edgeworth (1744–1817), Samuel Galton (1753–1832), James Keir (1735–1820), Joseph Priestley, William Small (1734–75), James Watt (1736–1819), Josiah Wedgwood, John Whitehurst (1713–88) and William Withering (1741–99). The *ODNB* lists their professions as 'manufacturer and entrepreneur' (Boulton), 'physician and natural philosopher' (Darwin), 'author and political campaigner' (Day), 'educational writer and engineer' (Lovell Edgeworth), 'chemist and industrialist' (Keir), 'theologian and natural philosopher' (Priestley), 'physician and natural philosopher' (Small), 'engineer and scientist' (Watt), 'master potter' (Wedgwood), 'physician and botanist' (Withering) and 'maker of clocks and scientific instruments, and geologist' (Whitehurst), so between them they represent a wide variety of sciences and disciplines. Only Galton does not appear in the *ODNB*, but he was an arms manufacturer and a Quaker (Wikipedia). One would expect these men to have left their mark on the English language with terms for the new inventions or innovations they brought about, particularly the core members of the group, Darwin, Boulton, Watt, Wedgwood and Priestley (Uglow 2002: xiv). The results of my searches were, however, disappointing: no first usages were found for Boulton, Day, Small or Watt, and possibly only one each for Galton and Whitehurst, while only the word *overstimulated* is first attested for Edgeworth. The first quotation for this word derives from the book *Practical Education* (1798) which Edgeworth had written together with his daughter Maria Edgeworth, who was also an educationalist and who is represented as a first user of words in the *OED* much more frequently than her father (see Section 4.3). Three first words were found for Keir, *perlated, porphyrization* and *unsolubility*, all in dictionaries of chemistry and hence not in daily use (compare Section 4.2). Only Darwin (64),

Withering (48), Wedgwood (21) and Priestley (15) are represented as
first users of new words in any numbers.

The first words attributed to Darwin are a somewhat curious mixture
of technical words, such as *to aerate* 'to oxygenate (blood or haemo-
lymph)' (1794), *carbonic* (1791), *hydrogen* (1791), *odorosity* and *saporosity*
(1794) and *subaquatic* (1789), and poetical words like *to car* 'place or carry
in a car' (1791), *haloed* (1791), *to lantern* (1789), *pansied* (1789) and *tintless*
(1789). The majority of the words in the latter category derive from his
didactic poem *The Loves of Plants*, first published in 1789 and reissued as
part of *The Botanic Garden* in 1791. The following quotation illustrates the
nature of the text and Darwin's didactic approach to science:

(15)   HENCE orient NITRE owes it's sparkling birth,
       And with prismatic crystals gems the earth,
       O'er tottering domes in filmy foliage crawls,
       Or frosts with branching plumes the mouldering walls.
                                     (*The Botanic Garden* 1791: 143–6)

The work is heavily annotated and the notes to this passage contain a
reference to his fellow Lunarian Joseph Priestley: 'Dr. Priestley discovered that nitrous air or gas which he obtained by dissolving metals in
nitrous acid, would combine rapidly with vital air, and produce with
it a true nitrous acid.' This same note contains the first quotation in
the *OED* for the word *azote*, 'the name given by Lavoisier . . . to the
gas now known as *nitrogen*' (1791). Whenever the *OED* refers to *The
Botanic Garden* for illustrations of more technical words, the quotations
derive from the annotations of the verse text. Darwin had also studied
medicine, and one of his other publications is *Zoonomia, or the Laws of
Organic Life* (1794–96). This work is frequently quoted by the *OED* for
first attestations of medical terminology, such as *exacerbescence, inexer-
tion, retropulsion* and *tonsillitis*. Some of Darwin's first words are mere
anglicisations of Latin terminology, such as *corol* (1791), which the *OED*
not very helpfully defines as 'Anglicized form of COROLLA', *glume* (1789),
for which earlier quotations had used *gluma*, and *moonleted* 'crescent-
shaped, lunate':

(16)   **1787** E. DARWIN tr. Linnaeus *Families of Plants* 385 *Isopyrum*...Capsules
       many, moonletted [L. *lunulatae*], recurved, one-cell'd.

Example (16) was taken from Darwin's translation of Linnaeus's *Families
of Plants*, but the list of firsts also contains a term from this text which
shows that Darwin adopted native plant names:

(17) **1787** E. Darwin tr. Linnaeus *Families of Plants* I. 182 *Selinum*...Milk Parsley.

Darwin's texts proved a good source of illustration for Webster's dictionary, for the *OED* reports that several first uses of words (for example, *to hibernate* and the noun *incitant*) were 'cited in Webster (1828)' (cf. Section 4.2). Also the rare word *ulcuscle*, 'a small ulcer' (1794), found its way into Webster's dictionary in 1847.

Withering's first words in the *OED* mostly derive from two sources, his *Botanical Arrangement of All the Vegetables Naturally Growing in Great Britain* (1776) and its third edition, *An Arrangement of British Plants* (1796). In this light, it is not surprising that the majority of the words can be divided into two categories, plant names (for example, *catchweed, cop-rose, fair-maid, hemp-nettle* and *pipewort*) and descriptive adjectives to classify them, such as *awned, club-shaped, midribbed, oak-leaved, salmon-coloured* and *umbrella-like*. But he is also credited with the introduction of the word *habitat* into English, though his definition in (18) suggests that the word was already in 'general' use.

(18) **1796** Withering *Brit. Plants* Dict. Terms (ed. 3) 62 *Habitatio*, the natural place of growth of a plant in its wild state. This is now generally expressed by the word **Habitat**.

There is also the word *herbarium*, which Withering adopted directly from Linnaeus:

(19) **1751** Linnaeus *Philos. Botan.*, **Herbarium** præstat omni iconi, necessarium omni Botanico.] **1776** Withering *Brit. Plants* (1796) I. 35 An Approved Method of Preparing Plants for an **Herbarium**.

Wedgwood's first words likewise primarily derive from two sources, the *Philosophical Transactions of the Royal Society* and his letters. The former are of a more technical nature (*apyrous, carbure, causticate, molybdenic* and *semi-vitreous*), all of which relate to his profession as a potter. Many of the latter were in more general use, such as *peg leg* (1769) 'an artificial leg, *esp.* a wooden leg' and *post time* (1772) 'the time at which mail is delivered or collected', though other words reflect the fact that he was a businessman: *order book* (1771), *stealage* (1769) 'losses due to stealing' and *unpacker*:

(20) **1768** J. Wedgwood *Let.* 13 June (1965) 64 He writes a good Hand, and will be more useful in that Respect than as an **unpacker**.

As a maker of fashionable pottery, Wedgwood is credited with a number of inventions in the *OED*, for example, *tableware*, according to the second illustration of the word in the *OED*:

> (21)   **1832** G. R. PORTER *Porcelain & Gl.* 16 The principal inventions of Mr. Wedgwood were 1. **His table ware**.

The first recorded instance of *tableware* dates from sixty years earlier, and first occurred in his own correspondence. *Staffordshire* in the sense of 'a service of Staffordshire ware', was first used by Wedgwood in 1765, and *rosso antico* is defined by the *OED* as 'The name given by Josiah Wedgwood (see WEDGWOOD) to the red stoneware produced at his Staffordshire factories'. Wedgwood is also the only one among the people discussed in this chapter who has an entry in the *OED* for his name:

> **1.a.** Used *attrib.* to designate the pottery made by Josiah Wedgwood (1730–95) and his successors at Etruria, Staffs. The best-known kinds are vases, plaques, medallions, etc., of fine clay lightly glazed, with classical designs in white relief on a blue or black ground. Sometimes spelt with lower-case initial. Now a proprietary name both in the U.K. (since 1876) and the U.S. (since 1906).

As the first quotation from 1787 shows, by the late 1780s 'Wedgwood' had already become an eponym, a word which the *OED* defines as 'a proper name used generically'. *Eponym* was first used in this sense in 1885, which confirms the fact, noted by Beal (2004: 27), that this is 'a method of word-formation which becomes prominent in the nineteenth century'. Contrary to expectations, however, James Watt does not have an entry in the *OED*, though the first cited instance for *watt*, from over sixty years after his death, does give credit to his name:

> **1882** SIEMENS in *Rep. Brit. Assoc.*, Presid. Addr. 6 The other unit I would suggest adding to the list is that of power. The power conveyed by a current of an Ampère through the difference of potential of a Volt is the unit consistent with the practical system. **It might be appropriately called a Watt, in honour of..James Watt**... A Watt, then, expresses the rate of an Ampère multiplied by a Volt, whilst a horsepower is 746 Watts, and a Cheval de Vapeur 735.

The last of the Lunar Men with any number of first words to his name is Priestley. Apart from a few words which occur in a religious context (*bonzery* 'a Buddhist monastery', *necessarian* 'a believer in necessity' and *vineity* 'vinous quality or property'), all his first words reflect his interest in physics: *alkalinity* (1788), *carbon* (1789), *causticity* (1772), *insulating* (1767) and *insulation* (1767), and *spirit lamp* (1767). Priestley's name has gone down into history as the man who isolated oxygen (Uglow 2003: 230), or 'dephlogisticated air', as he called it. The modifier *dephlogisticated* is indeed provided with a first instance from his work:

(22) **1775** Priestley in *Phil. Trans.* LXV. 387 This species may not improperly be called, *dephlogisticated air.*

The same applies to the related words *antiphlogistian* (1788), *phlogisticate* (1776), *phlogisticated* (1774) and *phlogistication* (1774). The word *phlogiston* is defined by the *OED* as 'a hypothetical substance', which is labelled as 'Now *hist.*', and under *oxygen*, first attested in 1788, the *OED* reads: 'Priestley, who isolated oxygen in 1774, held it to be air deprived of phlogiston, and called it *dephlogisticated air*'.

Both Wedgwood and Priestley, but also Watt, gave their names to science, and because of this they made their way into the *OED*. But so did Benjamin Franklin (1706–90), who is characterised in the *ODNB* as a 'natural philosopher, writer, and revolutionary politician in America'. He is commemorated in the *OED* in the word *Franklinian* (1767), first used by Priestley, who was an admirer of his. The *OED* also records the derivatives '**Fran'klinic** *a.* [see -IC], an epithet applied to electricity excited by friction; '**Franklinism** [see -ISM], frictional electricity; '**Franklinist** [see -IST], one who follows Franklin in his theory of electricity', with a first instance again being cited from the work of Priestley.

4.5 The language of dictionary makers

On the face of it, searching for words first attributed to Noah Webster produced the largest number of instances so far, 1078 (note, though, that this figure includes quotations from other Websters, such as the seventeenth-century playwright John Webster). However, on closer inspection it turns out that these instances rarely refer to his own usage. An exception is the first quotation for *aspergill* (1864) which is defined as an 'Anglicized form of Aspergillum', a 'kind of brush used to sprinkle holy water' used in the Roman Catholic Church. Most first instances refer to Webster's dictionaries, *A Compendious Dictionary of the English Language* (1806), *An American Dictionary of the English Language* (1828, 1832 and later revised editions), *Webster's International Dictionary*, *Webster's New International Dictionary* and the *New International Dictionary of the English Language*. The latter dictionaries were produced long after his death in

1843, and, as the preface to my own copy of *Webster's Universal Dictionary* (1970) records, the presence of his name in the title is no more than a tribute to the fact that 'the great American dictionary compiler has provided a major basis of lexicography in the English language'. It is therefore impossible to use the information provided by the *OED* as evidence of his contributions to the English language or of his own usage for that matter. If first instances – and at times even only instances, such as *aggrandizable* which is illustrated only with '**1864** in WEBSTER' – are attested from dictionaries (for example, *parodic* and *palaeologist*, both of which are also illustrated with present-day examples), this hardly serves to illustrate actual usage (see Section 4.2), as it is the purpose of dictionaries to record usage rather than, as seems to be the case here, to introduce new words.

The presence of Webster in the *OED* clearly presents a problem, but so does Murray, though it is a problem of a different nature. Of the handful of first words to his name (see Section 4.3), only *tailorless* (1876) reflects everyday usage, and it occurs in a letter quoted in his granddaughter's biography of him:

(23) **1876** J. A. H. MURRAY *Let.* in K. H. E. Murray *Caught in the Web of Words* (1977) x. 192 We are not quite *tailorless* and so not obliged to go *trouserless*.

The same quotation might have served as evidence for the word *trouserless*, which, however, does not have an entry in the dictionary. The reason for this can't have been lack of illustrations, for a full-text search of the *OED* produced various instances from before Murray's death in 1915. In addition to the five words attributed to Murray there must be more of them, though they occur without his name attached to them; I've already referred to the words deliberately created by Murray as well as the illustrations for the words *arrival* and *a*, which were merely marked as 'Mod.' (on the oddity of this label, see Brewer 2007: 224–5). Murray's presence in the *OED* is therefore primarily professional, making up for a lack of illustrations, and this is why he decided not to grace them with his own name.

Murray finds himself in good company, for one of his major predecessors as a lexicographer, Samuel Johnson, likewise occupies a strange position in the *OED* – as he did in his own *Dictionary of the English Language* (1755). To start with the *OED*, with seventy-two first words, and given his status as a literary writer, he seems rather underrepresented in the *OED*. As with Webster, for many of his first words evidence is cited from the *Dictionary*, such as *adjunctive* and *mouldily*:

(24) **1755** JOHNSON, *Adjunctive*, 1. He that joins. 2. That which is joined.

(25) **1755** JOHNSON *Dict. Eng. Lang.*, *Mustily*,..mouldily.

But Johnson, like Wedgwood (compare Section 4.4), also makes his appearance in the definitions of words, as a Simple Search ('definition') for his name shows (270 hits at the time of searching). See, for instance, the definition of the word *aleconner*:

> An examiner or inspector of ale: 'An officer appointed in every court-leet, and sworn to look to the assize and goodness of bread, ale, and beer, sold within the jurisdiction of the leet.' Phillips 1706. 'Four of them are chosen annually by the common-hall of the city; and whatever might be their use formerly, their places are now regarded only as sinecures for decayed citizens.' **Johnson** 1755. Still a titular office in some burghs.

And also that for the verb *to group*:

> **1.a.** *trans.* To make a group of, to form into a group; to place in a group *with* (something). Also *to group together*.
> **Johnson** 1755 gives the sense 'to put into a croud, to huddle together'. This meaning, if it existed, is now obs.; cf. GROUP *n.* 2.

As the illustration of the word *aleconner* shows, Johnson isn't alone in being referred to like this in the *OED*: see, for instance, the following illustration for the third sense of the noun *berth*:

> **3.** Hence, 'A convenient place to moor a ship in' (Phillips); the place where a ship lies when at anchor or at a wharf.
>
> **1706** PHILLIPS, *Birth* and *Berth* [see above]. **1731** BAILEY, *Birth* and *Berth* [as in Phillips].

Edward Phillips (1630–c.1796) was likewise a lexicographer, and the year 1706 refers to the sixth edition of his *New World of Words: Or, Universal English Dictionary* (1658). An even more useful resource for the compilers of the *OED* were Nathan Bailey's dictionaries of 1721 and 1730. Bailey and Johnson were frequently resorted to for definitions of words, as in the case of *apotheosis*:

> [a. L. *apotheōsis* (Tertull.), a. Gr. ἀποθέωσις, n. of action f. ἀποθεό_ειν to deify, f. ἀπό off, (in comb.) completely + θεό_ειν – to make a god of, f. θεός god. The great majority of orthoepists, from **Bailey** and

Johnson downward, give the first pronunciation, but the second is now more usual.]

As for Johnson's own *Dictionary*, he is frequently cited as having based it on illustrations which he obtained from 'the wells of English undefiled' (1755: C1^r), the period before the Restoration (1660) which for him represented the golden age of the English language. One of the innovations in Johnson's dictionary was the use of quotations to illustrate the meanings of the words (Sledd and Kolb 1955: 41), which later similarly became one of the main features of the *OED*. Johnson, however, specified that he would 'admit no testimony of living authours', the reason being that he did not want to be accused of partiality by including some writers but not others, and he adds:

> nor have I departed from this resolution, but when some performance of uncommon excellence excited my veneration, when my memory supplied me, from late books, with an example that was wanting, or when my heart, in the tenderness of friendship, solicited admission for a favourite name. (1755: B2^v)

It turns out that he did not quite stick to this resolution and that there are two people in particular whose performance Johnson apparently considered to be of such 'uncommon excellence' that he included quotations from their work in his *Dictionary*. Keast (1957) discovered that there are many contemporary quotations in the dictionary which derive from Richardson – three from *Pamela* and as many as ninety-six from *Clarissa* – as well as over fifty from his own writings! The words he adopted from *Clarissa* are not, however, from the novel itself but from an 'ample Collection . . . of Moral and Instructive Sentiments' which Richardson had attached to the third and fourth editions of the novel, published simultaneously in 1751. This list came in very handy 'to the harrassed lexicographer', as Keast (1957: 439) notes, for 'it offered a concentrated set of ready-made illustrations' for the dictionary.

4.6 Concluding remarks

As I mentioned, Richardson was evidently an innovator in his use of vocabulary, which is confirmed by the data presented in Section 4.3. Johnson, by contrast, was rather conservative in his usage (compare Tieken-Boon van Ostade 1991a), and Beal (2004: 20) notes that he 'was an important conservative influence in the mid-eighteenth century'. As we will see in Chapter 6, this is evident from the people whose language was directly influenced by him, but according to Beal Johnson's conservativeness is particularly clear in his dictionary, and, as the *Dictionary* was extremely authoritative, she argues that this is one of the main reasons there were so few new words in the language at the time. She also argues that during much of the eighteenth century there had been less need to expand the English lexicon (Beal 2004: 17), in contrast to the Early Modern English (EModE) period, when English was in the process of taking over from Latin as the language of scholarship. This goes some way towards explaining the 'trough' as she calls it in the development of the English lexicon after 1500, though I have argued in Section 4.1 that other reasons need to be reckoned with as well. The results of the Industrial Revolution and other developments during the LModE period already begin to show in the data presented in Table 4.1; these data do not, however, confirm Beal's 'peak of lexical innovation' for the decades 1830 to 1850 (2004: 21), which in my figures are part of a more general process of lexical increase.

As I have demonstrated above, many of the new additions to the English lexicon reflect current societal and technological developments. In particular, the increase in terminology for the latter, according to Beal, led to similar comments as those found during the EModE period, when writers complained of the use of inkhorn terms; Beal (2004: 24) quotes the poet William Barnes (1801–86), 'a staunch advocate of dialect', saying that 'the Latinish and Greekish wording is a hindrance to the teaching of the homely poor, or at least the landfolk'. Fairman, writing more recently, would indeed agree with him (see Chapter 2).

The quotation from Barnes dates from 1878, and it supplies a post-dating for the *OED* for the use of the word *landfolk*, the last quotation for which dates from 1865. In the present chapter I have dealt with lexical innovations, and with ways in which it is possible to study an individual author's contribution to the LModE lexicon. Words also disappeared from the language, and *landfolk* is a case in point: it no longer occurs in the BNC, so Barnes may have been among the last to use this word. There are many other words first found in the LModE period which disappeared again soon afterwards. The many words with the feminine suffix *-ess* illustrate this, as we now no longer refer to female artists, barristers or professors like that. One way to study this development systematically would be by performing Simple Searches in the 'definitions' area for 'not now' or 'now obsolete'/'now obs.'. These searches produced 84 and 37 + 122 items at the time of writing this chapter, such as *monoculus*, for which the *OED* notes that 'The genus name was published by Linnaeus in *Systema Naturæ* (ed. 10, 1758) I. 634, but it is **not now** in use' and the meaning '†2. A child's plaything or toy. (**Now obs.**, except as . . .' for *bauble*, the last quotation for which is from Southey (1814). Using these search terms also provides insight into developments of meanings that particular words underwent in the course of the LModE period. One example is the word *bitch*, in the sense 'applied opprobriously to a woman; strictly, a lewd or sensual woman', which is said to be '**Not now** in decent use'. In all this, however, one would have to reckon with the different meanings that might be implied by the use of the word 'now': for as long as the *OED* is in the process of revision, it is important to keep track of where in the *OED* the data comes from, before or after the letter M, which applies to any evidence derived from the current online version of the *OED*.

Further reading

The following chapters or sections deal with LModE vocabulary: Bailey (1996: 139–214), Beal (2004: 14–65), Görlach (2001: 136–94) and (1999a: 92–138). In addition, see *CHEL* Vol. III Chapter 5 (Nevalainen 1999) and Vol. IV Chapter 2 (Algeo 1998).

Much has been written on the *OED*, and many studies might be recommended, such as Sir James Murray's biography (Murray 1977), as well as studies of the *OED* proper: Schäfer (1980), Willinski (1994), Mugglestone (2003) and (2005) and, most recently, Brewer (2007) as well as her website *Examining the OED* (Weblinks).

Research questions

1. Study the date charts for any words of your own choosing, and compare your results with those found for *idyl* discussed above. What recommendations would you like to make to the *OED* editors?

2. Do a 'first cited author' search in the *OED* for any author other than the ones discussed here and describe your findings from the perspective of their personal background or interests (study their biographies in the *ODNB*).

3. Check the number of quotations from different LModE female writers (Fanny Burney, Mrs Thrale, Mary Brunton, Jane Austen, George Eliot or others) in the *OED* Online using 'first cited author'. Compare your results with full-text searches for these authors. On female writers in the *OED*, see *Examining the OED* (Weblinks), 'Top female sources' and 'More female sources'.

4. Do a full-text search in the *OED* for the word *chum*. Analyse the information retrieved along the lines discussed in Section 4.3. Also check the word's present-day currency in the BNC.

5. Do an advanced search in the *OED* for the suffixes *un-* and *-ess*,

combined with any of the authors discussed (or any other author of your own choosing), and analyse the results. Any first or only usages? How current are the words today?

6. Carry out a full-text search in ECCO for any of the new words discussed in this chapter to test their currency at the time. What about the nature of the texts in which the words occur?

7. Check all the eighteenth-century words discussed here as well as in the eighteenth-century chapter in Mugglestone (2006) against contemporary dictionaries in ECCO, e.g. Martin (1749), Johnson (2nd edn 1755–56). Any differences in later editions?

8. Analyse the first usages of the authors mentioned above (or any others, such as Captain James Cook), and classify them according to the nature of the English lexicon as outlined by Murray in his introduction to the *OED*.

9. Do a Full-Text Search for any of the Lunar Men in the *OED* and compare the results. What do the results tell us about the nature of the source material used for the *OED*?

10. Do a Simple Search ('definitions') in the *OED* for the members of the Lunar Society. Any results?

Notes

1. According to the website of the *OED* Online ('Dictionary facts'), the dictionary contains 1,861,200 citations. At approximately ten words per citation, this would amount to around 18.5 million words.

2. In the course of the ongoing revision process, defects such as these are currently being addressed by the *OED* editors. For details, see Chapter 8 of Brewer (2007).

3. Brewer (2007) notes that the *OED* Online is available in most UK public libraries. Elsewhere, availability is mostly through subscription only.

4. For a discussion of the gender bias of the *OED*, see Willinsky (1994). That Fanny Burney now occupies a third position in the above list of first users for the eighteenth century indicates that in the current revision process of the *OED* this gender bias is being corrected; see, however, *Examining the OED* (Weblinks).

5. In the revision process of the *OED*, example (14) has unfortunately been omitted.

5 Grammar and grammars

5.1 Introduction

Chapter 5 of *The Language of Thackeray* opens with the words that there is 'little difference between Thackeray's grammatical usage and our own, and a full-length study of his grammar would be unprofitable' (Phillipps 1978: 115). Yet it continues with twelve pages of grammatical features that attracted Phillipps's comment, such as the lack of *do* in negative sentences and questions, the 'curious' use of *shall* to express hypothetical situations, the fact that 'the subjunctive mood is used more frequently than today', that comparatives and superlatives of adjectives with more than one syllable had *-er* and *-est* rather than *more* and *most*, and the occurrence of 'odd formations' such as *sweeperess* and *bankeress* (compare Section 4.3). In Jane Austen's case, apart from dealing with her language, Phillipps (1970) also analysed her attitudes to grammar. While her own use of grammar, he notes, is of a high standard – so much so that, 'when minor solecisms crept in, she often corrected these in later editions' of her novels (1970: 13) – Jane Austen made use of grammatical variation as an instrument by which to characterise her protagonists, much as Dickens was to do after her (Brook 1970: Appendix). 'To be blatantly ungrammatical in the novels,' Phillipps concludes (1970: 145), 'is to be ungenteel.' Some examples are the use of past participle forms for past tenses, as in:

> (1) I should have **gave** it all up in despair. (1811, *Sense and Sensibility*; Phillipps 1970: 147)

Lucy Steele, who utters these words, is here shown to be a 'vulgar' character, but servants were depicted similarly through their language use. Example (2), for instance, shows a lack of concord between subject and finite verb.

(2) The horses **was** just coming out. (1811, *Sense and Sensibility*; Phillipps
      1970: 158)

In Chapter 4, I discussed Jane Austen's skills in representing the language of people from different social backgrounds, and it is evident from
examples (1) and (2) that her abilities in this respect were not limited to
the use of vocabulary.

Baugh and Cable ([1951] 1993: 287–8) claim that the rise of the
passive progressive (*the house is being built*) was the only grammatical
innovation that took place during the LModE period. LModE grammar,
however, was far from fixed. This is evident from the study by Rydén and
Brorström (1987) of *be* or *have* with mutative intransitive verbs in eighteenth-century English, as in *your letter is arrived* vs. *your letter has arrived*.
My own analysis of periphrastic *do* in the eighteenth century similarly
shows a great deal of sociolinguistic and stylistic variation (Tieken-Boon
van Ostade 1987), and this continued during the nineteenth century.
Not only are there many major and minor grammatical differences –
both in terms of syntax and in morphology – between the language of
LModE speakers and those of today, we also see writers like Jane Austen,
Thackeray and Dickens exploiting these differences in ways that reflect
variation along sociolinguistically significant lines. Baugh and Cable
here refer to the grammatical *system* underlying the English language,
which was extended with a construction that had not previously been in
use (see further Section 6.4); at the level of *usage*, however, the language
continued to be variable and subject to change, and the fact that this variation was perceived to be of sociolinguistic significance long before the
rise of sociolinguistics as a discipline is of great interest.

Phillipps compares Jane Austen's grammar and her uses of it with
the views expressed by normative grammarians, Lowth and Murray
in particular. The rise of normative grammar occurred during the
eighteenth century (Baugh and Cable [1951] 1993: 252–81; Tieken-
Boon van Ostade 2008a), and normative attitudes to language grew
stronger with the enormous output of grammars of English, from the
1760s onwards. As explained in Chapter 1, the nineteenth century is
consequently associated with the notion of prescriptivism, according to
which a model of correct language use was imposed on speakers and
writers of English, so much so that, according to Beal (2004: 123), we
are now stuck with 'a legacy of "linguistic insecurity"' instead of what
writers like Jonathan Swift (1667–1745) had in mind at the beginning
of the LModE period, a language that could be 'Corrected, Improved
and Ascertained' or, indeed, fixed, that would no longer be subject to
variation.

Normative grammarians believed that there was only one form of correct English, and they argued their case by drawing on 'reason, etymology, and the example of Latin and Greek' (Baugh and Cable [1951] 1993: 275); Lowth's grammar (1762), which indeed proceeds along these lines, developed into one of the most authoritative English grammars of its time. One reason for its popularity was the way in which Lowth focussed on grammatical errors committed by what he called 'our best Authors'. This normative approach to grammar became very popular, and left its mark on many grammars after him. Murray's grammar, published more than thirty years later in 1795, is a good example of this, and many of his rules are straightforward copies from Lowth (Vorlat 1959), which was why it was criticised by Cobbett in his *Grammar of the English Language* (1818) (Aarts 1994: 324). Phillipps (1970: 173) refers to Murray when discussing Jane Austen's attitudes to grammar, but, as this grammar was published when she was already twenty, it would be more likely that she had learned English grammar from Lowth, either directly or indirectly, through *The Accidence; or First Rudiments of English Grammar* by Ellin Devis (1746–1820). Devis's grammar had first been published in 1775 as an introduction to Lowth, and it was the first to be aimed at women only (Percy 1994: 123). Jane Austen's education had been rather erratic (Nokes 1997: 79–86), and it seems likely that if she was taught any grammar, it would have been done at home by her mother rather than at school, as was becoming increasingly common (see Chapter 1). Given the period in which she lived, though, with its strong interest in linguistic prescriptivism, it may have been more the spirit of the age that influenced her writing than any particular grammar.

Görlach, in his introductions to eighteenth- and nineteenth-century English, complains of the lack of empirical research on LModE syntax (Görlach 2001: 106 and 1999a: 71). To make up for this, he resorts to the information provided by the grammars of the period, though he is aware of the complicated relationship between actual usage and grammatical description. Because of their prescriptive function, normative grammars would be unlikely to present accurate analyses of contemporary usage, and in any case it takes a while before new developments are reflected in a grammar. This was the case for the use periphrastic *do* in the eighteenth century (Tieken-Boon van Ostade 1987: 230), as well as for that of the subjunctive (Auer 2006). More research is, however, available on LModE than Görlach seemed to think, and one example is the analysis of the language of Captain James Cook by Percy (1996), which shows an increasing awareness of linguistic propriety in the journals of the voyages of discovery he made. This was not so much the result of any exposure to the grammars of the period but to a similar linguistic self-consciousness – both his own and that of the editor of his third journal, John Hawkesworth (c. 1720–73) – as with Jane Austen.

Increasingly, empirical studies on the grammar of LModE are published, as can be seen by the recent collection of papers, all corpus-based, by Kytö et al. (2006), and many more are expected to follow due to the current popularity of the period. Meanwhile, earlier studies of writers' idiolects, such as those by Phillipps (1970, 1978) and Brook (1970) on Jane Austen, Thackeray and Dickens, could be used to supplement the more empirical data that is in the process of being collected and analysed at present. While these studies are obviously not representative of general usage, they do show how variable the language was, and also to what extent literary authors were aware of the ways in which they could exploit this linguistic variability for the purpose of representing speech naturalistically (see also Chapter 2). This linguistic awareness may well be resorted to in order to acquire insight into the then current attitudes to language, and the information presented, though offering no more than laymen's views of the language, could usefully supplement that found in the grammars of the period.

With the LModE period being largely associated with linguistic prescriptivism, it is usually believed that the normative grammars had an enormous influence on the language. It is, for instance, generally assumed that the grammars were responsible for the disappearance of double negation from the language – from standard English that is, as the majority of English dialects today still contain this feature. The same applies to the double comparative and superlative constructions such as *more worser* (see, for example, Beal 2004: 88). But the actual influence of the grammars is frequently overrated: both double negation and the use of double comparison were already on the way out well before any strictures against their use appeared in the normative grammars. In some cases, such as the use of *shall* and *will*, it has been shown that 'seventeenth- and eighteenth-century prescriptions were largely complied with in the nineteenth century' (Facchinetti 2000: 130), and Adamson (2007) similarly shows that we owe the correlation between the pronouns *who* and *which* with the gender of the antecedent to the influence of the grammars of the period, but such influence was by no means universal. The split infinitive is a case in point. Arising in the nineteenth century, it developed into one of the greatest shibboleths in the English language (Beal 2004: 112), and yet its use today seems to be on the increase. During the late 1960s, Mittins et al. (1970) performed a large-scale acceptability test of a number of usage problems. Many of these features were first commented on in the normative grammars from the eighteenth century; despite a long tradition of adverse criticism, Mittins et al. nevertheless noted an increased acceptability for most of them over the years. Even if the normative grammars did not prove as successful as they are usually assumed to be, what they did bring about was an awareness of the need for grammatical correctness, a need which was felt most keenly by those eager to move up the social scale. To answer this need, there was an enormous increase in published grammars from the early 1760s onwards (Tieken-Boon van Ostade 2008a).

This chapter will deal with real usage as well as with the way in which novelists drew upon current linguistic variation to mark the language of their characters as typical of particular social classes. At the same time, it will go into the relationship between LModE grammarians' linguistic strictures and actual usage, and it will also discuss their influence, whether merely alleged or real, on the language of the period. The chapter will end by showing how dynamic research on LModE grammar currently is, providing us with an increasingly better view of the language of the period.

5.2 Sociolinguistic stereotypes and markers

In Chapter XVI of Thackeray's *Adventures of Philip on his Way through the World* (1862), the following comment may be found:

(3) 'Is that *him*?' said the lady **in questionable grammar**. (Phillipps 1978: 119)

What is questionable about the lady's grammar is that it would have been more correct if she had said 'Is that *he?*' instead. The prejudice against *it is me* is as old as the normative tradition in English grammar, and according to Leonard's (1929) glossary of items criticised by eighteenth-century grammarians it originates with Lowth. It is a good example of the kind of arguments adopted by the grammarians for or against a particular construction – here the application of analogy with Latin. 'The Verb *to Be* has always a Nominative Case after it,' Lowth wrote when advocating 'it was I' (1762: 105). The rule was copied verbatim by Murray (1795: 113), as a result of which it gained general currency, despite the fact that Leonard believed Lowth to have 'misinterpreted the trend in usage'. Though Mittins et al. note an acceptance rate of only 25 per cent of the construction, the use of *It is I/he/she/we/they* today would be considered stilted and unnatural, which reflects a considerable change in attitude towards this construction compared to that in Thackeray's time.

One of the features of non-standard grammar in Dickens's novels is double negation, which is very common with his lower-class characters.

With Jane Austen, its occurrence is likewise 'always a sign of vulgarity', as in the following sentence uttered by a waiter:

(4) No, ma'am, he did **not** mention **no** particular family. (1817; *Persuasion*; Phillipps 1970: 186)

Many scholars believe that the disappearance of double negation from standard English was due to the influence of the normative grammarians, but Nevalainen and Raumolin-Brunberg (2003: 71–2) have shown that double negation was already on the way out during the EModE period. The same is true for another 'double' construction, the use of double comparatives and superlatives, no longer in general use either when first condemned by the grammarians (González-Díaz 2008). Some interesting examples may be found in the following passages, which, like example (3), show through explicit linguistic comment that both features served as linguistic stereotypes at the time: both Dickens and Thackeray employed the double comparative as a means of 'conscious characterization of the speech of a particular group' (Wardhaugh 2006: 145):

(5) 'What do you think I see in this very arbour last night?' inquired the boy.

'Bless us! What?' exclaimed the old lady, alarmed at the solemn manner of the corpulent youth.

'The strange gentleman – him as had his arm hurt – a-kissin' and huggin' – '

'Who, Joe? None of the servants, I hope.'

'**Worser** than that,' roared the fat boy, in the old lady's ear.

'Not one of my grandda'aters?'

'**Worser** than that.'

'**Worse** than that, Joe!' said the old lady, **who had thought this the extreme limit of human atrocity**. 'Who was it, Joe? I insist upon knowing.' (1836–37; Dickens, *Pickwick Papers*)

(6) Miss Horrocks was installed as housekeeper at Queen's Crawley, and ruled all the domestics there with great majesty and rigour. All the servants were instructed to address her as 'Mum,' or 'Madam' – and there was one little maid, on her promotion, who persisted in calling her 'My Lady,' without any rebuke on the part of the housekeeper. 'There has been better ladies, and there has been **worser**, Hester,' was

Miss Horrocks' reply to this compliment of her inferior. (1847–48; Thackeray, *Vanity Fair*)

The reason why grammarians nevertheless discussed double negation and double comparison is the widespread use of these forms by non-standard speakers, such as servants and nannies, whose language, it was felt, might contaminate that of the children of socially aspiring families (Tieken-Boon van Ostade 2008b). Such double constructions were already employed as social stereotypes in the eighteenth century, for both Smollett and Fanny Burney used them in their novels to respresent the language of ungenteel characters such as the captain in example (7), the Welshman Mr Morgan in (8) and Madame Duval, Evelina's French aunt who causes her considerable social embarrassment throughout the novel, in (9):

(7) When I was about to perform the ceremony, the captain cried with some emotion, 'No, no, d–me! I'll have **no** profanation **neither** . . .' (1748; Smollett, *Roderick Random*)

(8) 'Cot is my Saviour, and witness too,' said Morgan, with great vehemence, 'that I am **more elder**, and therefore **more petter** by many years than you.' (1748; Smollett, *Roderick Random*)

(9) and a look of much discontent from Madame Duval, who said to me in a low voice, 'I'd as soon have seen Old Nick as that man, for he's the **most impertinentest** person in the world, and **isn't never** of my side.' (1778; Fanny Burney, *Evelina*)

Examples (5) and (6) illustrate other grammatical features that were considered characteristic of non-standard English at the time, such as past tense *I see* which in Jane Austen's novels is used only by servants (Phillipps 1970: 109), *him as had his arm hurt*, which is also characteristic of Jane Austen's 'vulgar' characters, and the lack of concord between verb and complement after existential *there* in *There has been better ladies*.

The features discussed here were all employed as sociolinguistic *stereotypes* by the authors discussed, which suggests that they must have been perceived as such at the time. Wardhaugh (2006: 145) also distinguishes sociolinguistic *markers*, features which are 'clearly related to social groupings and to styles of speaking'. One example is the use of the form *don't* in the third person singular which, like *ain't*, 'was common and entirely acceptable . . . in the familiar speech of the educated and upper classes', according to Phillipps (1978: 121). The problem with the use of *he don't* and *ain't*, however, is that on the one hand they characterise the language of the lower classes, as in examples (10) and (11) produced by a waiter in *David Copperfield* (1849–50):

(10) 'My eye!' he said. 'It seems a good deal, **don't it**?'

(11) 'Lord bless my soul!' he exclaimed, 'I didn't know they were chops. Why, a chop's the very thing to take off the bad effects of that beer! **Ain't it** lucky?'

On the other hand, these forms were also used and 'even cultivated in the best society', according to Görlach (1999a: 60). The double function of these forms, both as markers of lower-class and of upper-class language, makes them tricky forms to use for real speakers but also for fictional ones. It may therefore not come as a surprise that *ain't* doesn't occur in Jane Austen's *Sense and Sensibility* (1811), *Mansfield Park* (1813), *Pride and Prejudice* (1813), *Emma* (1816), *Northanger Abbey* (1817) or *Persuasion* (1817), as these novels have the social aspirations of middle-class women as their main topic. *Don't* in the third person singular is found only three times in *Sense and Sensibility*, in the language of Mrs Jennings, who is described in the novel as 'Lady Middleton's mother ... a good-humoured, merry, fat, elderly woman, who talked a great deal, seemed very happy, and *rather vulgar*':

(12) Well, it **don't** signify talking ... Why **don't** he ... sell his horses, let his house, turn off his servants, and make a thorough reform at once?

Third person singular *don't*, according to Uhrström (1907: 21), was already 'very common in Richardson's time', and he provides evidence from *Pamela* (1740–41). My own analysis of *do* in eighteenth-century English has shown that third person singular *don't* indeed occurs in the language of upper- as well as lower-class speakers, as in:

(13) to engage myselfe where she **don't** like (1711; Lady Mary Wortley Montagu, Letters, Halsband 1965–7, Vol. I, 89)

(14) that **don't** argufy. (1751; Smollett, *Peregrine Pickle*)

But I have also found it in the language of people with overt as well as less overt social aspirations, such as Betsy Sheridan (Tieken-Boon van Ostade 1990: 81–2), and this similarly explains its presence in the language of Mrs Jennings in (12). Possibly, the same applies to the use of *ain't*, which occurs three times in Thackeray's *Book of Snobs* (1846–7). The forms attracted the criticism of the grammarians in the early nineteenth century, when the anonymous author of *The Vulgarities of Speech Corrected* (1826) writes that they are not to be 'admitted into correct and elegant conversation'. For all that, Phillipps (1984: 69) notes that third person singular *don't* 'was acceptable colloquially at least down to the 1870s'.

In nineteenth-century English, the use of the subjunctive likewise was a sociolinguistic marker. Phillipps (1970: 154) notes that, thanks to the normative grammarians, the subjunctive mood survived. What he means by the term 'subjunctive mood' is primarily the use of the morphologically marked or inflectional subjunctive, as in (15), (16) and (17), where it signals possibility or non-factuality:

(15) perhaps it **were** better not to force her (1813; Jane Austen, *Pride and Prejudice*)

(16) how soon it **be** possible to get them there (1817; Jane Austen, *Persuasion*)

(17) if she **remain** with him. (1813; Jane Austen, *Mansfield Park*)

According to Phillipps, 'Jane Austen seems to have used the subjunctive in appropriate contexts when she thought about it', and in cases where speakers in her novels do not use the subjunctive appropriately this signals their careless use of grammar and thus their low social status (1970: 155, 157). Dickens employs the subjunctive similarly in his novels, for Brook (1970: 247) observes that usually the indicative occurs after *if*, as in (17), but that 'when a character apes gentility, the subjunctive flourishes'. Possibly, the use of the subjunctive was regarded as a marker of gentility even in the eighteenth century, for Bishop Edward Synge consistently used it even when he wrote to his daughter Alicia. Synge appears to have been extremely self-conscious linguistically speaking, as one of the main purposes of the letters, about a hundred of them written between 1746 and 1752, was to instruct his daughter in matters of letter writing, including spelling and grammar (compare Section 2.1). The Synge letters were written when normative grammar was still in its infancy, and lacking a grammar which he might have recommended to his daughter, Synge attempted to instruct her himself, both explicitly and, as in the case of the subjunctive, implicitly, setting his own usage as an example.

The subjunctive underwent a curious development during the LModE period. While its use had rapidly decreased since the end of the sixteenth century, it began to rise slightly during the second half of the eighteenth century and into the nineteenth, when there was a sharp decrease from around 1870 onwards (Auer and González-Díaz 2005; Grund and

Walker 2006). The temporary rise of the subjunctive has been associated with the influence of normative grammar, and though this may explain the increased use during the nineteenth century, when linguistic prescriptivism was at its height and its effects must have been felt, in the second half of the eighteenth-century it must have been because of the strong linguistic sensitivity among social climbers rather than the actual effect of the grammars themselves. This is evident in the language of Robert Lowth and his correspondents: in Lowth's own usage, there is an increase of the subjunctive around the time when his grammar was newly published, and with his correspondents we found a similar linguistic awareness that they were writing to a celebrated grammarian (Auer and Tieken-Boon van Ostade 2007). Grund and Walker (2006: 97) note an interesting gender difference in the nineteenth century: while 'male writers overall use the subjunctive slightly more than female writers do', there is a decrease in usage among the men but an increase among the women. Grund and Walker don't offer an explanation for this, but it may be due to the fact that women tend to be linguistically insecure. This is, for instance, the case with Betsy Sheridan (Tieken-Boon van Ostade 1990), who used forms like *It is I* and *whom* in object position even when corresponding with her sister, all in agreement with the pronouncements of the normative grammarians of the period. To me, this is evidence of stylistic hypercorrection, as she used linguistic forms that would have been, even in the second half of the eighteenth century, inappropriate to the style of intimate letters, which she herself regarded as being pretty close to actual speech. The pattern identified by Grund and Walker may similarly be characteristic of the language of women, who, given the emphasis on correct language, would have been eager to use a grammatical feature like the subjunctive correctly, even when it was in the process of decline (see further Chapter 6).

5.3 Grammatical strictures vs. actual usage

In July 1857, a Mrs Henrietta English wrote a letter to Sam Beeton, Isabella's husband, which contained the following sentence:

(18) you can always see her, but have you not yet **wrote** to Her? (Hughes 2005: 192)

The use of *wrote* as a past participle stands out immediately, as, by the norms of present-day standard English at least, it should have been *written*. Lowth commented on this usage in his grammar as follows: 'We should be immediately shocked at *I have knew, I have saw, I have gave,* etc.: but our ears have grown familiar with *I have wrote, I have drank, I have bore*, etc., which are altogether as barbarous' (1762: 90). Variation in usage between what we now strictly distinguish as past tense and past participle forms of strong verbs was very common during the eighteenth century. In a case study of the verb *write*, Oldireva Gustafsson (2002) demonstrates that usage of past participle *wrote* increased considerably between the first and the second half of the century. Phillipps (1970: 147) shows that Jane Austen herself used *ate, eat* and *broke* as past participles, but also that she used the past participles *went, took* and *gave* to mark the language of servants and 'vulgar characters' as non-standard. The case of Henrietta English is therefore interesting. Despite her name, she was a Frenchwoman by origin, who, having survived the French Revolution, married a footman called Robert English. Though her grammar is 'scrappy' according to Hughes (2005: 191), her use of *wrote* might in fact be quite correct from the point of view of the social class she belonged to, as she would have learned her English from the servants along with whom she and her husband were employed when she first arrived in England. Lowth's comment that 'our ears have grown quite familiar' with forms like participial *wrote* is quite interesting. It is unlikely that, writing about a hundred years before Mrs English, he would be referring to the language of servants here, particularly in view of the form's general currency in the second half of the eighteenth century. Oldireva's data derive from letters, and my own analysis of Lowth's letters has shown that he used such forms himself as well (Tieken-Boon van Ostade 2002). In his grammar he had also noted that the usage he disapproved of 'prevails greatly in common discourse' (1762: 85–6), as indeed it did in the letters to his wife, which obviously represented 'common discourse' on paper.

In Chapter 3, I quoted Osselton ([1984] 1998), who presented arguments for the existence of two standards of spelling, a public and a private one. In grammar, too, the language of letters is characterised by greater variation in usage than the printed texts of the time. As the language of letters represents different degrees of formality (see Chapter 7), we may expect to find grammatical forms that are disapproved of in the normative grammars predominantly in the most informal letters, addressed to close friends and relatives. Similar cases to the examples already discussed are the use of *them* as a demonstrative, *you was, between you and I* and preposition stranding:

(19) **them** admirers you speak of (1710; Lady Mary Wortley Montagu, Letters, Halsband 1965–67: Vol. I, 61)

(20) I felt almost as if **you was** an old acquaintance (1811; Jane Austen, *Sense and Sensibility*)

(21) This was a day eagerly expected **by Dempster, Erskine, and I** (1762–63; Boswell, *London Journal*, Pottle 1950: 152)

(22) I shall otherwise have no Copy to correct **by.** (1758; Lowth to Robert Dodsley)

While examples (19) and (22) are taken from letters, (20) represents direct speech and (21) is from a private journal. Like participial *wrote*, these usages, along with many others, were condemned by the normative grammarians, some in the eighteenth century and others, such as the split infinitive (see Section 5.4), not until the nineteenth, but they all have in common that they were once perfectly acceptable, even in the language of the most highly placed people. Demonstrative *them* is listed among Dickens's features of non-standard grammar (Brook 1970: 244), which suggests that by his time, its usage had been considerably demoted. Görlach (1999a: 176) quotes a grammar by a certain George Edmonds, called, significantly, *Complete English Grammar, with a Supplemental Grammar of Ettiquette* (1837). Edmonds labelled *them* for *those* as a '*vulgar* or *vulgarish* blunder'. *You was*, according to Phillipps (1970: 159), was 'fairly frequent, and not necessarily vulgar, in Richardson's novels', but it was 'condemned by the grammarians, and in [Jane Austen's] novels only people like the Steeles have it'. Lowth had indeed condemned it as a grammatical error of the worst kind, calling it 'an enormous Solecism' (1762: 48), despite the fact that he used *you was* himself, though only in his informal letters. He was less fierce in his condemnation of preposition stranding, illustrated by (22), of which he noted that it

> prevails in common conversation, and suits very well with the familiar style in writing; but the placing of the Preposition before the Relative is more graceful, as well as more perspicuous; and agrees much better with the solemn and elevated Style. (Lowth 1762: 127–8)

This distinction agrees neatly with his own usage. In the course of time, the stricture against preposition stranding was formulated increasingly strongly. Yañez-Bouza (2008) quotes a grammar from 1796 saying that 'the preposition *should always precede* the relative pronoun with it governs' (Coar 1796: 179), which is a far cry from Lowth's careful stylistic distinction in usage. Despite the increasing fierceness of the pronouncements by normative grammarians, preposition stranding continued in general use. The following randomly selected instances illustrate this:

(23) which my mother, being on the watch, heard distinctly, and was sadly alarmed **at** (1816; Austen, *Emma*)

(24) You have not acquired ... anything like that amount of exact knowledge which I looked **for** (1854; Dickens, *Hard Times*)

(25) to be one of the most dismal sports ever entered **into** by a bachelor. (1847–48; Thackeray, *Vanity Fair*)

Though preposition stranding is still part of Crystal's 'Grammatical Top Ten' (1995: 194), Burchfield, in his 'final verdict' of the construction, is more lenient:

> In most circumstances, esp. in formal writing, it is desirable to avoid placing a preposition at the end of a clause or sentence, where it has the appearance of being stranded. But there are many circumstances in which a preposition may or even must be placed late ... and others where the degree of formality required governs the placing. (1996: 619)

After more than two hundred years of increasing prescriptivism, Lowth's distinction finally appears to have been sanctioned.

Between you and I is considered to be 'a common vulgarism' in the language of Dickens's characters (Brook 1970: 245), and this would apply to any construction with a subject pronoun following a preposition. A century earlier, such constructions had been branded as 'a female inaccuracy' by Walpole – attributing the pronouncement to 'a friend of his'. My analysis of eighteenth-century usage has shown that this allegation was wrong, as the construction was found in the language of men and women alike, though, interestingly, not in that of Walpole himself (Tieken-Boon van Ostade 1994). In the second edition of a satirical piece called *Lexiphanes* (1767), subtitled '... An Attempt to restore the ENGLISH Tongue to its ancient Purity', its author, Archibald Campbell (c.1724–80), defends himself against comments in the *Critical Review* on his use of *between you and I* in the first edition by saying that it was only a 'very trivial slip, if it be one', and that 'tho' it must be confessed to be ungrammatical, [it] is yet almost universally used in familiar conversation' (2nd edn 1767: 123). Mittins et al. (1970: 111) discovered that the acceptability of *between you and I* during the late 1960s was among the lowest of the structures they analysed, and this is confirmed by Burchfield (1996: 106), who notes:

> The nation is divided in its use of *between you and me* and *between you and I*. Let me begin by declaring that the only admissible construction of the two in standard use in the 20c. is *between you and me*.

5.4 The normative grammarians' influence

Not only was there an increase in the production of grammars during the second half of the eighteenth century, when four times as many English grammars were published as during the first half (Tieken-Boon van Ostade 2008a), the syntax sections in the grammars also grew considerably. This is due to the fact that after the 1740s the grammarians developed an interest in actual usage. The attention to syntax continued to grow because the grammars became more and more normative in view of the need for a model of linguistic correctness, particularly for those desirous of improving themselves, socially but also, inevitably, linguistically. To illustrate this, Lowth, having criticised Johnson for 'comprising the whole Syntax in ten lines' in the grammar preceding the dictionary (Lowth 1762: v), dealt with syntax in some sixty pages in the first edition in his grammar and more in later editions. And so did Murray sixty years later. New strictures kept being formulated, grammatical ones, like the split infinitive but also lexical ones, like the confusion between *errant* and *arrant*, so much so that the third edition of Fowler's *Modern English Usage* (1926) contains 862 pages (Burchfield 1996).

As already discussed, it is usually assumed that normative grammars had an enormous influence on the language. Increasingly, however, studies are devoted to the relationship between changing patterns of usage and the pronouncements of the prescriptive grammarians, as a result of which actual influence can be properly assessed. One example is the use of *shall* or *will* as a marker of the future, the stricture for which can be traced all the way to Wallis (1653: 94–5):

> *Shall* et *will* indicant Futurum . . .
>
> In primis personis *shall* simpliciter praedicentis est; *will*, quasi promittentis aut minantis.
>
> In secundis et tertiis personis, *shall* promittentis est aut minantis; *will* simpliciter praedicentis.

In this form, or with minor variations, the rule is found in many eighteenth-century grammars, which testifies to Wallis's influence – or, indeed, the way in which grammarians imitated each other (Tieken-Boon van Ostade 1985). Buchanan (1762: 116), for instance, provides little more than a straightforward translation from Wallis:

> Shall and will denote the Future Time, or the Time yet to come. Shall in the first Persons, as I shall, we shall, simply expresses the future Action; but in the second and third Persons; as, you shall, he shall, they shall, it promises, commands, or threatens.

> Will, in the first Persons, as, I will, we will, promises or threatens:
> But in the second and third Persons, as, thou wilt or you will; ye will
> or you will, he will, they will, it barely foretells.

Around 1680, according to Schlauch (1959: 143), there had been a 90 per cent preference for *will* in the first person and 10 per cent for *shall*. My analysis of Lowth's letters, written between 1748 and 1785, suggests that usage had changed, with an overall preference of nearly 70 per cent for first-person *shall*. According to Fries (1925), this was due to the influence of the grammarians. Arnovick (1997: 144) notes that 'vernacular usage [that is, common everyday language] was mixed', and this seems to be confirmed by Lowth's usage, but *shall* had many different meanings (Facchinetti 2000: 115), which may be illustrated with an example from Lowth:

> (26) I think *I shall* be in Town on Thursday: for *I will* sett out early Monday Morning. (1755; Lowth to his wife)

Though both *I shall* and *I will* refer to future events here ('on Thursday', 'early Monday Morning'), *I will* additionally expresses an intention, with arriving in London as a result. The normative stricture thus represents an oversimplification of actual patterns of usage, but nevertheless it had a clear impact on language use, for according to Phillipps (1970: 125) the rule is 'generally applicable to Jane Austen's usage', while Facchinetti (2000: 128) likewise writes that first-person *shall* for the future predominates throughout the nineteenth century, not only with English but also with Irish writers.

Interestingly, Irishmen were regularly singled out by the grammarians for failing to distinguish between *shall* and *will* correctly. While Johnson (1755) had been the first to criticise the usage of 'foreigners and provincials', Webster (1789), and Fogg (1796) after him, had been more explicit: 'The Scots and Irish, even of the first rank, generally use *will* for *shall* in the first person; by which means, they substitute a *promise* for an intended *prediction*' (Webster 1789: 236–7). Webster added that 'the errors in the use of the auxiliary verbs before mentioned, are not English; that they are little known among the inhabitants of South Britain, and still less among their descendants in New England' (1789: 240). He thus carefully pointed out that Americans belonged to neither of Johnson's categories of faulty users. If the Irish ever had belonged to this category, by the nineteenth century, according to Facchinetti, their usage wholly agreed with the normative stricture of the eighteenth-century grammarians. Mittins et al. (1970: 13) note a 56 per cent acceptance rate of 'I will be twenty-one tomorrow', while in 1925 Fries had already observed 'a tendency in American usage to eliminate *shall* forms' (Fries 1925: 1015). The normative grammarians thus ultimately did have had a lasting effect here.

An example of the ineffectiveness of a normative stricture despite increasing fierceness and long-lasting attack is that against the use of what Molencki (2003) calls the 'counterfactual perfect infinitive' as in the following examples, which illustrate that the perfect infinitive can occur after a simple past or a perfect construction in the main clause:

(27) I thought to **have written** last week (Lowth, new ed., 1769: 149)

(28) It would have been no difficult thing for Cedric . . . to **have placed** himself at the head of a third party. (1819; Scott, *Ivanhoe*; Molencki 2003: 191)

According to Molencki, proscription started with Priestley and Lowth, with Priestley calling the use of *have* in sentences like (28) 'superfluous', even if 'strictly grammatical', while Lowth was stonger in his pronounce-ment ('certainly vicious'), though only so in the 1769 edition of the grammar. Proscription continued throughout the nineteenth century, though former usage was unaffected, both in British and American English, and Molencki (2003: 192) cites a more liberal attitude adopted in a usage guide from 1995, which admits 'that the double perfect infini-tive often occurs in colloquial spoken English'.

In EModE, there was a lot of variation between different forms of the gerund, for which Nevalainen and Raumolin-Brunberg (2003: 65) list the following variants (spelling modernised):

(29) a. for the making of that little house
     b. for buying of grain
     c. of meeting you
     d. by continual charging of money
     e. towards the further discovering this villain's forgeries.

Variation is attributable to the changes affecting the gerund in the course of its history – that is, 'a gradual transition from a full abstract noun to a verbal structure'. Lowth had identified the problem in his grammar, noting that 'there are hardly any of our Writers, who have not fallen into th[e] inaccuracy' of treating the gerund as if it were 'of an amphibious species, partly Nouns, and partly Verbs', as in the case of (29e). His attempt to solve the problem, according to Görlach (2001: 115), 'is eminently clear – but his guidance does not appear to have had much influence'. In trying to clarify the phenomenon, Lowth had distinguished between the verbal noun, which has 'an Article before it, and the Preposition *of* after it', as in (29a), and the gerund proper, which only contains the participle followed by the object (29c). Thus, either *by the observing of which* or *by observing which* are correct, and 'not, "by observing of which;" nor, "by the observing which:" for either of those two uses would be a confounding of two distinct forms' (1762: 111–14). For all that, he himself occasionally made a grammatical slip in his letters, as in:

(30) no objection to **the** publishing ∅ a new Edition the grammar. (1781; Lowth to James Dodsley)

Jane Austen, according to Phillipps (1970: 131), similarly produced the kind of sentences that Lowth had condemned, though only of the type as illustrated in (30) above, that is, (29e). In Thackeray's language the same type is found, as in

(31) **the** very missing ∅ her. (Phillipps 1978: 117)

The question of the variation between genitival and object pronouns preceding the gerund, as in (32a and b), 'remained undecided' according to Görlach (1999a: 77).

(32) a. I hate him reading books
      b. I hate his reading books
      c. I hate the man reading books.

Mair (2006) discovered that after the verb *remember* a common case noun phrase, i.e. not in the genitive as in (32b), and ambiguous between being a subject and object as in (32c), followed by a gerund was on the increase in nineteenth-century English. The noun phrase in the possessive, however, was surprisingly rare during this period. Dekeyser comments on the ineffectiveness of the nineteenth-century grammarians' strictures with respect to what he calls the subject of the gerund, noting 'an ever widening cleavage between grammar and usage' (1975: 189).

The use of *who* for *whom* in Jane Austen's time was evidently considered to be 'vulgar', for in *Sense and Sensibility* it is associated with the non-standard language of Lucy Steele, as in:

(33) The name of the man on *who* all my happiness depends. (1811; Phillipps 1970: 171)

Some fifty years previously, we find Betsy Sheridan, always conscious of what was considered grammatically correct, using *whom* in object position consistently (Tieken-Boon van Ostade 1990). Lowth, who as expected exposed a number of errors in the use of this relative in his grammar (1762: 97n, 99n), is scrupulously correct in his own usage here, even to the extent of producing a sentence like:

(34) We have lost our good Friend D[r]. Chapman, *than whom* no man had better pretensions to long life. (1760; Lowth to Robert Dodsley)

This construction is dealt with in the second edition of his grammar (1763: 158–60), which also offers a fuller discussion of the proper use of *who* and *whom*. Today, the correct use of *whom* seems pedantic, particularly in sentences like (34), though Burchfield (1996: 848) still lists contemporary instances of *who* 'where strict grammar calls for *whom*' and of '*whom* used "ungrammatically" for *who*'. Already, for the nineteenth century, Johansson (2006) discovered that *whom* was rare in the language of science, trials and letters; apparently, it was considered too formal for these text types. Occasionally she encountered an instance of hyper-correct usage, as in:

(35) Then you saw a man **whom** you were told was Sir Roger coming out of the door? (1870–1900; Trials; Johansson 2006: 169)

It seems that the instance in (35) was produced by the extreme formality of the occasion, an examination in a courtroom. Görlach (1997), who discovered two peaks in the use of *than whom*, as illustrated by example (34), in the periods 1650–1750 and 1810–1910, notes that during the nineteenth century the grammarians' interest in the construction began to wane. Interestingly, the BNC still contains four instances of the construction.

In 1850, an Act of Parliament was issued specifying that the masculine pronoun *he* was to be adopted when the sex of the referent was unclear or irrelevant. During the 1970s and 80s, this led to strong opposition, particularly from women who felt excluded as a result, and alternative solutions were proposed: *he or she*, *s/he* and singular *they*. Singular *they* had actually been in general use throughout the LModE period, and according to Bodine (1975: 136) the Act of Parliament had been a response to the 'virtual explosion of condemnation of singular "they"' at the time, as in examples (36) and (37), in which *they* is used as a singular pronoun, referring to the singular if unknown referents of *anyone* and *who*:

(36) Anyone can do it if **they** try hard enough

(37) Who dropped **their** ticket?

The first grammarian to condemn this use of singular *they* was not Kirkby (1746), as Bodine claims, but, surprisingly perhaps, a female grammarian, Ann Fisher (1745), who had been plagiarised by Kirkby (Tieken-Boon van Ostade 1992). Burchfield (1996: 779), however, notes a continuous use of singular *they*, even by what he calls 'writers of standing', which suggests evident ineffectiveness of the rule. Mittins et al. (1970) show a 42 per cent acceptance rate of singular *they*, which has probably increased since they did their research as a result of efforts to avoid sexist language.

There will be many more normative strictures which were relaxed after the LModE period. A systematic analysis of the list of grammatical strictures provided by Leonard (1929: 251–307) in the light of today's usage would demonstrate the extent to which this was the case. A final example is the question of concord between the indefinite pronoun *none* and the verb, i.e. whether it should be *none is/was* or *none are/were*. The *OED* provides the following comment: 'Many commentators state that *none* should take singular concord, but this has generally been less common than plural concord, especially between the 17th and 19th centuries'. Who these commentators were is not specified. Leonard (1929) notes that in the eighteenth century Johnson was one of them but that in advocating singular concord he was evidently 'misinterpreting the trend in usage', which agrees with the comment found in the *OED*. Leonard also mentions Baker (1770), Priestley (1761) and Murray (1795), all of whom allowed either. Dekeyser (1975: 73) quotes G. W. Moon's *Common Errors in Speech and Writing* (1875), who reacted against current usage by 'fiercely opposing a plural concord' on the grounds that *none* is singular. Moon was, however, in a minority, for according to Dekeyser most of the nineteenth-century grammarians he consulted were in favour of plural concord. Now, however, usage appears to have reversed, for a search for these forms in the BNC shows that the singular forms are about twice as frequent as the plural ones. A Google search, however, shows approximately equal numbers for both (see Table 5.1 below). Usage, as represented by that found on the internet, is clearly very much divided, despite the fact that Burchfield (1996: 526) still prescribes the singular 'where possible'.

The question of singular vs. plural concord is also dealt with by Smitterberg (2006), who studied partititive constructions, such as *a bit/part/number/group/glass of* + noun. Particularly when the noun in the complement is a collective noun, such as *people*, variation occurs, as in

Table 5.1 Singular or plural concord with *none*.

	BNC	Google
None were	56	611,000
None are	47	790,000
None was	110	626,000
None is	95	856,000

(38) and also when the head of the complement is the word *number*, as illustrated by (39).

> (38)   the unwillingness, which a particular **class** of people **feel**

> (39)   when ... the **number** of labourers **is** increased.

The clause in (38) is a variant of the example provided by Smitterberg, which contains the noun *persons* rather than *people*:

> (38)   a. the unwillingness, which a particular **class** of persons **feel**.

This example also shows variation in the occurrence of singular and plural verb forms, i.e. *feel* vs. *feels*. Smitterberg found more instances of plural concord towards the end of the nineteenth century, despite the fact that the plural of verbs in clauses like (38a) 'was more heavily censured in the first half of the nineteenth century than after 1850' (2006: 261–2). As in the cases discussed above, this suggests that ultimately usage continued irrespective of the pronouncements of the grammarians, and also that occasionally the battle against a different pattern of usage was eventually given up. With *number*, there is today a distinction between whether the preceding article is definite or indefinite, with *a number of* according to Burchfield (1996: 534) 'normally governing a plural verb both in BrE and AmE', and with *the number of*, as in (39) above, the singular. This situation was already to a certain extent apparent in the nineteenth century, when, as Smitterberg discovered, usage was divided only with respect to *a number of*, which might occur both with a singular and with a plural verb though with a preference for the plural form, just like today.

5.5 Current research on LModE grammar

Much recent research on LModE grammar reports on results obtained from corpus analyses. An example is *Nineteenth-Century English* (Kytö,

Rydén and Smitterberg 2006), in which almost all articles made use of CONCE, the one-million-word Corpus of Nineteenth-Century English, developed by Kytö and others. The articles deal with topics never previously explored in such depth for the period in question, so the material presented is both new and innovative in drawing upon this recently compiled corpus. The articles discuss the use of partitive constructions and of the subjunctive already referred to (Sections 5.2. and 5.4) and the question of whether the rise of the passive as a typical characteristic of scientific prose, as in (40) is a nineteenth-century phenomenon.

> (40) a piece of leaf . . . **was divided** into four equal parts. (1850–70; Faraday; Oldireva Gustafsson 2006: 124)

Other articles deal with the distribution of the relativisers *which*, *that* and *who*, which had been a topic of concern during the early eighteenth century but which by the nineteenth century unexpectedly, according to Johansson (2006: 179), came to show a preference for the *wh*-strategy; and with a special type of the gerund (discussed in Section 5.4, compare (29c)), which now seems more common in written than in spoken discourse; see (41).

> (41) though I have still persisted **in doing without a fire**. (1800–30; Sarah Hutchinson; Rudanko 2006: 233)

The articles in Kytö et al. (2006) show ongoing change during the nineteenth century but also stability in usage. An example is the analysis by Rudanko of a low-frequency construction like the *that/those + of* construction, which may be illustrated by (42):

> (42) I know of one instance, **that of** Mrs. Clarkson. (1800–30; letter by Robert Southey; Rudanko 2006: 187)

An instance of ongoing change is that of adjective comparison, of which Kytö and Romaine show that there was variation between the inflectional or the older form (*happier, happiest*) and the periphrastic or newer form (*more/most elegant*). The results of the analysis show 'a steady increase in the use of the inflectional forms throughout the nineteenth century', approaching PDE usage towards the end of the period (Kytö and Romaine 2006: 212). Though this is not mentioned as a possible factor in the change described, the normative grammars possibly played an important role here, for Bax (2008) has shown that in the course of the eighteenth century the grammar rules offered increasingly clear-cut guidance in the matter; he also notes that the birth of today's prescriptions in the use of comparatives and superlatives, as found in Quirk et al.'s *Comprehensive Grammar of the English Language* (1985), occurs in the eighteenth century.

Another example of where a change in usage is identified without being linked to possible influence of prescriptivism was dealt with by McFadden (2007), who discussed the use of *be* and *have* with mutative intransitive verbs. Throughout the eighteenth century there was a lot of variation between the two, so that sentences like (43) and (44) occur alongside each other:

(43) Your Letter of the 26th **is** just **come** to my hands (1755; Lowth to his wife)

(44) that **have** not **come** to my hands. (1758; Lowth to Robert Dodsley)

In their study of *be/have* variation between 1500 and 1900, Rydén and Brorström (1987) show that *have* progressively replaced *be* with verbs like *arrive, come, improve, pass* and *return*. McFadden noted that during the second half of the eighteenth century usage definitively 'tips' in favour of the *have* construction, as had also been demonstrated by Rydén and Brorström (1987: 200), and he wondered what 'the magic' was that caused this tip. As in the case of adjective comparison, the trick may have been the onset of the influence of the normative grammars. Perhaps Lowth's grammar played a role here, as he was the first to condemn examples with *be* rather than *have* (1762: 63, footnote), followed by various other grammarians including Cobbett (1818) (Rydén and Brorström 1987: 209n). There was apparently no opposition to the use of the *have* construction among the grammarians, unlike in the case of the new passive progressive construction, which produced a lot of comment (Pratt and Denison 2000; see Section 6.4).

5.6 Concluding remarks

Studies like those in *Nineteenth-Century English* as well as McFadden (2007) demonstrate the complexity of the research questions tackled. Some of the usage patterns correlate with gender, a topic which will be discussed in the next chapter. The result of these papers, according to Kytö et al., is to 'invite rather than preclude further research' (2006: 2). The book sets a pattern for studies along the same lines that could look for inspiration among the work done on the language of individual authors carried out in the 1970s by Brook and Phillipps. Such studies would help us decide whether their description of the language of Jane Austen, Dickens and Thackeray shows merely idiosyncratic patterns of usage or whether these authors' language conformed with more general trends and developments of the period in which they lived. Evidence of the fact that the LModE period is a fruitful period for further research into its use of grammar may be found in the publication of the proceedings of the special conference devoted to its language (Dossena and Jones 2003; Pérez-Guerra et al. 2007; Tieken-Boon van Ostade and van der Wurff forthcoming), and of which more are expected to be produced in the next decade or so. Whatever such future research will discover, it will confirm that throughout the LModE period people increasingly came to experience a heightened sense of linguistic self-consciousness. Their use of grammar will have been affected accordingly.

Further reading

For general overviews of LModE grammar, see Bailey (1996: 215–61), Beal (2004: 66–123), Görlach (2001: 98–129) and (1999a: 65–91), as well as *CHEL* Vol. III Chapter 4 (Rissanen 1999) and Vol. IV Chapter 3 (Denison 1998). On grammar in relation to usage, see Vol. IV Chapter 6 (Finegan 1998). For a study of grammars and grammar writing in the eighteenth century, see *Grammars, Grammarians and Grammar Writing in Eighteenth-Century England* (Tieken-Boon van Ostade (ed.) 2008) as well as Tieken-Boon van Ostade (2000b), and on Lindley Murray's grammar in particular Tieken-Boon van Ostade (ed.) (1996). Vorlat (2007) presents a useful introduction to normative grammar writing. Nineteenth-century grammatical production is dealt with by Michael (1991 and 1997) and Görlach (1998); Görlach, moreover, suggests interesting topics for further research on the subject.

Research questions

1. Fogg does not appear in the *ODNB* or in Wikipedia. Write an entry for him for Wikipedia in which you pay attention to his contribution to our current knowledge on the grammatical tradition in the LModE period (see also Chapter 2, Research Question 6), and do the same for Robert Baker (see Research Question 7 in this chapter).
2. Look up Devis's grammar (1775) in ECCO. What marks its particular focus on Young Ladies, as the title suggests? (Compare her use of examples with those in Lowth's grammar.)
3. Adamson (2007) refers to several eighteenth-century grammars as sources for her argument that *who* and *which* came to correlate with gender as a result of current strictures on usage. What do other grammars in ECCO have to say on the subject?

4. Study the use of non-standard grammar in the novels by Thomas Hardy and George Gissing (Project Gutenberg), Mary Brunton (Chadwyck Healey Eighteenth-Century Fiction database) and others (compare Tieken-Boon van Ostade and Faya Cerqueiro 2007).

5. Study the occurrence of *he/she/it don't* and *ain't* in the novels of Dickens, Thackeray and other writers from the period along the lines discussed in this chapter (Project Gutenberg). Also consult the list of novels by minor nineteenth-century novelists in Hodson and Milward (2007).

6. What features from *The Vulgarities of Speech Corrected* (1826) other than those dealt with in this chapter are made use of in nineteenth-century novels?

7. Study Robert Baker's use of the subjunctive in *Reflections on the English Language* (1770), and discuss whether his usage reflects any aspirations to gentility he might have experienced. Baker is not listed in the *ODNB* or in Wikipedia, but he supplies a lot of biographical information in his own preface.

8. Compare Baker's strictures (see eTable of Contents in ECCO) with those in Burgess's *Five Hundred Mistakes of Daily Occurrence* (1856) and Burchfield's edition of *Fowler's Modern English Usage* (1996).

9. In his *Encyclopedia of the English Language*, Crystal provides a Grammatical (rather: ungrammatical) Top Ten, comprising the following usage problems: *between you and I*, split infinitives, placement of *only*, *none* + plural verb, *different to/than*, preposition stranding, first person *shall/will*, *hopefully*, *who/whom* and double negation.
   a. How are all these features dealt with in a single eighteenth-century grammar?
   b. How is any one of these features treated by different grammars from the period? (ECCO)

10. How do grammarians other than Kirkby or Fisher deal with the problem of singular *they*? (Use ECCO for the eighteenth century and Google Book Search for the nineteenth.)

6 Language and social networks

6.1 Introduction

Chapter 5 dealt with the relationship between the rise of prescriptivism and the influence of the normative grammars on actual usage. There are instances where grammatical strictures were effective in that variation came to an end, as in the use of past participle *wrote* alongside *writ* and *written*, or with *you was*, which was strongly condemned by the grammarians. Though *you was* was quite common in eighteenth-century English, by Jane Austen's time it had been demoted to non-standard usage (see Section 5.3). There was indeed an enormous peak in the occurrence of *you was* in novels from the period just previous to its condemnation by Lowth, as illustrated in Figure 6.1 (Tieken-Boon van Ostade 2002: 95), which suggests a link with the normative grammarians' influence:

After it was condemned in the standard language, *you was* continued in non-standard usage down to today, as example (1) from the BNC illustrates:

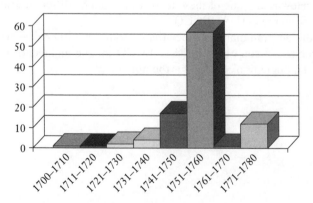

Figure 6.1. *You was* in eighteenth-century novels.

(1) **A06** 1260 Like sunnink reely glamorous that everyone wants an' I can't see woss so wrong wiv vat. 'Cos I ain't gonner get no kitchen wiv pitcher winders an' some geezer wiv a pipe **like you was on abaht** am I now?

At the end of the eighteenth century, we also find *you was* in the language of the members of the Clift family, who came from Cornwall. As already discussed, William, the youngest, quickly got rid of his local dialect after he moved to London in 1792, wishing to be assimilated into the London middle classes and working hard to adjust his language accordingly. Austin (1994) describes his earlier use of dialectal features, such as *where* for 'whether' and *was a week* (or its variant *was Sennight*) for 'a week ago', as in:

(2) Be pleased to let me know in your next letter, **where** you have had any letter from Brother Thomas (1792; William to Elizabeth Clift; Austin 1994: 295)

(3) John Adams the Footman left us last monday **was Sennight**. (1792; William to Elizabeth Clift; Austin 1991: 33)

The use of *do* in the third person singular present tense (*he do* or *he don't*) also gradually disappeared from his letters, as he would soon have discovered that this was a tricky form to use, given his social aspirations (see Section 5.2). *You was*, however, is a different case, for Austin continued to find it in his language throughout the period she analysed. But we also find singular *you were* from 1797 onwards, five years after his arrival in London. *You was* served as a kind of bridge in the introduction of singular *you were*, which after all used to be plural until the singular pronoun *thou* had lost general currency (Tieken-Boon van Ostade 2002; see Nevalainen 2006: 78–80). William Clift was indeed fairly quick in adopting the new standard form, and in his continuing use of *you was* in his letters home he may simply have been accommodating – unconsciously – to his dialect-speaking relatives.

There is another interesting feature in his language. Almost immediately upon his arrival in London – after less than a month, according to Austin (1994: 303) – William Clift dropped his use of *'d* in his letters, despite the fact that *'d* was still part of epistolary spelling (see Sections 3.2 and 3.3). Austin believes that this was due to the fact that his language had been corrected by John Hunter when he was copying manuscripts for him. In using the expanded form in his letters, Clift was actually hypercorrecting, as the *-ed* spelling was not appropriate to the style of his letters. Interestingly, he soon reverted to the use of *'d* again in his letters. Could this be, Austin asks, because Hunter had 'intimated that such contractions might be used in private writing?' (1994: 304). Hypercorrection is typical of people who are linguistically insecure, such as members of the lower-middle classes, and it is striking that Clift overcame his linguistic insecurity in this respect. Austin even notes that 'after 1800 Clift stops using abbreviations altogether, even in letters that exist only in draft form'.

6.2 Social and geographical mobility

The example of William Clift makes an interesting case study. Coming from the provinces and discovering new opportunities for himself after he arrived in London, he quickly adapted to the new linguistic norm he encountered there. The new norm he aimed for, however, was not that of the class of servants in whose company he usually found himself but that of John Hunter, whom, according to Austin (1994: 306), he worshipped like a hero. William Clift was no exceptional case. There was a lot of geographical mobility throughout the LModE period. During the eighteenth century, London had an enormous attraction to people born elsewhere, such as James Boswell (Edinburgh), John Gay (Barnstaple), Samuel Richardson (Mackworth, Derbyshire), Robert Dodsley (Mansfield, Nottinghamshire), Henry and Sarah Fielding (who went to school in Salisbury, Wiltshire), Samuel Johnson and David Garrick (both from Lichfield, Staffordshire), Robert Lowth (Winchester), Laurence Sterne as well as Richard and Elizabeth Sheridan (all three from Ireland) and Fanny Burney (King's Lynn, Norfolk) (Tieken-Boon van Ostade 2006: 243–4). Sometimes we can see what kind of linguistic consequences such moving about had on the people concerned. In his *Life of Johnson*, for instance, Boswell records his anxiety at being identified as a Scotsman when he was introduced to Dr Johnson in 1763: "'Don't tell where I come from" – "From Scotland," cried Davies [their mutual acquaintance] roguishly. "Mr. Johnson, (said I) I do indeed come from Scotland, but I cannot help it"' (Chapman 1953: 277). I have already referred to the criticism Betsy Sheridan got on her provincial pronunciation when visiting a friend in London (Section 2.1).

With the opening of the public railway lines in the early nineteenth century, first from Stockton to Darlington in 1825 and from Liverpool to Manchester five years later, travel increased considerably, not only within the country itself but also abroad. In 1842, Charlotte and Emily Brontë (whose father had been born in Ireland) attended a school in Brussels, and Mrs Beeton similarly spent time in Heidelberg as a young girl for her education. Later, she and her husband made various trips to Paris for the sake of their publishing business. Thackeray, who had been born in Calcutta (India), spent time in France as well as in Ireland, and Dickens visited America twice between 1842 and 1868. In short, the world was becoming smaller as people were taking increasing advantage of the opportunities offered to them by new modes of transport. A person who did not travel much was Jane Austen, and it is her 'sedentary life', as Rydén and Brorström (1987: 204) argue, that explains the difference in usage of the *be/have* paradigm between her and a writer like Dickens, whose life was 'one of social mobility and variability and filled with experiences such as those of a journalist and parliamentary reporter'. Jane Austen's usage of *have* was as low as 22.5 per cent whereas that of Dickens was 87 per cent, considerably higher than the average of 66.5 per cent for the period as a whole (see also Section 5.5).

Travel abroad made people aware of the existence of different languages, as a result of which they would pick up new words and introduce them into their own language (see Section 4.3 for examples of this). Travel in their own country made them realise that they spoke differently from people living elsewhere, and that they would have to adapt their own language if they moved permanently and wished to be part of the new community they had joined. I have already referred to the fact that Mrs Beeton is believed to have had a Cockney accent (Section 2.1), but it is more likely that she adapted her accent after her marriage when she moved to Pinner, a London suburb, particularly because with their publications she and her husband aimed at a middle-class market. For her husband, things may have been different, for reasons I will go into in Section 6.5.

Geographical mobility often involved social mobility too: John Gay, who came from a background of drapers, moved to London hoping to find a position at Court; Lowth rose from being a deacon in Winchester, through Durham, where he was a canon, and his first bishopric in Oxford to his most prestigious post as Bishop of London; William Clift's father had been a journeyman miller, while William's own career planted him firmly into the middle classes; Betsy Sheridan commented on the fact that her brother Richard, who had written plays like *The Rivals* (1775) and *School for Scandal* (1777) and who also became a politician, was 'a little *grand*' (Lefanu 1960: 186) and this may have been evident from his speech as well (compare Section 2.2). Social aspirations like those of Richard Sheridan – who felt a lifelong embarrassment by the fact that his father Thomas had started his career as an actor – inevitably had an effect on their language, and it was for this purpose that Lowth's grammar was put to good use, assisting people in acquiring the linguistic norms of the social class they aspired to. Thomas Sheridan, moreover, published his pronouncing dictionary and Cobbett his grammar to try to offer equal opportunities to all through improved language use. For the historical sociolinguist, socially and geographically mobile people are of particular interest, because they are the ones who introduce new usages into the communities to which they belong.

6.3 Social networks and linguistic change

Socially and geographically mobile people can play an important role as the instruments of linguistic change, and a research model that helps explain this is that of Social Network Analysis. Deriving from the social sciences, this model was adopted and further developed for linguistic analysis by James and Lesley Milroy in their study of the Belfast vernacular (Milroy 1987). There are, broadly speaking, two types of social networks, open ones and closed ones. Open social networks are usually characterised by the existence of many loose ties between the network members themselves and with speakers from other social networks. Closed networks, by contrast, consist of speakers who are closely bound to each other, in the sense that everybody knows everybody else and generally in many different capacities. In a closed network, people may be each other's neighbours, relatives, friends and colleagues all at the same time, whereas in open networks people are often tied to each other either in the capacity of neighbours or relatives or friends or colleagues. Open networks tend to occur among the middle classes, and closed networks among the lower as well as the highest social classes.

From a linguistic perspective, closed networks are characterised by what Milroy (1987) calls a 'norm enforcement mechanism'. In other words, such networks have their own norms by which they distinguish themselves from other social networks, linguistically or otherwise. Language therfore serves as a means of identification against the rest of society. Closed networks are usually found in traditional societies, inner-city areas like those in Belfast investigated by the Milroys and rural speech communities. The linguistic norms of closed networks are usually conservative, and tend to resist change. Middle-class networks, which are usually characterised by an open structure, abound in ties and thus in opportunities to adopt and spread new linguistic features. The language of open social networks is not as a rule conservative but is open to change. Even middle-class networks may contain more or less closed clusters of speakers with their own linguistic norms that are resistant to change and thus relatively conservative. A LModE example is the cluster centred around the writer Henry Fielding (1707–54), which included his sister Sarah and their friends James Harris and Jane Collier (1715–55) (Tieken-Boon van Ostade 2000a). These people had multiple ties with each other, as relatives (HF + SF), as friends from their school days in Salisbury (all four), living in the same house (HF + SF after the death of Henry's wife) and in writing literature together (HF + SF + JH, SF + JC, JC + JH). Another link, though an indirect one, was the one between Sarah Fielding and Jane Collier in that Jane's brother Arthur had taught Sarah Latin and Greek. The situation described here came to an end upon Henry Fielding's death in 1754 and that of Jane Collier a year later; subsequently, James Harris came to play a more important role in Sarah Fielding's life, stimulating her Greek scholarship. The change in linguistic model that resulted accordingly is evident in her language. Sarah Fielding and Jane Collier also formed a cluster with Samuel Richardson, who was not part of the larger network cluster because of his literary rivalry with Henry Fielding. That Richardson, as a printer, served as Sarah Fielding's model is also evident from her language: in her use of capitalisation in her letters she appears to have accommodated to him. Possibly, Richardson had a similar influence on Jane Collier, but I have not yet come across any letters by her that could be studied to this end.

Social networks are a thing of all times and places. Bergs (2005) has studied the language of the fifteenth-century Paston family from the perspective of this research model, and he has, for instance, shown that differences in the language of two brothers can be explained by the fact that one stayed at home while the other travelled, and was thus exposed to usage patterns that he encountered elsewhere. Imhoff (2000) was able to explain the differences in conservative and more innovative language use in two medieval Spanish villages with the help of the social network model. He notes that immigration leads to the breaking of ties, and Milroy and Milroy (1985b: 378) write that there is 'relatively rapid change in areas where pre-existing strong networks are disrupted'. The Milroys also argue that 'innovations seem to hop from one centre of population to another', and that they frequently travel by road and by railway (1985: 380). With the Industrial Revolution, which led to considerable migration and consequently the break-up of social networks, we may thus expect a lot of linguistic change throughout the LModE period. But it is due to the normative grammars and dictionaries of the period that this change did not go completely unchecked. It is no coincidence that the large-scale increase of prescriptive grammars coincides with large population movements, both geographically and socially.

People who migrate break the ties with the network they originally come from, but they also form bridges with new networks. These bridges are important, as changes may travel along them. Such people are called 'linguistic innovators', and in order to study linguistic change it is helpful to identify these potential linguistic innovators, people who are socially and linguistically mobile. For a change to spread into a social network it needs to be adopted by people who occupy an important role within that network and who are thus in a position to function as a linguistic model. People who follow the norm set by these 'early adopters' can be called 'followers'. How a particular change spread along a social network may be illustrated as follows. As already discussed in Section 6.2, the poet John Gay, who moved from a lower middle-class provincial background to London and had high social aspirations when he got there, is a good example of someone who was geographically mobile and who also had social ambitions. The network he became part of consisted of writers like Pope, Swift and Lady Mary Wortley Montagu, but he remained a marginal network member. In his biography of Gay, Nokes (1995) depicts him as someone who regularly came up with new ideas which would be adopted by someone else who subsequently gained the credit for them. This happened, for instance, when Lady Mary Wortley Montagu picked up the idea for a series of 'town eclogs' from him (Weblinks), and acquired renown for it herself. In this case, Gay was the innovator and Lady Mary the early adopter. Something similar is found for his language. Bijkerk (2004) has shown that Gay was the first to use the epistolary formula *yours sincerely*, which is now a common formula expressing politeness but in those days signalled intimacy (Tieken-Boon van Ostade 1999); after it was adopted, once again, by Lady Mary Wortley Montagu, it gained greater currency.

According to Milroy and Milroy (1985b: 365), only weak ties can function as bridges and are thus able to convey innovations from one network to another, but in my own analysis of eighteenth-century social networks I have found examples where strong ties can lead to linguistic change, too. Samuel Richardson, like Gay, was someone who was geographically and socially mobile – originating from Derbyshire and becoming a printer's apprentice in London, he married his master's widow in 1721. Being a successful novelist brought him considerable fame and the attention of fellow writers, but he nevertheless remained on the edges of the literary social networks of the time. This may well have been due to his character, for Zirker (1966: 85) describes him as a

> shy, diffident man who found it difficult to meet people socially . . . [he] was unable to meet such men as Garrick, Johnson, or Fielding on equal terms, and he retreated to the more congenial circle of feminine admirers and mild-mannered men who were willing to pay court to him.

With Johnson he did contract a strong tie, which dates from the time he helped Johnson when he was in financial need. Johnson, in return, held Richardson's literary abilities in high regard. Johnson was greatly admired as a writer in his time, and he occupied a central position in a network that largely consisted of his admirers. Richardson, however, was never more than a marginal member of Johnson's network. In other words, within Johnson's network he would have had only one strong tie – with Johnson himself – and a multitude of weak ties. If we can detect any linguistic change in Johnson's language and that of his social network, Richardson might have functioned as a linguistic innovator, with Johnson being the early adopter and other network members following Johnson's linguistic norm. I have found two instances of this (Tieken-Boon van Ostade 1991b). To begin with, there are the large number of words in Johnson's *Dictionary* for which he drew upon the language of Richardson, in particular the ready-made collection illustrating 'moral and Instructive Sentiments' from *Clarissa* discussed in Section 4.5. Secondly, Johnson's use of periphrastic *do* does not differ substantially from that of his contemporaries (Tieken-Boon van Ostade 1986), with the exception of *The Rambler*, which shows an archaic pattern of usage, much like that found in Richardson's language. In view of their friendship, Johnson had invited Richardson to contribute to *The Rambler*, a privilege he rarely extended. Johnson may well have allowed himself to be influenced by Richardson's style accordingly as, along with its author, he valued it highly. But because the strong tie between Johnson and Richardson was reciprocal, change could also travel the other way, and it did, for I have found an example of this in the field of spelling, particularly in the use of *'d* in participles and past tense forms of weak verbs (see Chapter 3). Richardson's use of this feature as I analysed it is particularly low: 27 per cent compared to a general usage of 40–50 per cent as recorded by Osselton ([1984] 1998) for the period as a whole. Johnson stopped using *'d* after 1738, well before he met Richardson. In this case, it was Johnson who was the linguistic innovator and Richardson the early adopter, and Richardson may have been instrumental in the spread of this new norm in his circle of 'feminine admirers and mild-mannered men who were willing to pay court to him', as Zirker called them. Sarah Fielding certainly appears to have been influenced by him in her spelling (see Section 3.4).

Johnson's language was widely imitated, through the *Dictionary* (Section 4.5) but also through *The Rambler* and even his private letters. Bax (2005) has coined the term 'Ramblerian' to define the style adopted by Johnson in *The Rambler*, which is usually referred to as 'heavy' by other scholars. Characteristic of this style are what Bax (2005: 170) describes as 'emphatic prepositions, abstract noun phrases and Latinate borrowings' as well long noun phrases. Examples are the following:

(4) **In** his medical capacity he seems to rise Daily

(5) the **coldness** of my complement, the **liveliness** of your fancy etc.

(6) He had at last, by the daily **superaddition** of new **expedients**, contrived a door which could never be forced

(7) When a writer has with long toil produced **a work intended to burst upon mankind with unexpected lustre, and withdraw the attention of the learned world from every other controversy or inquiry,** he is seldom contented to wait long without the enjoyment of his new praises. (1751; *Rambler* 146)

Fanny Burney has been criticised for being influenced by Johnson's language. Cecil (1945: 223), patronisingly, writes about 'her prejudiced, enthusiastic, feminine spirit', her 'unpretentious talent' and her 'homely and sociable little personality' when he notes that, after the publication of her first novel *Evelina* (1778), she adopted 'stately "Johnsonese" – all abstraction and polysyllables and antitheses' for her later work. This is confirmed by Bax's analysis, and also by my own study of periphrastic *do*, which shows a much more old-fashioned usage in her novel *Camilla* (1796) than in *Evelina*: less than 30 per cent *do*-less negative sentences in *Evelina* (only with *know* and *doubt*, the verbs that continue longest in this construction) as against 75 per cent in *Camilla* (mostly with verbs other than *know* or *doubt*) (Tieken-Boon van Ostade 1986). This illustrates that language change is rarely straightforward or unidirectional, but that conservative influences play a role due to the status of particular people in society. These conservative influences can often be associated with the role played by a single person, Dr Johnson in this case. The model of social network analysis helps explain what is going on in such instances and why.

6.4 Social networks and linguistic influence

In the Streatham Circle, a literary salon presided over by Mrs Thrale in her residence in Streatham Park which ran until shortly after her husband's death in 1781, Johnson occupied a central position, along with its hostess. Other important members were, apart from Mrs Thrale's husband and her daughter Queeney, the painter Sir Joshua Reynolds (1723–92), Queeney Thrale's music teacher Giuseppe Baretti (1719–89), the writer and politician Edmund Burke (1729/30–97), Charles Burney and David Garrick (Bax 2000: 277). Boswell, though Johnson's declared biographer, was not part of the group: he and Mrs Thrale were not friends, possibly because of their rivalry for Johnson's affection. After the publication of her first novel in 1778, Fanny Burney was included in the circle as well. By means of a network strength scale, developed on the basis of the one drawn up by Milroy (1987) in order to calculate the integration of network members into their social network, Bax shows that Johnson was the most central network member. Being in a position to set a linguistic norm, Johnson thus qualifies for an early adopter, and the other network members as followers of his norm. As, at best, a marginal network member, Boswell might qualify for the role of linguistic innovator. I have already referred to Johnson's influence on Fanny Burney, but Mrs Thrale's language was also subject to his influence. In the course of her correspondence with him, she changed her spelling of words in *-ic/ick*, as in *publick, enthusiastick, frolick* and *musick*, showing a consistent preference for the old-fashioned spelling *-ick*, whereas she used to write these words with *-ic* (Tieken-Boon van Ostade and Bax 2001). As discussed in Section 3.2, the spelling of words in *-ick* can be called Johnsonian, in the sense that it was prescribed in the *Dictionary* (of which the Thrales possessed a copy), while Johnson used it in his letters, too. Boswell, however, did not use the Johnsonian spelling, for he had learned in the late 1760s that the *-ic* spelling had become common practice (Pottle 1966: 359).

Boswell's use of *do* confirms that Johnson's language did not serve as a model for him. Both in his informative prose and in the language of his letters, his language shows greater similarities with that of Addison than with Johnson in this respect (Tieken-Boon van Ostade 1996b). Boswell had referred to Johnson's style as being characterised by 'inflated rotundity and tumified Latinity of Diction' (Quennell 1972: 174). Addison had been widely regarded as a model of good writing during the first half of the eighteenth century (Wright 1994), and his influence spread through the popularlity of *The Tatler* and *The Spectator*, which continued to be read well beyond the time of their publication. Boswell had been 'taught to admire Addison's prose' in school (Pottle 1950: 3), and in his letters he frequently referred to Addison's work, which confirms the high opinion he had of him. While Addison was the most influential linguistic model until around 1750, his role was taken over by Johnson in the second half of the century. This is evident, for instance, from the fact that Addison was among the authors most frequently criticised in Lowth's grammar of 1762 and later editions. Johnson's influence continued into the nineteenth century, as according to Phillipps (1970: 151) Jane Austen 'owes much ... to Dr Johnson'. One example may be her unusually conservative use of the *be/have* paradigm, already commented on (Section 6.2; Rydén and Brorström 1987: 201). Other than Fanny Burney, however, she evidently 'knew how to lighten the rather ponderous tendencies of a balanced, Latinate cast of sentence with the leaven of sprightly colloquial English', and as a grammatical example of this Phillipps (1970: 151–2) mentions her use of preposition stranding (see Section 5.3).

Applying the concept of Social Network Analysis may help explain the existence of linguistic models on a macro level, but it may also show how the language of individual people was influenced by other members belonging to the same network. Lowth, best known among linguists for his grammar, was also first and foremost a language user. Analysing his letters to different correspondents (called 'out-letters' by Baker 1980) as well as those addressed to him (the 'in-letters') helps to reconstruct the different social networks he was part of. Three major networks, or network clusters, can be distinguished: one around the year 1755 when he was away in Ireland and when attempts were made by his patrons to obtain a bishopric for him; one consisting of his family and friends who kept in touch with him with news from home; and a third network, or rather a coalition, which he tried to establish when he had been nominated Bishop of London in 1777 (Tieken-Boon van Ostade 2008c). A coalition could be defined as a 'strategic alliance' which someone would try to set up along 'with specifically selected other actors, for particular purposes, for a particular period of time' (Fitzmaurice 2000: 273). The coalition Lowth attempted to form included all the famous men of the period: the current as well as the previous Prime Minister, the one a Tory and the other, like Lowth himself, a Whig; the Lord Chancellor; the Lord Mayor; the Speaker of the House of Commons; the Lord Primate of Ireland; and Sir Joshua Reynolds, president of the Royal Academy. Lowth attempted to ally himself with these men by presenting them with a copy of his *Isaiah,* which had been published in 1778, the year after his appointment. It was something on which he spent an enormous amount of money, possibly as much as £250–300.

The extent to which Lowth was successful in this attempt is hard to measure, as we only have his correspondence as evidence. With Reynolds he did establish some kind of a relationship, though merely as acquaintances rather than as friends; another relationship he struck up was with Sir David Dalrymple (1726–92), a Scottish judge and historian. Dalrymple sent Lowth three books in return, and a lengthy correspondence ensued. The relationship, however, never became very close, as we can tell from the way Lowth signed his letters: all conclusions which included the word *affectionate* in one form or another or greetings to the addressee's wife indicate a close personal relationship, as in:

(8) We & our little **folks** [his children] are, I thank God, all well; & join
     in our best respects to M^{rs}. Speed & Yourself.

> I am very
>
> > sincerely, Dear S^r. Your most **Affectionate**
> >
> > humble   Servt.
> >
> > > Robt. Lowth. (1760; Lowth to Samuel Speed)

His letters to Dalrymple he continued to sign as 'S^r. Your most
Obedient/humble Servt.'. The analysis of address terms is of great use in
establishing the relationship between writer and addressee. This is true
for Lowth, but also for the Methodist minister John Wesley (1703–91)
(Baker 1980). The relationship between writer and addressee is one
of the variables that determines the relative formality of an utterance,
along with such things as the topic, the setting or the medium (speech
or writing) in which the communication occurs (Traugott and Romaine
1985). In Lowth's case, usage which he himself, in his own grammar at
least, considered to be ungrammatical correlates with the informality of
the style of his letters (see Chapter 5), and we similarly find so-called
informal spellings in the letters to his wife and his close friends (see
Chapter 3). There are also certain words that occur in his most intimate
letters only, such as *'tother* in the following letter to his nephew John
Sturges:

(9) I was talking with our good friend the B^p. of Chester **'tother** day of
     the present state of Ecclesiastical affairs (1778).

Another example is the word *folks*, as in (8), which is only found in the
letters to his wife. We can also see Lowth adopting different spellings on
the basis of the example he found in letters from people he corresponded
with, such as *immediatly* which is substituted by *immediately* from 1768
onwards. Lowth's linguistic self-consciousness can be linked to his class
consciousness. This is what made him write his grammar to begin with,
to offer his son Thomas Henry the best opportunities of making a career
for himself (Tieken-Boon van Ostade 2008d).

The application of the social network model to another LModE
network, the Bluestocking Circle, shows equally interesting results.
The Bluestockings, according to Sairio (2008: 133), were a 'circle of
learned and virtuous men and women whose salons and assemblies
were dedicated to polite conversation and who collaborated in literary and scholarly ventures'. The circle flourished around the middle

of the eighteenth century, and it included people like Elizabeth Montagu, Elizabeth Vesey (c.1715–91), Frances Boscawen (1719–1805), Elizabeth Carter, Catherine Talbot (1721–70) and Hester Chapone (1727–1801). Other members were Lord George Lyttelton (1709–73), William Pulteney, Earl of Bath (1684–1764), Mrs Thrale, Hannah More and Dr Johnson. Sairio studied the use of preposition stranding as well as its more acceptable counterpart, pied-piping, in a corpus of letters by members of the Bluestocking network, in order to discover whether prescriptivist attitudes to language had influenced that of the Bluestockings. She found that pied-piping, as in a rewritten version of example (22) in Chapter 5,

(10)   I shall otherwise have no Copy **by** which to correct [the proofs],

did indeed increase, but that this development was already set in motion before the normative grammarians could have had any influence. Mrs Montagu used the preferred form in her letters to members of the aristocracy, which shows that the grammatically correct form was believed to represent the then current norm of correctness. In her younger days, Mrs Montagu had been a member of a salon run by Lady Margaret Bentinck, Duchess of Portland (1715–85), and Sairio believes that through contacts like this she developed her ideas of what type of usage to imitate. That this linguistic modelling didn't just take place subconsciously is evident from the fact that her letters contain instances of where she corrected a sentence with preposition stranding into one with pied-piping. All this suggests that the language of the aristocracy was an important linguistic model to socially ambitious people. It is this model, rather than that of the middle classes, that formed the basis of many of the prescriptions in the normative grammars from the eighteenth century.

In Section 4.3, which reports on searches in the *OED* for lexical innovations for the nineteenth century, the two writers at the top of the list were Coleridge and Southey. Could we therefore also call them linguistic innovators in a Social Network sense? To qualify for this label they would have to be characterised as socially and/or geographically mobile, and to have been marginal members of the social networks they belonged to. Pratt and Denison (2000) deal with this issue, and they argue that Coleridge and Southey belonged to a close-knit social network of writers. The members of this network, which included people like the Wordsworths, Charles Lamb (1775–1834), Percy Bysshe Shelley (1792–1822), Mary Shelley (1797–1851), John Keats (1795–1821) and Walter Savage Landor, all knew each other, regularly corresponded together and were often in close proximity of each other. They had similar social and educational backgrounds, shared cultural and political sympathies, as well as literary ambitions, and had a very similar style of writing. They employed, for instance, what Pratt and Denison refer to as 'a complicated "Language of Allusion"', which seems to have functioned as a sign of group membership. A similar use of allusions is found in the correspondence of Dr Johnson and Mrs Thrale (Bax 2002) and in that of Walpole and his Eton friends (Henstra 2007), which suggests that it served as an important binding mechanism between friends. Pratt and Denison discovered that the Southey–Coleridge Circle is associated with the introduction of a new construction into English, the passive progressive, as in:

(11) His tooth was being pulled out.

Though the construction is first found in the 1770s, it subsequently became a feature of the language of the Southey–Coleridge Circle. Instances were subsequently found in the language of various members, such as Southey (1795), Coleridge (1797), Mary Shelley (1817), Shelley (1819), Lamb (1823) and Landor (1829). Pratt and Denison believe that the construction even became 'a linguistic sign of group identity', and that it 'spread slowly outwards from that circle at first, only later becoming more acceptable in print' (2000: 416–17). This suggests that Southey and Coleridge were early adopters here, not linguistic innovators, and that the other users followed their norm. That Mary Shelley is listed as the next user in this list may be significant, and I will return to the question of the special position of women in relation to linguistic change in Section 6.5. But how the passive progressive entered the social network, or in other words who the real linguistic innovators were, is still a mystery.

6.5 Social network analysis and the language of women

In her study of the language of Wordsworth and Coleridge, Austin (1989: 3) notes that Dorothy Wordsworth 'was undoubtedly a great influence on both poets', and that this is one of the complicating factors in trying to distinguish between the language of the two men. With all three being members of a close-knit social network that showed similar linguistic usage throughout, this is not very surprising. It is nevertheless unlikely that Dorothy Wordsworth would have had the role of early adopter in the network, as women rarely functioned as linguistic models in those days. Sarah Fielding presents a similar case, despite the fact that she was a writer and a scholar of repute (Tieken-Boon van Ostade 2000a). Lady Mary Wortley Montagu, however, stands out here, as I've discussed in Section 6.3, due to the fact that, until she and Pope fell out, she generally fulfilled a role similar to that of the well-known male writers in her circle.

When studying the Belfast vernacular, the Milroys dicovered that women sometimes behaved linguistically like men (Milroy 1987). This was the case in the area in which there was a lot of male unemployment, and where the women went out to work instead. Such women had more multiplex network ties and were consequently more strongly integrated into the social network than the men. Their language accordingly showed more vernacular features than that of the men, due to the fact that the women were more subject to the norm enforcement mechanism of their social network. It is therefore not so much a person's sex that acts as a variable correlating with a person's linguistic behaviour as their degree of integration into a social network. This would equally be the case in social networks today that exhibit a traditional role division between men and women as in pre-industrialised society, in which women were not usually as highly educated as the men of their social class. They did not normally have the kind of jobs which would enable them to contract multiplex network ties, by which they would be subject to stronger network integration and greater exposure to the network norm as well as to the need to adhere to it.

Gender differs from sex as a variable in relation to the way in which men and women are expected to behave in society and do so accordingly, in that it is a woman's duty to at stay at home and look after her family rather than go out to work. In the LModE period, women did not usually receive much formal education, and it would not be until well into the nineteenth century that they could go to university (Section 1.4). Lady Mary Wortley Montagu and Sarah Fielding – and many other women of their time (Clarke 2000) – were exceptional, in that somehow or other they did obtain the kind of education that put them into the same category of the men in their social class. Fanny Burney was not as ambitious as these women with respect to her education. In her biography of Mrs Beeton, Hughes writes that Sam and Isabella Beeton had 'a companionate marriage based on respect, love, and an unspoken assumption of absolute equality' (2005: 324). From a present-day perspective, Isabella's brief life can be described as a working woman's career. Hughes argues that Isabella's position was not exceptional at the time, and it would be interesting to discover whether this was reflected in her language and that of other women like her. The early New England factory women studied by Kiełkiewicz-Janowiak must have been like the women in Milroy's study of the Belfast vernacular: they 'left their homes and native villages to work in the textile industry', and many of them 'sought to continue education during their stay in a mill town' (Kiełkiewicz-Janowiak 2002: 195, 77). Their language must consequently have shown characteristics that were more similar to that of the men of their class than the women who did not go out to work or educate themselves further. Bäcklund (2006: 35) discovered a greater increase in the course of the nineteenth century in the use of modifiers of the kind illustrated in (12) and (13) by women than by men, and attributes this to 'an adaptation on the part of the female writers to a more male style of writing'.

(12)   a man **of quick impulse and energetic action**

(13)   a man **of known musical talent.**

It would be interesting to find out if more such differences can be detected. Gender roles were changing at the time due to women's suffrage movement (Bäcklund 2006: 18), and this is confirmed by linguistic evidence.

Modern sociolinguistic studies often show that female informants conform more closely to standard English in their usage than men. Historical studies confirm that women are frequently in the vanguard of linguistic change: this was true for eleven of the fourteen features analysed by Nevalainen and Raumolin-Burnberg (2003) in their study of EModE letters. This study also demonstrated that women never actually initiated linguistic change, but that they took the lead only after a change had been set in motion. There is in all this clearly a correlation with gender in the sense that due to limited educational and economic possibilities women were less strongly integrated into their social networks. Rather than being as much subject to the norm enforcement mechanism of their social networks as their male counterparts, they would adopt network external features, and in particular those that were in the process of becoming part of the standard language. At the same time, sociolinguistic studies show that women, like the lower middle classes, tend to be linguistically insecure (Coates 1986: 71–2); it is this that makes them adopt a feature once it is clear that it is going to be part of the standard. From this perspective, it might be argued that the eleven features identified by Nevalainen and Raumolin-Brunberg in which women's language is more advanced than that of men are instances of hypercorrection. The same applies to the use of periphrastic *do* by Lady Mary Wortley Montagu, usage of *do*-less negative sentences in her essays, as in *I question not*, is only 2 per cent, compared to the average figure of 25 per cent for the eighteenth century as a whole (Tieken-Boon van Ostade 1987: 136). Lady Mary Wortley Montagu, however, was far from linguistically insecure, and she was moreover the only born aristocrat among my eighteenth-century informants. As *do*-less negative sentences eventually disappeared from standard English, this is another example of how the language of the upper classes presented a norm of correct usage (compare Section 6.4).

6.6 Concluding remarks

There are several studies in Kytö, Rydén and Smitterberg (2006) that show that women were ahead of ongoing linguistic changes, for example in the use of the subjunctive (see Section 5.2) and in the greater use of *that* in restrictive relative clauses (Johansson 2006: 140). Arnaud (1998) has similarly shown that women were more advanced in their use of the progressive; Mary Shelley is a case in point (Section 6.4). Sairio (2006) noticed a function in the use of the progressive that is typical of women's letters, that is, in the expression of immediacy, as in:

(14) I **am writing** at Mrs Boscawen's table, who desires her best compts. (1761?; Elizabeth Montagu to Edward Montagu)

However, this usage occurs in letters from male members of the Bluestocking Circle as well. Arnaud, who identified the same preference for the progressive in Jane Austen's most intimate letters, attributes the spread of the progressive to a change from below in that the usage is adopted unconsciously due to contact with servants. A similar case is the spread of *please* as a courtesy marker discussed in Section 4.3, the first instances of which occur in representations of the language of servants. Rather than calling women linguistic innovators, as Johansson (2006: 172) does in her study of relativisers in nineteenth-century English, from the perspective of the research model of social network analysis the servants, as the very marginal members of middle-class social networks, were the true linguistic innovators. It will be interesting to analyse in detail what role they played in bringing about other instances of change from below during the LModE period. The middle-class women, as the ones who were most in touch with servants − maids, nannies, housekeepers − would have acted as instruments in giving greater currency to the new forms. All this might also explain Johansson's finding (2006: 178) that they made greater use of the informal, colloquial feature of preposition stranding at a time when this construction was stigmatised.

Further reading

The Social Network model is dealt with in detail by Milroy (1987); for social network analysis in a historical context, see Milroy and Milroy (1985b) as well as the special issue of *European Journal of English Studies* edited by Tieken-Boon van Ostade, Nevalainen and Caon (2000). In addition, the social networks of different eighteenth-century individuals are discussed by Bax (2000, 2002, 2005), Henstra (2008) and Sairio (2006, 2008). The Lunar Men as a network are the subject of Uglow (2002), though Uglow doesn't deal with their language (compare Section 4.4). Epistolary formulas in eighteenth-century letters are the subject of various studies, for example, Austin ([1973] 1998), Tieken-Boon van Ostade (1999) for the eighteenth century and Phillipps (1984: 133–67) for the Victorian age, in particular the aristocracy. On regional and social variation in language, see *CHEL* Vol. III, Chapter 6 (Görlach 1999b).

Research questions

1. Describe your own social network or network cluster. Would you characterise it as open or closed? On what grounds? If closed, what features, linguistic or otherwise, are typical of the network that serve as a means of identification to you and the other members?
2. Do an advanced search in ECCO that combines, for instance, 'Priestley = author' and 'Darwin = full text' and vice versa, and repeat this for all the members of the Lunar Society (see Chapter 4). How closed would you say their social network was? How can the relationships between these men be identified as a correlate with the number of times they refer to each other in their published work?
3. From the lists of eighteenth- and nineteenth-century letter collections published in *Historical Sociolinguistics and Sociohistorical Linguistics* (see Correspondences in Weblinks), select one letter writer and study their use of epistolary formulas (opening as well as closing ones). How do different formulas correlate with different social relationships?
4. Study the occurrence of *yours sincerely* in different collections of letters from the eighteenth and nineteenth centuries (see the lists referred to in Research Question 3). When does this formula cease to express informality? What new forms are adopted instead?
5. Study the use of *-ic/ick* in the letters of any member of Johnson's circle (see the relevant list referred to in Research Question 3). (Check that the editor did not normalise or modernise the spelling.) Any changes over the years?

6. Select one LModE author whose correspondence has been published. Study the author's entry in the *ODNB* and determine whether he or she was socially and/or geographically mobile. Select a batch of letters from a short period of the author's correspondence (see the list referred to in Research Question 3) and try to determine the author's position in the social network (linguistic innovator, early adopter, follower).

7. In the introduction to his edition of John Wesley's correspondence, Baker (1980: 48) identifies a kind of hierarchy of terms of address, for which see Section 7.2 below. Select one LModE correspondence and try to determine to what extent the author in question made use of a similar system and how this enables you to describe his or her social network.

8. Identify letters, or parts of letters, in a correspondence that deal with a particular topic. In what way or ways would the language of the letters (lexicon, style) correlate with the topic?

9. Isolate variant spellings in any LModE correspondence (see Chapter 3). Analyse the extent to which the variation found corresponds with the relationship between writer and addressee. What are their relative positions in their social network?

10. Study the use of the progressive in an early nineteenth-century correspondence. What different forms of the progressive do you identify? Any differences in usage according to addressee/style of writing?

7 The language of letters and other text types

7.1 Introduction

In Chapter 3 of Jane Austen's *Northanger Abbey* (1817) the good-looking Mr Tilney tells Catherine Morland, the novel's heroine:

> 'I shall make but a poor figure in your journal to-morrow.'
> 'My journal!'
> 'Yes, I know exactly what you will say: Friday, **went to** the Lower Rooms; **wore** my sprigged muslin robe with blue trimmings – plain black shoes – **appeared** to much advantage; but **was** strangely **harassed by** a queer, half-witted man, who would make me dance with him, and distressed me by his nonsense.'
> 'Indeed I shall say no such thing.'

Evidently, Tilney not only knew that young ladies kept diaries, or journals as he calls them,[1] but he was also familiar with the typical language used to record everyday events, for example, sentences from which the subject would be elided, as in the above 'went to', 'wore', 'appeared', 'was harassed by'. Depending on the purpose of the journal, as well as on the inclinations of the writer, its language might be more or less elliptical. Fanny Burney's journal takes the form of letters addressed to her sister Susan, and so does Betsy Sheridan's, who wrote to her sister Alicia in Dublin, and their sentences rarely show any signs of typical journal language:

(1) Indeed, my dearest Susy, I know not how to express the *fullness of my contentment* at this sweet place (1778; Troide et al. 1988–, Vol. III: 83)

(2) I sent off my journal in a sort of hurry yesterday as I was afraid you would be uneasy if you were longer without hearing from me. (1785; Lefanu 1960: 47)

In addressing their writing to someone, these authors are in effect talking on paper. Some journal writers need an addressee, real or otherwise, and at the start of her journal Fanny Burney created a fictitious 'Nobody', which gave occasion to a pun:

> (3) To Nobody, then, will I write my Journal! Since To Nobody can I be wholly unreserved – to Nobody can I reveal my every thought, every wish of my Heart. (1768; Troide et al. 1988–, Vol. I: 2)

She soon, however, abandoned what Troide calls her 'girlish attempts at the "sublime" style' that characterise the language of (3) in favour of a more colloquial style that looks like real talk. One reason that her diaries are of great value for historical linguists is that they include a lot of dialogue, as in (4):

> (4) Sunday morning, when I went into the Library [at Streatham Park, see Section 6.4], Mr. Thrale called out: 'Why, Miss Burney, this will never do!'
> 'What Sir?' cried I.
> 'Why You grow Thinner & Thinner! You have hardly any *waist* left already! What account can I give of you to Dr. Burney?'
> 'Ay, well, cried Mr. Lort, drily, – she will be *all* spirit, & *no* substance, by & by, for she *Eats* nothing; – however, it will be all the better for the *World*, one way or other!' (1778; Troide et al. 1988–, Vol. III: 122)

Though there is of course no way to check this, the dialogue sounds natural; in her own time, Fanny Burney had quite a reputation for recording direct speech faithfully, like Boswell for his *Life of Johnson* (Tieken-Boon van Ostade 2000b: 443–4).

Journals like Fanny Burney's represent one type of document that gives us access to the spoken language from before the time when it was possible to record speech. In *Everyday English 1500–1700*, Cusack (1998) includes various other documents that do likewise: Abuse, Depositions and Presentments. In addition, her collection contains Accounts, Journals, Letters, Memoirs and Wills. Though she doesn't call them so, these documents are instances of 'text types', a relatively new concept in historical linguistics. Görlach (1992: 738) defines text types as 'specific linguistic pattern[s] in which formal/structural characteristics have been conventionalized in a specific culture for certain well-defined and standardized uses of language'. In other words, people can readily identify a text type as such, knowing what its structural and linguistic characteristics are, as in the case of Mr Tilney's reference to the journal in *Northanger Abbey*. Görlach identified more than a thousand English text types, such as dedicatory letters, cooking recipes, advertisements, church hymns, jokes, administrative texts, scholarly texts, grammar books, private letters, journalism and newspaper reports, drama, poetry, narrative texts, book reviews, obituaries and essays (see Görlach 2004). In this chapter, I can treat only a limited number of text types; my selection includes Depositions, Journals, Memoirs, Newspapers, Letters, Recipes and Wills, and as the private letter was a major LModE text type, I will start with Letters.

7.2 Letters

According to Cusack (1998: 190), 'for most people in the sixteenth and seventeenth centuries, letters are substitute speech, a means of communication when the other person is absent', and this was true for the LModE period, too. Betsy Sheridan, for instance, told her sister: 'To you my dear Love I write as I talk in all modes and tempers' (1788; Lefanu 1960: 123), and Isabella Mayson, during the days of her courtship, wrote to her fiancé Sam Beeton, 'I take advantage of this after dinner opportunity to enjoy myself and have a small chat with you on paper' (Hughes 2005: 102). Kiełkiewicz-Janowiak (2002: 189–90) notes about the correspondence between Aaron Burr (1756–1836) and his daughter Theodosia (1783–1813), whom she classifies as New England aristocrats, that 'stylistically it is reminiscent of modern telephone conversations':

(5) Pray how do you advance? Heavy business, is it not? I beg you will perform your promise, and write me the history of it (1803; Theodosia to Aaron Burr)

(6) I told you the negotiation should not be long. It is finished – concluded – for ever abandoned – liber sum. (1803; Aaron to Theodosia Burr)

Such letters represent the writers' vernacular or ordinary everyday language, and are therefore a possible alternative to the spoken language studied by modern sociolinguists (Tieken-Boon van Ostade 2005). But not all letters can be taken as substitute speech, as particularly during the eighteenth century letters paradoxically had to be given the impression of being produced spontaneously. Letter writing was considered to be an 'Art', and the best letters, according to Anderson and Ehrenpreis (1966: 273), were not 'thoughtless outpourings' but the result of considerable effort. Tillyard (1994) quotes Emily and Caroline Lennox, two eighteenth-century aristocratic sisters, on this:

Emily and Caroline saw themselves as self-conscious letter writers with 'formed' styles. Like polite conversation, letter writing was an accomplishment with its own complex rules, as Caroline revealed when she told Emily how ashamed she was that [her son] Ste Fox wrote like a child at the age of seventeen. 'His letters are quite a schoolboy's. He is well, hopes we are, and compliments to everybody. Adieu. Yours Most Sincerely.' Emily's daughter, in contrast, received Caroline's praise for epistolary skill. 'I wrote to your daughter Emily . . . She is a delightful correspondent, her style quite formed . . .'. (Tillyard 1994: 93)

Studying such contrived letters is a historical version of what is known as the Observer's Paradox: in modern sociolinguistics, due to how data is collected (mostly through interviews), the presence of the investigator acts as a bar against obtaining access to the object of analysis, the speaker's vernacular language. In historical sociolinguistics, it is the medium − writing, and often carefully monitored writing at that − that prevents researchers from approaching a writer's most vernacular style.

Letters, therefore, are *not* speech, and should be analysed accordingly. But like speech, they show evidence of a writer's communicative competence or the ability to vary in style − and consequently in language use − depending on the formality of the utterance. Relative formality is largely determined by the situation, the topic and the relationship with the addressee (see Section 6.4), and I have already shown above that this makes LModE letter writers vary in spelling as well as in grammar. Such variation is as systematic as that found in modern sociolinguistic analysis of speech. Studying the language of letters has, moreover, produced new insights into the development of the English language. Nevalainen and Raumolin-Brunberg (2003), for instance, have shown on the basis of their Corpus of Early English Correspondence (c.1410−1681) that double negation disappeared from English well before the normative grammarians started criticising it (see Section 5.2). The disappearing process therefore took place irrespective of any influence from above such as grammars or usage guides, but it was motivated, consciously or unconsciously, by the speakers themselves. Why it disappeared is possibly due to the development of more literate styles of writing: double negation is a typically oral feature. Another example of the importance of the language of letters to our knowledge of earlier phases of the English language is that we now know, for instance, that *yours sincerely* started out as a formula expressing intimacy between writer and addressee rather than distance, as it does today (Section 6.3). How or why the formula changed still needs to be investigated.

Letters have a form that is easy to recognise: Nevalainen (2004: 181) defines a letter as 'consisting of written communication typically addressed to one or more named recipients, and identifying the sender and conveying a message'. In doing all this, the letter writer makes use of formulaic language, particularly at the beginning and at the end, as in a letter by Sarah Fielding to James Harris, which starts with 'Sir,/I am much obliged to you for the Favour of yours', that is, his letter, and it ends with 'I am Sir with sincere Respect/ your obliged and Obed^t./ hum^ble. Servant/ S Fielding' (1758; Battestin and Probyn 1993: 141). A typical, though very short example is the following letter from John Wesley, which contains all the essential ingredients of a letter, if only barely so: the date, the opening and closing addresses, contents and the writer's signature (Baker 1980: 52):

(7)   Aug. 13. 1774

    My dear brother

        All is well. I am,

                    Yours affectionately

                        J. Wesley.

On the basis of his analysis of Wesley's correspondence, Baker (1980: 48) drew up a hierarchically arranged set of opening formulas:

Sir/Madam

Dear Sir/Dear Madam

My dear Mr. −/Mrs. −/Miss X

My dear brother/sister

Dear James/Jane, etc.

Dear Jemmy/Jenny, etc.

Standard closing formulas consisted of three elements: the address ('I am, Dear Sir'), the 'compliments' or 'services' ('your most obedient humble servant') and the signature (Baker 1980: 59). Such formulas are of a typically 'courtly' nature (McIntosh 1986), but they were used by men and women alike. Variations in the middle section of the closing formula, such as the substitution of 'obedient' by 'affectionate', are an important clue to the nature of the relationship between writer and addressee, and to changes in this respect. The language used in the body of the letter may be expected to correlate with the epistolary formulas selected: the more formal the formula, the less variation will be found in the language and the more closely the language adheres to that of the standard as defined in the grammars and dictionaries of the period.

Sarah Fielding's repetition of the word 'Sir' in the closing formula quoted above was prescribed by the letter-writing manuals, which informed writers of how to write an appropriate letter. Such formulas, according to Austin ([1973] 1998), are many centuries old, and their continuity is partly due to the influence of guidebooks like *The Complete Letter Writer* (Anon., 2nd edn 1756). These manuals similarly gave instruction on how to write different types of letters, offering, as the title-page of *The Complete Letter-Writer* informs the reader, 'DIRECTIONS for writing Letters on all Occasions, in a polite, easy, and proper Manner; with a great variety of Examples, from the best Authors, in BUSINESS, DUTY, AMUSEMENT, AFFECTION, COURTSHIP, LOVE, MARRIAGE, FRIENDSHIP, &c'. Many letter writers simply copied the example letters, so such letters obviously do not represent their own language. Sequences of letters are of interest in that they can be analysed similarly to actual conversations (Fitzmaurice 2002), though taking place at a distance in time as well as space; they can also bring to light the operation of linguistic influence within a social network to which writer and addressee belonged (Section 6.4).

As letters concern both a writer and an addressee, they are typically characterised by the use of so-called 'involvement strategies' (Sairio 2005: 24). This results in a frequent use of first person pronouns ('ego involvement') and second person pronouns (as part of 'interpersonal involvement'). Sairio believes that the higher the involvement between writer and addressee, the more evidential verbs such as *think, know, believe* and *suppose* are found, as well as degree adverbs (*very, so, quite, pretty, really*) and first and second person singular pronouns. To illustrate this, a passage may be cited from a letter by Mary Jackson Lee (1783–1860), one of Kiełkiewicz-Janowiak's New England women:

(8) **I really** think of **you** with astonishment **my** dear husband **you**, who need to profess not to love letter writing, not to understand it, to have become **such** an adept in the business for it ~~really~~ discovers no inconsiderable talent to be able to write **so** much & render all **you** write **so** interesting when **you** have no incidents with which to enliven **your** epistles. (1813; Kiełkiewicz-Janowiak 2002: 143)

Even Mary Jackson Lee, upon rereading her letter, noticed the high degree of involvement expressed, and she struck out one instance of the word *really*.

Apart from particular epistolary formulas and the use of involvement features, the nature of the relationship between letter writer and addressee can be deduced from the occurrence of contractions like *won't*, *can't*, *don't* and *I'll*. These forms are of interest as they reflect pronunciation, but according to the letter-writing manuals they were not supposed to be used; nor were abbreviations, shortened forms that do not reflect pronunciation but that are typical features of letter writing because they speeded up the writing process, such as y^e., y^t., y^n. and *Affect.* for 'the', 'that', 'than' and 'Affectionately'. Forms like these were considered to show disrespect to the addressee and excessive familiarity; see, for instance, the following passage from the chapter on 'Directions and Observations on EPISTOLARY CORRESPONDENCE' in Carter's *Practical English Grammar* (1773):

> WHEN you are writing to your Superior, . . . be particularly careful in not omitting any Letter belonging to the Words you write; as, *I've, can't, don't, wou'd*, &c. Instead of *I have, cannot, do not, would*, &c. for such Contractions appear disrespectful and too familiar. (Carter 1773: 140)

In Lowth's letters, the presence of such contractions correlates with his relationship with the addressee, but I also encountered an extraordinarily high incidence of contractions and abbreviations in the letters he received from Edward Pearson, his secretary while he was – briefly – Bishop of St Davids in 1766. As Lowth was Pearson's superior, these features indicate the kind of easy familiarity that might be typical of the relationship between a boss and his secretary. A greater variation in spelling as well as the occurrence of spelling features that are typical of letters rather than of printed texts similarly correlates with informality in the relationship between writer and addressee (see Chapter 3). What is furthermore of interest is that long <s> continues in nineteenth-century letters long after it ceased to occur in printed books (Section 3.2), though only in words like *busineſs* and *likeneſs* (Mugglestone 2006: 281).

Essential first-hand experience of transcribing LModE letters – and, next, of studying their language – can be acquired through electronic collections like that of the letters and other papers of the naturalist Sir Joseph Banks (1743–1820), published online by the State Library of New South Wales (Weblinks). Banks participated in various voyages of discovery with the explorer Captain James Cook, and according to the New South Wales Library website 'practically anyone who wanted to travel to New South Wales, in almost any capacity, consulted Sir Joseph Banks'. The collection covers the letters by many different people,

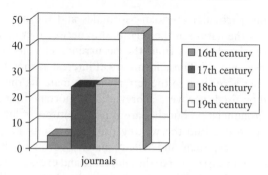

Figure 7.1 An overview of journals published between the sixteenth and nineteenth centuries (based on Ponsonby 1923: 45–54).

including Joseph Priestley and William Clift. Banks hadn't been a very diligent student when he was young, and this is evident in the language of his letters as an adult. Many of the letters in the collection belong to the category of business letters, which differ considerably in terms of personal involvement from private letters such as those illustrated in examples (5)–(8).

7.3 Journals

Journals, according to Cusack (1998: 158), 'commit to paper the events of a day'. She adds: 'They are private documents, aiming at no reader other than oneself at some future time, looking back to review past events and experiences.' I have already shown that this definition does not apply to all journals, in any case not to those of Betsy Sheridan and Fanny Burney, and another example is the diary of the New Englander Mary Jackson Lee, who kept a journal which her husband could read after returning from his travels (Kiełkiewicz-Janowiak 2002: 54). Such diaries are of a hybrid nature, in the sense that they were directed at a specific if closely related addressee, and they should more appropriately be called journal letters. Cusack (1998: 158) notes that journal writing was popular during the seventeenth century, and if Ponsonby's (1923) survey is still anything to go by this popularity increased during the LModE period (see Figure 7.1). Since the publication of Ponsonby's overview, many more journals have been published, such as those by Mrs Thrale (called *Thraliana*), Boswell and Betsy Sheridan, as well as Martha Ballard, Elizabeth Barrett Browning (1806–61) and John Ruskin (1819–1900). An updating of Ponsonby's survey is definitely called for.

Journals were kept by men and women from different social

backgrounds: Ponsonby's survey includes a lady in waiting, a yeoman farmer, a clergyman, a schoolmaster, a novelist, a diplomat, a shop assistant (male), a Mrs Brown and Lady Mary Coke (1727–1811), who is described in the *ODNB* merely as a 'letter writer and noblewoman' and who was a friend of Horace Walpole. In journals that were strictly intended for the writer's personal use, one might expect to find less carefully unmonitored writing than in the case of letters (or journal letters) in that there would be no addressee to whom writers would be required to accommodate their language (see Chapter 6). When looking for evidence of the vernacular, one needs to to reckon with the typical characteristics of the language of journals, such as ellipsis of the subject, as already discussed in Section 7.1, but also of other features:

- economy of allusiveness in referring to people, places and circum-stances familiar to the writer
- omission of verbs
- special patterns of organising a journal entry
- co-ordination rather than subordination
- the absence of second person forms (in the absence of a direct addressee).   (Cusack 1998: 161–3)

A preference for co-ordinated sentences is similarly a characteristic of the spoken language. Like letters, the language of journals shows instances of involvement, though, obviously, ego involvement only. We might therefore similarly expect to find a high incidence of evidential verbs and degree adverbs, but the expected occurrence of first person pronouns may be hampered by the tendency to elide the subject. What is more, we might expect to find typically gendered language, as the writer would be writing primarily for him or herself alone. An example of this is Boswell's *London Journal* (Pottle 1950), in which he records his encoun-ters with prostitutes, using fairly explicit language in the process:

(9) I picked up a girl in the Strand; went into a court with the intention to **enjoy** her in **armour** [a condom]. But she had none. I **toyed** with her. She wondered at my **size**, and said if I ever took a girl's **maidenhead**, I would make her **squeak**. I gave her a shilling . . . (1762; Pottle 1950: 49–50)

Despite Boswell's candidness, we must reckon with the possibility of personal inhibitions in language use even in a diary intended for – more or less – private reading, as Fanny Burney, for instance, was hesitant to use any relatively explicit terms to refer to her stepmother's pregnancy:

(10) … teazing me with *particular* questions, on **a** *particular* **subject**, which related to a *particular* case, concerning Mama − Can you not guess *what*? (1768; Troide et al. 1988−, Vol. I: 19)

She even refrained from writing down the 'particulars' relating to a love affair which resulted in the marriage of a friend:

(11) Nevertheless − she − was married last Saturday! − Good Heaven − what a romantic Life has this beloved friend Lived! − I dare not commit **particulars** to paper. (Troide et al. 1988−, Vol. I: 222)

Such prudishness, if that is what it was, increased in the course of her lifetime, for when she revised her journals later in life, Fanny Burney, by then Madame d'Arblay, rigorously cut out and overscored what she considered to be potentially offensive passages. The editors of her journals endeavoured to recover the obliterated passages, and an analysis of them gives an interesting insight into how she came to view earlier events but also into her own changed language use. Fanny Burney, who lived well into the Victorian age, may be considered an early case of someone whose usage was influenced by current attitudes to language, which, for instance, resulted in tabooing even a common word like *trousers* (Brook 1970: 189). These were commonly referred to by the word *unmentionables*:

(12) **1836–7** DICKENS *Sk. Boz, Shabby-Genteel People*, The knees of the unmentionables..began to get alarmingly white. (*OED*)

An interesting journal that may be used to illustrate the typical language of diaries is Martha Ballard's diary, already referred to in Chapter 2 for possible evidence on local pronunciation. The following entry, which follows the one in which she reports the delivery of a daughter to a Mrs Floid, is a typical one:

(13) Cloudy. Came from Floids about Day Br^k, Left her Comfortable. Received my fee. mr Floid Breakfasted here. Cyrus & Hannah Set out for Sebastac^k. I Slept ye afternorne, feele Better. moon full this D^y 11^h 1^m aftern. (1785)

As expected, the pronoun *I* is barely used here, and its only instance serves to clarify what would have been an ambiguous sentence. Later entries become more elaborate, and we see the pronoun *I* and its oblique forms appear as a result as well:

(14) Clear, Pleasant day. mr Waid workt here. I did **my** washing, Sally Did
      the house work. Cyrus Conducted **me** to See mr Dingley and famely.
      I find him poorly, his wife better. Hannah unwell. mr Ballard Came
      there for **me** at 8h Evn. mr Gill Came in Soon after him for **me** to go
      and See his wife who is in Labour and was Safe Delivered of a Daug^t
      between 10 and 11h Evn. Old Lady Brooks, mrss Capin and Dagt
      Lambard were assistants, they all returnd from there. **I** tarried all
      night. (1798)

Other typical features of diary language, such as the lack of verbs, are
still evident in (14) (*his wife better*), while subordination is indeed almost
completely absent.

Examples (13) and (14) illustrate what Cusack calls 'special patterns
of organising a journal entry'. Martha Ballard starts most of her entries
with a comment on the weather, relevant information for someone who
travelled as much as she did. An analysis of this feature would throw light
on the terminology used to refer to the weather in colloquial everyday
English of the time. Another 'special pattern' of Martha Ballard's diary
is the marking of deliveries in the margin, as in:

(15) Birth Theop^s Hamlins 2^{nt} Son & 4th Child. (1795)

There was a financial reason for this, as she was essentially keeping an
account of the babies she had delivered, which was her source of income.
Examples (13) and (14) also illustrate that, as with informal letters (see
Section 7.2), abbreviations and contractions had an important function
in diary writing. An example is the word *delivered*, which is far more
frequent in its abbreviated form in the diary (118 instances) than its full
form (8).

Martha Ballard's diary can be searched for words that would be
typical of the profession of a midwife. Doing so produces interesting
results. The word *baby*, for instance, does not occur; instead, *child* (935),
son (3290) and *daughter* (410) are used. Though not all these instances
refer to newborn babies, do these figures suggest that more boys were
born than girls? Another interesting feature is that *fine* collocates far
more frequently with *son* (104) than with *daughter* (16), which, as *daughter*
rarely collocates with anything where newborn babies are concerned,
possibly reflects on the greater preference for boys as a future economic
security factor than girls.

If words like *pregnant* or *pregnancy* were taboo for Fanny Burney, what
about a midwife like Martha Ballard? *Pregnant* is indeed attested in
the diary, though only twice; the more colloquial *with child*, with one

occurrence only, is equally rare, and another possible alternative, *expecting*, is not found at all. According to Fairman (2007), in his corpus of letters by unschooled writers the word *big* is used instead, but this word is not part of Martha Ballard's register either. The question of what words she would have used instead deserves further analysis. The diary, in any case, is a fruitful source for the study of the kind of colloquial medical terminology used by healers like Martha Ballard, who was not educated in the medical profession in any way similar to her male counterparts. That the word *delivery* only occurs from 1791 onwards suggests that she did pick up some more learned medical terms in the course of practising her profession.

7.4 Memoirs

Memoirs, according to Cusack (1998: 254), differ from journals in that writers of journals look back on the events of the day expecting the entries to be of future use, while in memoirs the events are looked at from a distance with the purpose 'of making a story out of some particular past time in [a writer's] life'. Compared to letters, memoirs, but also journals, typically deal with past events, and the language of these text types differs accordingly. To begin with, memoirs are written in the past tense, but, like journals, they are written from a first-person perspective. What memoirs have in common with journals is that there is no addressee, so that the pronoun *you* does not occur. Cusack (1998: 255) notes that it is not uncommon for memoirs to have a printed version. In this light, the language of memoirs may be more carefully planned than that of journals (or, indeed, private letters), either with a view to presenting an account for an external readership or to having the text published. Memoirs will therefore contain less evidence of vernacular usage than journals or informal letters.

An example of a published memoir that has also come down to us in manuscript is that of Laurence Sterne. As explained in Section 3.3, the memoirs had been written in 1767, allegedly for his daughter Lydia, who published them in 1775 (Monkman 1985: vii). The differences between the two versions are considerable, and led Monkman, the editor of the text, to ask the question of what Lydia had done to the manuscript. The text was evidently written spontaneously, though Sterne's interlineations suggest that he revised it afterwards. Example (16), the opening sentence, illustrates the differences found:

(16)a. Roger Sterne ^{Grandson to Arch Bishop Sterne} Lieutenant in Handy:sides
     Regiment, married to Agnes Hobert, widow of an Officer, I think

a Captain of a good Family: her Family name, I believe was Nuttle
– Tho' upon Recollection, That was the name of her Father in Law
(MS)

(16)b. ROGER STERNE, (grandson to Archbishop Sterne) Lieutenant in
Handaside's regiment, was married to Agnes Hebert, widow of a
captain of a good family: her family name was (I believe) Nuttle –
though, upon, recollection, that was the name of her father-in-law
(printed version).

A number of these differences do indeed seem attributable to Lydia, such
as some misreadings (*Hebert* for *Hobert*), the 'improvement' of particular
phrases (but also of some facts), and the suppression of certain dates
(Monkman 1985: xiii). But there are also many spelling and punctuation differences that must be attributed to the printer or typesetter, such
as the removal of extra initial capitals and the expansion of contractions,
the normalisation of genitival *'s* and the standardisation of place names,
the normalisation and standardisation of the spelling variation of the
-ed ending of weak verbs (MS *carryd, orderd, furnish d, unhinged, supplyed,
fetch'd*) and of compounds (MS *Arch Bishop, Birth Day, a Drift, small Pox*),
and the correction of unacceptable or old-fashioned spellings (MS *Father
in Law, Mony, Designe, untill*) (Tieken-Boon van Ostade 1998: 463–4).
The spelling differences between the two versions suggest that much
had changed since Sterne had learned to spell as a child. Interestingly,
the pronoun *I* is barely used by Sterne, despite the fact that, according
to Cusack (1998: 257), memoirs 'are, by definition, written in the first
person singular'.

Lowth's memoirs, by contrast, were never published.[2] Compared to
Sterne's memoirs, which comprise some 1400 words, the text is very
short indeed: only 521 words. The text may, indeed, not have been
written for publication. It has all the ingredients of a memoir, in that it
mentions his parents, his marriage to Mary Jackson, his children, his
education, his career, including his various bishoprics, and his publications. In listing all these, he occasionally adds an expression of feelings,
such as 'Had the honour of a Conference with the King of Prussia, by his
Majesty's orders', 'Thomas Henry Lowth born Dec[r]. 16.1753: he died
(Fellow of New Coll. Oxf[d]. Rector of Thorley Hants), June 7. 1778: **a
most excellent Youth!**' and, on the publication of the grammar which
made him famous, 'Many Editions since in 12[mo]. all corrected with some
alterations, additions, &c by y[e]. Author. The number of Copies printed
in the whole including the Edition of 1780 (or 1781) amounted to about
34.000'. This information is all we have on the print runs and hence the
evident popularity of his grammar.

Being largely a list of the main events of his life, this short text abounds with names of people and places, and like a journal most sentences lack a subject, the opening sentence starting with the only subject in the piece which, as in the case of Sterne, is not the pronoun *I*.

> (17) Robert Lowth Son of William Lowth B.D. Prebendary of Winchester, & Margaret Daughter of Robert Pitt of Blandford Esqr. was born in his Father's Prebendal house in the Close Winchester, Novr. 27.1710.

The intended audience appears to have been his heirs, not so much the general public, and it is interesting to see that there are annotations on the manuscript of the memoir in a later hand, possibly a relative.

7.5 Depositions

Cusack defines depositions as 'statements from court cases, where witnesses, or occasionally the accused person, give an account of what they saw, heard or did' (1998: 92). Consequently, this text type is among the more promising ones for the identification of LModE speech. However, it should be borne in mind that the witnesses' words were recorded by a clerk and that they may have been edited in the process. The text therefore possibly does not represent the exact words of the deponent, though some clerks may have attempted to do so. Trials, moreover, according to Johansson (2006: 139), 'contain formal legal language ... such as specific formulae for questions and answers', while often the answer will repeat part of the question. Thus, Johansson notes, pied-piping might occur when preposition stranding would be expected (compare Section 6.4), with the form actually attested being merely a repetition of the question asked:

> (18) What were the symptoms **of which** he complained? These were the symptoms **of which** he complained. (1870–1900; Trials)

In such cases the context of features needs to be considered carefully. Other characteristics typical of trials are that they contain 'frequent references to time, place or the situation in question', and that 'relative clauses occurring in the dialogues often refer to people or individuals ... in order to identify them' (Johansson 2006: 138–9).

One important resource for studying the language of LModE depositions is the website containing the proceedings of the Old Bailey of London (see Section 2.1). Though the Observer's Paradox must be reckoned with here even more than in the case of letters (Section 7.2), the accounts still allow us to analyse linguistic features that are impossible to obtain in any other way. As many trials concern rape, for instance, the database allows us to study the use of euphemisms to avoid naming sexually explicit terms. One example is the use of the word *impudence* which occurs in the ordinary sense in the court proceedings but also as a substitute for 'penis', as in:

(19) Did he say any thing to you? – No, Sir, he stuffed my mouth with his hand, he put his **impudence** into me. What do you mean his private parts? – Yes. (1783; Sexual Offences: Rape)

Not surprisingly, perhaps, this meaning of the word is not found in the *OED*. Other euphemisms used to refer to the sexual act in the course of rape accusations are *the Thing, such practices, committing the same fact with me, doing some indecencies, using bad practices, vile actions, very ill usage, wicked things, that accursed Abomination, finding X in his body, all that beastly stuff, a venereal affair,* and *pulling his y – d* ['yard'] *out.*

Trials, according to Kytö and Romaine (2006: 204), score high on three different dimensions, the 'involved', 'narrative' and 'non-abstract' dimensions. Example (19) illustrates how these dimensions are reflected in language: the deponent makes a narrative statement (in this case, relating details concerning a rape) which describes high personal involvement (the rape occurred to the person in question: '*my* mouth', 'into *me*') as well as a concrete instance (the accused putting his penis into the victim's body). The terms 'involved', 'narrative' and 'non-abstract' refer to the multi-dimensional register analysis set up by Biber (1988). According to this approach, spoken and written registers differ with respect to certain linguistic features that are considered to be part of different dimensions, such as informational vs. involved production, narrative vs. non-narrative concerns and abstract vs. non-abstract information. A relatively higher or lower occurrence of these features distinguishes one text type from another along the dimensions studied. Thus, a spontaneous conversation would be more involved and less abstract than a scientific paper in that it would contain more evidential verbs, degree adverbs and first and second person singular pronouns (see Section 7.2). Biber's analysis is based on PDE text types, and trial records are included under the heading 'Spontaneous speeches' (1988: 69). His results show that trial records are fairly similar to face-to-face conversations for the dimensions narrative and abstract/non-abstract, but that they differ considerably where involvement is concerned, with face-to-face conversations scoring higher on this scale. He also found that for this dimension letters and spontaneous speeches score very similarly.

His results therefore suggest that neither letters nor trial records should be uncritically identified with face-to-face conversation, but also that letters may be taken as approximations of spontaneous speech in this respect. The findings presented by Kytö and Romaine indicate that the language of nineteenth-century trials shows a similar pattern to that of present-day spontaneous speech, though they also report on odd collocations of features, such as a high frequency of first person pronouns as well as of passive constructions. Passives are usually characteristic of less involved styles, and to find them together is unexpected. It would be interesting to investigate all this further on the basis of the material from the Old Bailey proceedings.

Johansson (2006: 166) notes that 'in Trials, speakers of different social ranks or roles are represented, mainly judges, or other members of the legal profession, and doctors and servants as witnesses'. She thus suggests that it is possible to study the use of particular linguistic features in the light of 'different social roles and professional backgrounds'. The variable gender will be of less interest here, as women would only appear in a limited number of social roles, such as servants and midwives, who only appear as witnesses or as people accused, never on the other side of the bar. For all that, apart from looking at gender-related language differences, it would be interesting to study the question of whether what are considered to be typically women's language (WL) features, such as super polite forms, the use of emphatic language, empty adjectives and hypercorrect grammar and pronunciation (Coates 1986: 112–14), should be reformulated as features of powerless language. Coates reports on a study of present-day courtroom language which showed that 'the use of WL features . . . does not correlate with sex of speaker' and that there were 'male witnesses [who] used a high proportion of WL features', too (Coates 1986: 113). Being in the role of a witness or in that of the accused calls for different linguistic behaviour, and this may have also been the case for LModE.

7.6 Wills

Wills may be defined as 'written documents which express the testator's personal wishes in regard to the distribution of property after his or her death' (Cusack 1998: 318). Bach, in an article on EModE wills, notes that wills 'have only rarely been studied from the point of view of pragmatics including discourse analysis' (1995: 127), nor are wills part of CONCE. It is perhaps not hard to see why: the language of LModE wills is highly formulaic, so much so that the question arises as to what extent the language of wills represents that of the testator him- or herself. It is precisely the formulaic nature of the language that gives them an archaic flavour. Cusack (1998: 319) raises the question of the authorship of wills: 'Who actually wrote the original will, the testator or an amanuensis?' During the EModE period, wills were usually written by amanuenses. Whether this was also the case for the LModE period I do not know, as there has been, to my knowledge, no study of wills from this period like that by Bach (1995).

Wills can easily be obtained – for a small fee only – from the National Register of Archives (NRA; Weblinks), so that the hand in which they are written can be verified. Jane Austen's will, for instance, was written by herself and addressed to her sister Cassandra, while Robert Lowth's will is not in his own hand but has come down to us in the form of a record copy. According to Cusack (1998: 320), 'If the language in the will is the testator's own then we have material of particular sociolinguistic value.' This is indeed the case with Jane Austen's will, though even in Lowth's will there is much that may have originated as text produced by the testator himself. If Lowth had dictated his will to an amanuensis, we would have evidence of speech, if highly formal, but if he submitted it as a document, which subsequently got lost, we would be dealing with writing, though equally formal as in case the will had been speech based.

There are long and short wills. Consisting of only ninety-nine words, Jane Austen's will is very short, whereas with 1470 words (excluding the inventory of his library) Lowth's will is much longer. But an even longer will is that of his wife's guardian, Thomas Cheyney (c.1694–1760). It consists of eighteen versions, drawn up between 1724 and 1759. Administering the will was consequently very complicated. Traditionally, according to Bach (1995: 137–8), wills consist of four parts:

1. the preamble: invocation of God, initial date, self-identification, justification (= death close), assertion of capacity to act (= sound mind), declaration of making will
2. religious part: bequest of soul, bequest of body, burial instructions
3. secular bequests: individual bequests, appointment of executor
4. assertion and confirmation of authenticity: scribal statement, signature, end date, witnesses.

Each of these parts may be illustrated from the first version of Cheyney's will (PRO, NRA Prob 11/866), as in examples (20) to (23):

(20) *Preamble:* **I** Thomas Cheyney, ffellow of the College near Winchester being by God's Will at this time of a sound mind, tho' labouring under

great bodily Infirmitys, which daily call upon **me** to remember **my** latter End, have with **my** own hand, in order to dispose of such things as a boutifull providence has besto'd upon **me**; wrote this **my last Will and Testament**, this thirteenth day of April An. D^{ni}. 1724.

(21) *Religious part (burial instructions only)*: **I** desire to be buried (with as little Charge as decently may be) as near as conveniently **I** can to such a place as **my** ffather shall chuse for himself.

(22) *Secular bequests:* **I give and bequeath my** ffarm and Manor of Litton in the County of Somerset, together with all the Rights and Interests **I** have in them ... to **my** Kinsman M^r. Edwd. Esmonds of Hardwick in the County of Burks ... making **my** ffather, or Mother (if he be dead) the sole Executor of this **my** Will.

(23) *Assertion and confirmation of authenticity:* Tho: Cheyney ... Sign'd, seal'd, publish'd and declar'd ... in the presence of Robt. Pescod, Sen. Willm. Pescod, Robt. Pescod, Jun.

Unlike Cheyney's will, Lowth's will does include the bequest of his soul, which was traditionally one of the essential functions of a will (Bach 1995: 125):

(24) In the first Place **I** commend **my** Soul into the hands of **my** most Merciful Creator in humble hope of Pardon of **my** Manyfold Sins and acceptance with him through the Merits of Jesus Christ our blessed Lord and Saviour. (PRO, NRA Prob 11/1160, file ref. 190, 189)

Examples (20) to (24) illustrate various linguistic features that are characteristic of wills as a text type, in particular the formulaic nature of the text, which, with the exception of the personal details, could be found in the will of any other person: the use of doublets (*last Will and Testament, give and bequeath*), and the high level of personal involvement, as is evident in the use of the first person pronoun *I* and its variant forms. The same features may be found in Jane Austen's will, which is so short that it may be quoted in full:

(25) **I** Jane Austen of the Parish of Chawton **do** by this **my last Will & Testament give and bequeathe** to **my** dearest Sister Cassandra Elizth. every thing of which **I** may die possessed, or which may be **hereafter** due to **me**, Subject to the payment of **my** Funeral Expences, & to a Legacy of £ 50. to **my** Brother Henry, & £ 50 to M^{de} Bigeon – which **I** request may be paid as soon as convenient. And **I** appoint **my**

said dear Sister the Executrix of this **my** last will & Testament: / Jane
Austen/ April 27. 1817. (PRO, NRA Prob 1/78)

Though they may seem so today, these collocations are not tautolo-
gous: a will referred to 'real', or immovable, property such as land
and houses, while a testament was concerned with moveable property:
chattels and leasehold interests (see *OED*, s.v. *will* n¹, IV 23). The
distinction was abolished in the course of the nineteenth century. As
far as the doublet *give and bequeath* is concerned, the description of the
meaning of *bequeath* in the *OED*, 'so as to pass to the recipient after
one's death: To "leave" by will', suggests that its addition lends a more
permanent air to *give*.

Jane Austen's will illustrates the archaic language of wills, as with
hereafter, which in the sense of 'in the future' was no longer very
common, and the affirmative but clearly unemphatic use of *do*, which was
rare even in eighteenth-century English outside a legal context. Another
archaic usage is the occurrence of a double determiner, as in '**this my**
last Will & Testament' in (25) and the deictic use of the verb *said*, as in
'my **said** dear Sister'.

In Lowth's will the verb *said*, with forty instances, is the sixth most
frequently used word. Frequency lists can be compiled with the help
of concordancing programs such as MonoConc or Wordsmith Tools.
Usually, high-frequency words are function words, the ten most frequent such words in PDE being *the, and, to, of, a, I, in, was, he* and *that*
('Top 1000 words in UK English'; Weblinks). In the case of Lowth's will,
the ten most frequent words are *and, of, the, my, to, said, in, I, her* and *or*.
The high position of *my* confirms the high level of personal involvement
in wills; *her* collocates with his wife (12/20), his daughter (4/20) and his
sister (4/20), who, together with his son, were his principal beneficiaries.
Other interesting collocates are *dear*, which is found almost always with
wife and once with *children*, the deictic use of *said* with *my* (26), *the* (12),
their and *his* (1 each). *My said dear sister* is also found in Jane Austen's will.
A final example of interest here is the word *pounds*, which occurs seventeen times in Lowth's will, in thirteen instances of which it collocates
with *thousand* and three times with the word *hundred*. Lowth evidently
died a very rich man.

The analysis of wills therefore provides interesting linguistic evidence, but may also serve an important function in reconstructing the
testator's social network: the more someone inherited, the closer their
network tie was with the testator (see Chapter 6). Cheyney made provi-
sion for his servants as well, which suggests not only that he felt a considerable social responsibility for their welfare but also that he must have

been in close touch with them. It would be interesting to speculate on what effect such relationships would have had on his language (compare the origin of the courtesy marker *please* discussed in Section 4.3).

7.7 Recipes

Cooking recipes, according to Görlach (1992: 750), 'tend to be collected in books devoted to the purpose of cooking, or household management'. Between 1500 and 1850, the number of such books increased dramatically, which, interestingly, shows a parallel with the steep rise in the publication of English grammars since the 1760s (see Chapter 5). Their reading public was also similar: people who desired access to the 'polite' middle classes, and who needed tools for this, even cookery books. Another similarity is that writers of cookery books often 'copy from existing collections so that such compilations tend to be "improvements" of earlier cookery books' (Görlach 1992: 750). I've already commented upon Mrs Beeton's plagiarism of earlier works (see Section 4.3). LModE grammars likewise engaged, almost as a matter of course, in unacknowledged copying, though this was frowned upon towards the end of the eighteenth century (Tieken-Boon van Ostade 1996c).

It is only since the beginning of the eighteenth century that the word *recipe* could also be used to refer to cooking; until that time the word was used for medical prescriptions only (see *OED*, s.v. *recipe*). Modern recipes have a distinct form and language use: they are preceded by a list of ingredients, and the cooking instructions are usually put in elliptical language, with a minimum of personal and interpersonal involvement, unlike in the case of letters and depositions (see Sections 7.2 and 7.5). The kind of language used is also specific to the purpose of the text type, and as such characteristically restricted. In Chapter 4, I illustrated this with reference to the first usages in the *OED* ascribed to Mrs Beeton. Her well-known *Book of Household Management* (1859–61) is available online (Weblinks), and the website informs us that it 'was the first book to show recipes in a format that is still used today'. Her recipe for 'Irish stew' illustrates this:

(26) 721. INGREDIENTS – 3 lbs. of the loin or neck of mutton, 5 lbs. of potatoes, 5 large onions, pepper and salt to taste, rather more than 1 pint of water.

Mode. – Trim off some of the fat of the above quantity of loin or neck of mutton, **and** cut it into chops of a moderate thickness. Pare and halve the potatoes, **and** cut the onions into thick slices. Put a layer of potatoes at the bottom of a stewpan, **then** a layer of mutton and onions, **and** season with pepper and salt; proceed in this manner until the stewpan is full, taking care to have plenty of vegetables at the top. Pour in the water, **and** let it stew very gently for 2½ hours, keeping the lid of the stewpan closely shut the whole time, **and** occasionally shaking it to prevent its burning.

Time. – 2½ hours.

Average cost, for this quantity, 2s. 8d.

Sufficient for 5 or 6 persons.

Seasonable. – More suitable for a winter dish.

The sentences are all very short, and they are lightly linked by coordination. The most frequent sentence coordinator in (26) is *and* (5), with another coordinator being *then* (1). All the verbs in this recipe are verbs of action, and they mostly occur in the imperative: *trim, cut, pare, halve, put, season, proceed, pour* and *let.* The nouns and adjectives almost only refer to food items (*fat, loin, neck of mutton, potatoes, onions, pepper, salt, vegetables, water*), quantities or size (*lbs, large, pint, quantity, chops, moderate, thick, slices, layer, full*) or cooking utensils (*stewpan, lid*). In addition, we typically find manner adverbs such as *gently* and duration adverbials (*for 2½ hours, the whole time*).

A century before, in Hannah Glasse's *The Art of Cookery made Plain and Easy,* recipes looked very different. According to the BBC documentary 'Hannah Glasse: The First Domestic Goddess', broadcast in January 2007, it was the most popular cookery book of the eighteenth century, being reprinted thrity-three times within fifty years. At first, it appeared anonymously, with the title-page just mentioning that it was written 'By a lady'. ECCO includes twenty-three copies of it, which allow us to analyse how her recipes changed in the course of the years when new ingredients became available. The book was first published by subscription, and the subscription list gives a glimpse of Hannah Glasse's reading public. Most of her readers were women, and most of them came from the middle classes. Hannah Glasse was the first to include a recipe for an Indian curry, though the resulting dish hardly compares with curries as we eat them today:

(27)   *To make a Currey the* India *Way.*

Take two Fowls or Rabbits, cut them into small Pieces, and three or four small Onions, peeled and cut very small, thirty Pepper Corns, and a large Spoonful of Rice, Brown some Coriander Seeds over the Fire in a clean Shovel, **and** beat them to Powder, take a Tea Spoonful of Salt, **and** mix all well together with the Meat, put all together into a Sauce-pan or Stew-pan, with a Pint of Water, let it stew softly till the Meat is enough, **then** put in a Piece of Fresh Butter, about as big as a large Walnut, shake it well together, **and** when it is smooth and of a fine Thickness, dish it up **and** send it to Table; if the Sauce be too thick, add a little more Water before it is done, and more Salt if it wants it. You are to observe the Sauce must be pretty thick. (Glasse 1747: 52)

If the first sentence is rewritten into a proper list of ingredients, the recipe would be more similar to the format presented in Mrs Beeton's cookery book. The only significant difference is the final sentence, which rather than interpersonal involvement indicates the kind of polite address to the reader that would no longer be considered appropriate in a modern recipe. Instead, it might simply have read: 'The sauce must be pretty thick.'

The language of this recipe is very similar to Mrs Beeton's (and to that of recipes in general): sentences are short, mostly coordinated by *and* or *then*, action verbs occur in the imperative (*take, cut, brown, beat, mix, put, let, shake, dish up, send, add*), nouns and adjectives refer to food items (*Fowls, Rabbits, Onions, Pepper Corns, Rice, Coriander Seeds, Salt, Meat, Water, Butter, Sauce*), quantity or size (*small Pieces, large Spoonful, Tea Spoonful, Pint, a large Walnut*), cooking utensils (*Shovel, Sauce-pan, Stew-pan*), and there are mostly manner adverbs like *softly* and adverbials relating to duration (*till the Meat is enough*). Interestingly, the word *Walnut* here refers to quantity or size rather than to a food item, which illustrates the practical nature of Hannah Glasse's cookery book. Other examples are:

(28)   put into it two or three **Handfuls** of Flour (Glasse 1747: 53)

(29)   Take a Bit of Veal, the **Bigness of your Fist**. (Glasse 1747: 54)

A pair of scales may not have been easily available to middle-class housewives or their maids, and Hannah Glasse's recipes show that there was not really any need for them. Above, I commented on her strategy to avoid too much abruptness, which might have been interpreted as impoliteness at the time. A similar strategy is the use of *must*, as in (30) and (31), which at most expresses weak obligation, similar to that expressed by an imperative:

(30)   To clarify it, you **must** put it on a Stove that draws well (Glasse 1747: 53)

(31)   You **must** get the middling Sort of Crawfish. (Glasse 1747: 54)

Despite the formulaic language of recipes, there is a lot in the language of Hannah Glasse's cookery book that suggests idiosyncratic usage. There is, for instance, an interesting mixture of colloquial language, as in (32) and (33), and the attempt to write formal language, as the use of the subjunctive in (35) and (36) demonstrates:

(32) let it stew softly till the Meat is **enough** (1747: 52)

(33) it must be very thick and dry, and not the Rice **boiled to a Mummy** (1747: 52)

(34) When **your** Cullis is **done**, take out the Meat, and strain your Cullis through a silk Strainer (1747: 54)

(35) If the Sauce **be** too thick, add a little more Water before it is done (1747: 52)

(36) *Rules to be observed in all Made-Dishes.*

FIRST, that the Stew-pans, or Sauce-pans and Covers, **be** very clean (1747: 52)

(37) Take great Care it **don't** burn. (Glasse 1747: 45)

Enough in (32) clearly means 'tender, done', as in (34), but this sense is not included in the *OED*. *Mummy* in (33) is included in the *OED*, with the meaning 'pulpy substance'. Though it might easily be interpreted as such, *your* in (34) does not indicate interpersonal involvement; instead, it is a colloquial variant of the use of the weak demonstrative (Quirk et al. 1985: 283n). The use of *don't* in (37), as I argued in Section 5.2, would mark Hannah Glasse's language as typical of either the lower classes or the socially aspiring middle classes; alternatively, it could be a subjunctive form, depending on the exhortation in the main clause 'take great Care' (compare *be* in examples (35) and (36)).

Hannah Glasse's cookery book was directed at the middle classes, which is not only evident from the approach adopted or the language used but also from her frequent criticism of French cookery (for example, 'But if Gentlemen will have *French* Cooks, they must pay for *French* Tricks', Glasse 1747: ii). Görlach discusses a contemporary of Mrs Beeton, Charles Elmé Francatelli (1805–76), an Englishman of Italian descent, who 'rose to the position of maître d'hôtel to Queen Victoria, chef de cuisine at the Reform Club and manager of the Freemason's Tavern' (1992: 752–4). Francatelli wrote cookery books for people belonging to different social classes. His *Modern Cook* (1845) is aimed at a more general public, who were nevertheless, as his recipes show,

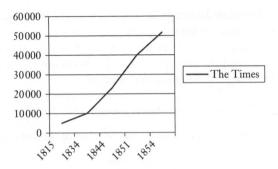

Figure 7.2 Increase in the circulation of *The Times* (first half nineteenth century), based on Görlach (1999a: 13).

familiar with the French vocabulary of cooking: *blond (of veal)*, *comsommé*, *bain marie*, *roux*, *julienne*, *quenelles* and *purée* – all printed in italics. But he also published *A Plain Cookery Book for the Working Classes* (1852), presumably, as Görlach suggests, in order 'to provide some practical guidance to those who severely needed it'. Görlach notes that Francatelli accommodated his language to that of his readers, though he also used language that was typical of his own class, thus in effect talking down to his readers. Though Beeton and Francatelli 'published in the heyday of the Victorian period', Görlach argues, there is also evidence in the recipes of the authors' idiolects, as I have likewise shown for Hannah Glasse's cookery book.

7.8 Newspapers

Newspapers were a new phenomenon during the LModE period. With the first newspaper, *The Daily Courant*, appearing in 1702, Görlach (2001: 207) notes that 'there were twelve London newspapers by 1712 and 52 by 1801', while there was also a significant increase in newspapers published in the provinces. For the nineteenth century, he quotes figures that show a tenfold increase in circulation of *The Times* (founded in the 1780s) during the first half of the nineteenth century (Figure 7.2). An overview of the many different newspapers set up during the period is provided by the British Library webpage 'Concise History of the British Newspaper since 1620' (Weblinks). The list records that the *Daily Telegraph* had been founded in 1772 as the *Morning Post* by John Bell (1745–1831), the printer who had abolished long <s> in print. After the tax on newspapers had been lifted in 1855, newspapers also came within reach of the working classes. They thus functioned as an important instrument in increasing widespread literacy, though they became the typical domain of the working-class man, 'while the women preferred light literature' (Aarts 1994: 323).

According to Görlach (2001: 207), newspapers as a new medium 'became a conglomerate of various text types'. The online database ZEN, or Zurich English Newspaper Corpus (Weblinks), includes many of them. The database comprises 1.6 million words taken from 349 complete newspaper issues published between 1661 and 1791. As different text types, it includes advertisements, announcements of births, deaths and marriages, foreign and home news, proclamations, reviews, shipping news and a category called 'lost-and-found'. Each of these are characterised by different linguistic features, though Görlach (2001: 208) notes that eighteenth-century advertisements are very different from what they are today. Searching ZEN for the keywords 'grammar' or 'dictionary', for instance, shows that new publications were only announced as such towards the end of the period covered. An example may be found in (38):

(38)   The Accidence, or First Rudiments of English Grammar, designed for the use of young Ladies, by Ellin Devis, the sixth edition, price 1 s. 6 d. (1791)

Evidently, the publication of new editions of grammars or dictionaries was not at first considered to be news worth reporting. Previously, the proper domain for this had been the *Monthly Review* and the *Critical Review*, founded in 1749 and 1756 respectively (Percy 2008).

ZEN allows for the analysis of the developing language during part of the LModE period of the text types included in newspapers. To give one example, in searching for the word *preparing*, it turns out that the so-called passival construction, which is the precursor of the passive progressive (see Section 6.4), an eighteenth-century innovation, may already be found among the very earliest records. See, for instance, (39):

(39)   We are inform'd that Bills are **preparing** ['being prepared] against the Sessions to try several of the mutinous Journeymen Taylors. (1721)

Fries (2007) studied the occurrence of foreign words in ZEN, and as a particularly interesting feature he mentions the use of legal terminology in parliamentary courtroom reports. Such terminology might be fruitfully compared with usage in the Old Bailey records (Section 7.5). Bailey (1996: 53) discusses the development of a special grammar for newspaper headlines, the lead in which was taken by the *New York Sun* (founded 1833). As typical features, he mentions the deletion of definite and indefinite articles, the use in headlines of participles instead of finite verbs and that of surnames.

According to Görlach (1999a: 146), the pressures of the medium led to considerable 'stylistic decay' in the course of the nineteenth century. The negative term *journalese* was first recorded in the *OED* for the year 1882, as the opposite meaning to 'plain English'. The other quotations listed similarly display negative sentiments: 'guilty of such journalese' and 'I refrained from putting any journalese into it'. It would be interesting to see whether the kind of usage problems referred to in Research Questions 6 (Chapter 1) and 9 (Chapter 5) arose as a consequence. Fowler, who claimed to read nothing other than contemporary newspapers (McMorris 2001), found the data for his *Modern English Usage* primarily in the writing of journalists (Burchfield 1996: vii–viii).

7.9 Concluding remarks

Of the text types discussed here, journals, memoirs, wills, recipes and newspapers are not included in CONCE, while of these five only journals and newspapers are part of ARCHER, or A Representative Corpus of Historical English Registers (Biber et al. 1998: 283). ARCHER, however, also includes letters and depositions along with various other text types. Conversely, these corpora include text types that have not been discussed in this chapter. Recently a website was launched providing access to British Parliamentary Papers (Weblinks). The database includes '1400 volumes of core 18th century official parliamentary publications that include sessional papers, bills, acts, debates, registers, reports and journals', and its website claims that 'by making previously obscure materials accessible, it releases potential to reassess the role of the 18th century parliament'. It will also make it possible to study the specific language of this particular text type. Unfortunately, however, access is restricted to UK academics, but this example illustrates that, when more such publications follow, it will be possible to make increasingly sophisticated linguistic analyses.

New text types bring about the development of new registers. Oldireva Gustafsson (2006: 110), for instance, notes that the new impersonal style in scientific English is a nineteenth-century development, and Kaunisto (2006) has similarly shown that the use of anaphoric *that/those* + *of*, as in (40), is more typical of the language of science – and of debates and history – than of trials and drama.

(40) Where neither parent was consumptive, the proportion in a small
      batch of well marked cases that I tried, was as high as 18 or 19 per cent.,
      but this is clearly too much, as **that of** the general population is only
      16 per cent. (1870–1900; Science; Kaunisto 2006: 189)

Kiełkiewicz-Janowiak (2002: 189) notes that in the nineteenth century,
we find the beginnings of 'stenographic English', producing *ditto, via* and
per, that has its origin in so-called 'mercantile English', and that called
for criticism in the press at the time. LModE business language is currently receiving a lot of scholarly attention, particularly in the work of
Dossena (for example, Dossena 2008) which focusses on the language
of the correspondence conducted by and for the Bank of Scotland. The
LModE period shows linguistic developments of considerable complexity, but it is due to the increasing availability of new resources and tools,
electronic and otherwise, that we will be able to analyse them in ever
greater and illuminating detail.

Further reading

See Görlach (2001: 196–212) and (1999a: 139–50); a comprehensive
study of text types may be found in Görlach (2004). For a study of the
correlation between particular linguistic features and text types, see
Biber (1988). An excellent introduction to corpus linguistics is provided
by Biber et al. (1998). The program Corpus Presenter is a very useful
tool for doing corpus analysis (Hickey 2003). An excellent and detailed
account of letter writing in the eighteenth century is offered by Baker
(1980), while the papers in Dossena and Tieken-Boon van Ostade (2008)
deal with a variety of aspects of the LModE letter. A selection of editions of LModE letters can be found in *HSL/SHL*, 'Correspondences'
(Weblinks).

Research questions

1. Select a letter from the Joseph Banks Collection (Weblinks) and
   carefully transcribe it. What particular features do you notice? Pay
   attention to the occurrence of long <s>, spelling, grammar and
   lexis. To what extent can the epistolary formulas serve as a guideline
   to the nature of the relationship between writer and addressee?
2. Different text types make use of different registers. Study the language of botany in the Joseph Banks correspondence and that of
   midwives in Martha Ballard's diary.
3. How does the language of midwives differ from LModE professional,

i.e. male, writers on medical matters? (ECCO, Google Book Search)

4. Many letters in the Banks Collection can be called business letters. What are the features typical of this genre of letters?

5. Tombstones can be considered a text type. Discuss the linguistic features of LModE graves (compare Research Question 2, Chapter 3).

6. Many wills, such as those of Thomas Gray and Dickens, are available online (Weblinks). Analyse their language.

7. Women's language features, such as the use of hedges (*sort of, kind of*), superpolite forms, emphatic forms (*so, very*) (Coates 1986: 112–13), have recently been redefined as powerless language (Section 7.5). Can you find evidence of this in the Old Bailey records?

8. Analyse the words and phrases that Fanny Burney obliterated from her diaries later in her life (Troide et al. 1988–). Can you identify any linguistic reasons why she did this?

9. Analyse the weather register as it transpires from Martha Ballard's diary.

10. Describe the register of LModE cookery (ECCO, Google Book Search, Mrs Beeton's *Book of Household Management* online).

Notes

1. According to the *OED*, the words *journal* and *diary* are largely synonymous (see also Cusack 1998: 163n), and both have been around about equally long, since the end of the sixteenth, beginning of the seventeenth centuries.

2. The manuscript of Lowth's memoirs is in the Bodleian Library, as part of MS Eng. misc. c.816, fols. 124–136.

References

Primary sources

Anon. (1707), *Spelling-Book for Children, with a Short Catechism*, [London].

Anon. (1756), *The Complete Letter Writer*, 2nd edn, London.

Anon. (1797), *A Vocabulary of such Words in the English Language as are of Dubious or Unsettled Accentuation; in which the Pronunciation of Sheridan, Walker, and other Orthoepists is Compared*, London.

Anon. (1826), *The Vulgarities of Speech Corrected*, London.

Bailey, Nathan (1721), *Universal Etymological English Dictionary*, London.

Baker, Robert (1770), *Reflections on the English Language*, London.

Batchelor, T. (1809), *An Orthoëpical Analysis of the English Language*, London.

Buchanan, James (1757), *A New English Dictionary*, London.

Buchanan, James (1762), *The British Grammar*, London.

Burgess, Walton (1856), *Five Hundred Mistakes of Daily Occurrence in Speaking, Pronouncing, and Writing the English Language, Corrected*, New York.

Carter, John (1773), *A Practical English Grammar*, Leeds.

Coar, Thomas (1796), *A Grammar of the English Tongue*, London.

Cobbett, William (1818), *A Grammar of the English Language*, New York.

Cooley, A. J. (1861), *A Dictionary of the English Language*, London.

Devis, Ellin (1775), *The Accidence; or First Rudiments of English Grammar*, London.

Ellis, A. J. (1869–89), *On Early English Pronunciation*, London.

Fenn, Ellenor (1798), *The Mother's Grammar*, London.

Fenn, Ellenor (1799), *The Friend of Mothers; Designed to Assist them in their Attempts to Instill the Rudiments of Language*, London.

Fogg, Peter Walkden (1792–96), *Elementa Anglicana; or, the Principles of English Grammar Displayed and Exemplified*, Stockport.

Glasse, Hannah (1747), *Art of Cookery, Made Plain and Easy*, London.

Johnson, Samuel (1755), *A Dictionary of the English Language*, London.

Lowth, Robert (1762), *A Short Introduction to English Grammar*, London.

Murray, Lindley (1795), *English Grammar*, York.

Owen, John (1732), *The Youth's Instructor in the English Tongue*, London.

Priestley, Joseph (1761), *The Rudiments of English Grammar*, London.

Routledge, Edmund (1866), *Everyday Blunders in Speaking*, London.

Savage, W. H. (1833), *Vulgarities and Improprieties of the English Language*, London.

Sheridan, Thomas (1780), *A General Dictionary of the English Language*, London.

Smart, B. H. (1810), *A Practical Grammar of English Pronunciation on Plain and Recognised Principles*, London.

Smart, B. H. (1836), *Walker Remodelled: A New Critical Pronouncing Dictionary of the English Language*, London.

Urmston, John (1710), *The London Spelling-Book: Being a More Easie and Regular Method of Teaching to Spell, Read and Write True English*, 4th edn, London.

Walker, John (1791), *A Critical Pronouncing Dictionary and Expositor of the English Language*, London.

Wallis, John (1653), *Grammar of the English Language*, Oxford.

Webster, Noah (1789), *Dissertations on the English Language*, Boston.

Secondary sources

Aarts, F. (1994), 'William Cobbett's *Grammar of the English Language*', *Neuphilologische Mitteilungen*, XCV: 319–32.

Adamson, Sylvia (2007), 'Prescribed reading: Pronouns and gender in the eighteenth century', *Historical Sociolinguistics and Sociohistorical Linguistics*, 7, http://www.hum2.leidenuniv.nl/hsl_shl/index.html.

Algeo, John (1998), 'Vocabulary', in *CHEL* IV: 57–91.

Anderson, Howard, Philip B. Daghlian and Irvin Ehrenpreis (eds) (1966), *The Familiar Letter in the Eighteenth Century*, Lawrence: University of Kansas Press.

Anderson, Howard and Irvin Ehrenrpreis (1966), 'The familiar letter in the eighteenth century: Some generalizations', in Anderson, Daghlian and Ehrenpreis (eds), 269–82.

Arnaud, René (1998), 'The development of the progressive in 19th century English: A quantitative survey', *Language Variation and Change*, 10: 123–52.

Arnovick, Leslie K. (1997), 'Proscribed collocations with *shall* and *will*: The eighteenth-century (non-)standard reassessed', in Jenny Cheshire and Dieter Stein (eds), *Taming the Vernacular: From Dialect to Written Standard Language*, London: Longman, 135–51.

Auer, Anita (2006), 'Precept and practice: The influence of prescriptivism on the English subjunctive', in Dalton-Puffer, Kastovsky, Ritt and Schendl (eds), 33–53.

Auer, Anita and Victorina González-Díaz (2005), 'Eighteenth-century prescriptivism in English: A re-evaluation of its effects on actual language usage', *Multilingua* 24: 317–41.

Auer, Anita and Ingrid Tieken-Boon van Ostade (2007), 'Robert Lowth and the use of the inflectional subjunctive in eighteenth-century English', in Smit, Dollinger, Hüttner, Lutzky and Kaltenböck (eds), 1–18.

Austin, Frances [1973] (1998), 'Epistolary conventions in the Clift family correspondence', in Rydén, Tieken-Boon van Ostade and Kytö (eds), 319–47.

— (1989), *The Language of Wordsworth and Coleridge*, Basingstoke: Macmillan.

— (1994), 'The effect of exposure to Standard English: The language of William Clift', in Stein and Tieken-Boon van Ostade (eds), 285–313.

— (ed.) (1983), *The Letters of William Home Clift 1803–1832*, Shaftesbury: Meldon House.

— (ed.) (1991), *The Clift Family Correspondence*, Sheffield: CECTAL.

Bach, Ulrich (1995), 'Wills and will-making in 16th and 17th century England: Some pragmatic aspects', in Andreas H. Jucker (ed.), *Historical Pragmatics: Pragmatic Developments in the History of English*, Amsterdam/Philadelphia: John Benjamins, 125–44.

Bäcklund, Ingegerd (2006), 'Modifiers describing women and men in nine-teenth-century English', in Kytö, Rydén and Smitterberg (eds), 17–55.

Bailey, Richard (1996), *Nineteenth-Century English*, Ann Arbor: University of Michigan Press.

Bainbridge, Beryl (2001), *According to Queeney*, London: Little, Brown.

Baker, Frank (1980), *The Works of John Wesley*, Vol. 25, *Letters* I, 1721–1739, Oxford: Clarendon Press.

Barber, Charles (1997), *Early Modern English*, 2nd edn, Edinburgh: University Press.

Battestin, Martin C. and Charles T. Probyn (eds) (1993), *The Correspondence of Henry and Sarah Fielding*, Oxford: Clarendon Press.

Baugh, Albert C. and Thomas Cable [1951] (1993), *A History of the English Language*, 4th edn, London: Routledge.

Bax, Randy C. (2000), 'A network strength scale for the study of eighteenth-century English', in Tieken-Boon van Ostade, Nevalainen and Caon (eds), 277–89.

— (2002), 'Linguistic accommodation: The correspondence between Samuel Johnson and Hester Lynch Thrale', in Teresa Fanego, Belén Méndez-Naya, Elena Seoane (eds), *Sounds, Words, Texts and Change*, Amsterdam/Philadelphia: Benjamins, 9–23.

— (2005), 'Traces of Johnson in the language of Fanny Burney', in J. C. Conde-Silvestre and J. M. Hernández-Campoy (eds), *Sociolinguistics and the History of English: Perspectives and Problems*, special issue of *International Journal of English Studies*, 5/1: 159–81.

— (2008), '*Foolish, foolisher, foolishest*: Eighteenth-century English grammars and the comparison of adjectives and adverbs', in Tieken-Boon van Ostade (ed.), 279–88.

Beal, Joan C. (2004), *English in Modern Times 1700–1945*, London: Arnold.

Benzie, W. (1972), *The Dublin Orator: Thomas Sheridan's Influence on Eighteenth-Century Rhetoric and Belles Letters*, Menston: The Scolar Press.

Bergs, Alexander (2005), *Social Networks and Historical Sociolinguistics: Studies in Morphosyntactic Variation in the Paston Letters (1421–1503)*, Berlin/New York: Mouton de Gruyter.

Biber, Douglas (1988), *Variation across Speech and Writing*, Cambridge: Cambridge University Press.

Biber, Douglas, Susan Conrad and Randi Reppen (eds) (1998), *Corpus Linguistics: Investigating Language Structure and Use*, Cambridge: Cambridge University Press.

Bijkerk, Annemieke (2004), '*Yours sincerely* and *Yours affectionately*: On the origin and development of two positive politeness markers', in Nevalainen and Tanskanen (eds), 297–311.

Black, Maggie and Deirdre Le Faye (2002), *The Jane Austen Cookbook*, Toronto: McClelland & Stewart.

Blake, N. F. (1981), *Non-Standard Language in English Literature*, London: Andre Deutsch.

Bliss, Alan (1979), *Spoken English in Ireland 1600–1740*, Dublin: The Dolmen Press.

Bodine, Ann (1975), 'Androcentrism in prescriptive grammar: Singular "they", sex-indefinite "he", and "he or she"', *Language in Society*, 4: 129–46.

Brewer, Charlotte (2007), *Treasure-House of the Language: The Living OED*, New Haven/London: Yale University Press.

Brook, G. L. (1970), *The Language of Dickens*, London: Andre Deutsch.

Burchfield, R. W. (rev.) (1996), *Fowler's Modern English Usage*, 3rd edn, Oxford: Oxford University Press.

Cajka, Karen (2008), 'Eighteenth-century teacher-grammarians and the education of "proper" women', in Tieken-Boon van Ostade (ed.), 191–221.

Carney, Edward (1994), *A Survey of English Spelling*, London/New York: Routledge.

Cecil, Lord David (1945), 'Fanny Burney's novels', in *Essays on the Eighteenth Century, Presented to David Nichol Smith in Honour of his Seventieth Birthday*, Oxford: Clarendon Press, 212–24.

Chapman, R. W. (ed.) (1953), *Boswell's Life of Johnson*, Oxford: Oxford University Press.

Charvat, William (1959), *Literary Publishing in America 1790–1850*, Philadelphia: University of Pennsylvania Press.

CHEL III: *The Cambridge History of the English Language*, Vol. III 1476–1776 (ed. Roger Lass) (1999), Cambridge: Cambridge University Press.

CHEL IV: *The Cambridge History of the English Language*, Vol. IV 1776–1997 (ed. Suzanne Romaine) (1998), Cambridge: Cambridge University Press.

Clarke, Norma (2000), *Dr. Johnson's Women*, London/New York: Hambledon Continuum.

Coates, Jennifer (1986), *Women, Men and Language* [2nd edn 1993], London/New York: Longman.

Crystal, David (1995), *The Cambridge Encyclopedia of the English Language* (repr. 1999), Cambridge: University Press.

Cusack, Bridget (1998), *Everyday English 1500–1700: A Reader*, Edinburgh: Edinburgh University Press.

Dalton-Puffer, Christiane, Dieter Kastovsky, Nikolaus Ritt and Herbert Schendl (eds) (2006), *Syntax, Style and Grammatical Norms: English from 1500–2000*, Bern: Peter Lang.

Dekeyser, Xavier (1975), *Number and Case Relations in 19th Century British English*, Antwerpen/Amsterdam: De Nederlandsche Boekhandel.

Denison, David (1998), 'Syntax', in *CHEL* IV: 92–329.

Dobson, E. J. (1968), *English Pronunciation 1500–1700*, London: Clarendon Press.

Dossena, Marina (2008), '"We beg leave to refer to your decision": Pragmatic traits of nineteenth-century business correspondence', in Dossena and Tieken-Boon van Ostade (eds), 235–51.

Dossena, Marina and Charles Jones (eds) (2003), *Insights into Late Modern English*, Bern: Peter Lang.

Dossena, Marina and Ingrid Tieken-Boon van Ostade (eds) (2008), *Studies in Late Modern English Correspondence: Methodology and Data*, Bern: Peter Lang.

Erisman, Marjon (2003), 'A matter of letters: Spelling in the correspondence of Lady Mary Wortley Montagu', MA thesis, University of Leiden.

Facchinetti, Roberta (2000), 'The modal verb *shall* between grammar and usage in the nineteenth century', in Kastovski and Mettinger (eds), 115–33.

Fairman, Tony (2003), 'Letters of the English labouring classes and the English language, 1800–34', in Dossena and Jones (eds), 265–82.

— (2006), 'Words in English Record Office documents of the early 1800s', in Kytö, Rydén and Smitterberg (eds), 56–88.

— (2007), '"She has four and big agane [and common prostitute Bad woman": "Ellipses" and other compositional strategies in the letters of writers with mechanical schooling: England, 1795–1834', paper presented at the Third Late Modern English Conference, Leiden, 2007.

Finegan, Edward (1998), 'English grammar and usage', *CHEL* III: 536–88.

Finkenstaedt, Thomas, Ernst Leisi and Dieter Wolff (1970), *A Chronological English Dictionary*, Heidelberg: Winter.

Fitzmaurice, Susan (1998), 'The commerce of language in the pursuit of politeness in eighteenth-century England', *English Studies*, 79: 309–28.

— (2000), 'Coalitions and the investigation of social influence in linguistic history', in Tieken-Boon van Ostade, Nevalainen and Caon (eds), 265–76.

— (2002), *The Familiar Letter in Early Modern English*, Amsterdam/Philadelphia: John Benjamins.

Fowler, H. W. (1926), *A Dictionary of Modern English Usage*, Oxford: University Press.

Fries, Charles C. (1925), 'The periphrastic future with *shall* and *will* in Modern English', *Publications of the Modern Language Association of America*, 40: 963–1024.

Fries, Udo (2007), 'Foreign words in early English newspapers', in Smit, Dollinger, Hüttner, Lutzky and Kaltenböck (eds), 115–32.

González-Díaz, Victorina (2008), 'On normative grammarians and the double marking of degree', in Tieken-Boon van Ostade (ed.), 288–310.

Gordon, Ian A. (1966), *The Movement of English Prose*, London: Longman.

Görlach, Manfred (1992), 'Text-types and language history: The cookery recipe', in Irma Taavitsainen (ed.), *History of Englishes: New Methods and Interpretations in Historical Linguistics*, Berlin: Mouton de Gruyter, 736–61.

— (1997), '. . . a construction than which none is more difficult', in Terttu Nevalainen and Leena Kahlas-Tarkka (eds), *To Explain the Present: Studies in the Changing English Language in Honour of Matti Rissanen*, Helsinki: Société Néophilologique, 277–301.

— (1998), *An Annotated Bibliography of Nineteenth-Century Gammars of English*, Amsterdam/Philadelphia: John Benjamins.

— (1999a), *English in Nineteenth-Century England: An Introduction*, Cambridge: Cambridge University Press.

— (1999b), 'Regional and social variation', in *CHEL* III: 459–538.

— (2001), *Eighteenth-Century English*, Heidelberg: Universitätsverlag C. Winter.

— (2004), *Text Types and the History of English*, Berlin: Mouton de Gruyter.

Grund, Peter and Terry Walker (2006), 'The subjunctive in adverbial clauses in nineteenth-century English', in Kytö, Rydén and Smitterberg (eds), 89–109.

Halsband, Robert (1956), *The Life of Lady Mary Wortley Montagu*, Oxford: Clarendon Press.

— (1965–67), *The Complete Letters of Lady Mary Wortley Montagu*, Oxford: Clarendon Press.

Hemlow, Joyce (1958), *The History of Fanny Burney*, Oxford: Clarendon Press.

Henstra, Froukje (2007), '*You was* and the problem of small numbers: some issues concerning social network analysis', paper presented at the Third Late Modern English Conference, Leiden, 2007.

— (2008), 'Social network analysis and the eighteenth-century family network: a case study of the Walpole family', *Transactions of the Philological Society*, 106/1: 29–70.

Hickey, Raymond (2003), *Corpus Presenter: Software for Language Analysis*, Amsterdam/Philadelphia: John Benjamins.

Hodson, Jane and Julie Milward (2007), *The Geoffrey Bullough Collection*, http://www.shef.ac.uk/library/special/bullough.pdf.

Hughes, Kathryn (2005), *The Short Life & Long Times of Mrs. Beeton*, London: Fourth Estate.

Hyde, Mary (1977), *The Thrales of Streatham Park*, Cambridge, MA: Harvard University Press.

Imhoff, Brian (2000), 'Socio-historic network ties and medieval Navarro-Aragonese', *Neuphilologische Mitteilungen*, 101: 443–50.

Johansson, Christine (2006), 'Relativizers in nineteenth-century English', in Kytö, Rydén and Smitterberg (eds), 136–82.

Jones, Charles (2006), *English Pronunciation in the Eighteenth and Nineteenth Centuries*, London: Palgrave Macmillan.

Kastovski, Dieter and Arthur Mettinger (eds) (2000), *The History of English in a Social Context*, Berlin/New York: Mouton de Gruyter.

Kaunisto, Mark (2006), 'Anaphoric reference in the nineteenth century: *that/ those + of* constructions', in Kytö, Rydén and Smitterberg (eds), 183–93.

Keast, William R. (1957), 'The two Clarissas in Johnson's *Dictionary*', *Studies in Philology*, 54: 429–39.

Kiełkiewicz-Janowiak, Agnieszka (2002), *'Women's Language?' A Socio-historical View: Private Writings in Early New England*, Poznan: Motivex.

Kytö, Merja and Suzanne Romaine (2006), 'Adjective comparison in nineteenth-century English', in Kytö, Rydén and Smitterberg (eds), 194–214.

Kytö, Merja, Mats Rydén and Erik Smitterberg (eds) (2006), *Nineteenth-Century English: Stability and Change*, Cambridge: Cambridge University Press.

Lass, Roger (1999a), 'Introduction', in *CHEL* III: 1–12.

— (1999b), 'Phonology and Morphology', in *CHEL* III: 56–186.

Lefanu, William (ed.) (1960), *Betsy Sheridan's Journal: Letters from Sheridan's Sister* (repr. 1986), Oxford/New York: Oxford University Press.

Legg, Marie-Louise (ed.) (1996), *The Synge Letters. Bishop Edward Synge to his Daughter Alicia: Roscommon to Dublin. 1746–1752*, Dublin: The Lilliput Press.

Leonard, S. A. (1929), *The Doctrine of Correctness in English Usage 1700–1800*, Madison, WI: University of Wisconsin.

McFadden, Tom (2007), 'Auxiliary "selection" and restrictions on perfect semantics: An Early English/Modern Scandinavian parallel', paper presented at the Sixth York-Newcastle-Holland Symposium on the History of English Syntax, Leiden, 2007.

McIntosh, Carey (1986), *Common and Courtly Language: The Stylistics of Social Class in 18th-Century English Literature*, Philadelphia: University of Pennsylvania Press.

McMahon, April (1998), 'Phonology', in *CHEL* IV: 373–535.

McMorris, Jenny (2001), *The Warden of English: The Life of H. W. Fowler*, Oxford: University Press.

Mair, Christian (2006), 'Nonfinite complement clauses in the nineteenth century: The case of *remember*', in Kytö, Rydén and Smitterberg (eds), 215–28.

Michael, Ian (1991), 'More than enough English grammars', in Gerhard Leitner (ed.), *English Traditional Grammars*, Amsterdam: Benjamins, 11–26.

— (1997), 'The hyperactive production of English grammars in the nineteenth century: A speculative bibliography', *Publishing History*, 41: 23–61.

Milroy, James and Lesley Milroy (1985a), *Authority in Language: Investigating Standard English* [3rd edn 1997], London: Routledge.

— (1985b), 'Linguistic change, social network and speaker innovation', *Journal of Linguistics*, 21: 339–84.

Milroy, Lesley (1987), *Language and Social Networks* (repr. 1989), Oxford: Blackwell.

Mittins, W. H., Mary Salu, Mary Edminson and Sheila Coyne (1970), *Attitudes to English Usage* (repr. 1975), London: Oxford University Press.

Molencki, Rafał (2003), 'Proscriptive prescriptivists: On the loss of the "pleonastic" perfect infinitive in counterfactual constructions in Late Modern English', in Dossena and Jones (eds), 175–96.

Monaghan, E. Jennifer (1983), *A Common Heritage: Noah Webster's Blue-Back Speller*, Hamden, CT: Archon Book.

Monkman, Kenneth (ed.) (1985), *Sterne's Memoirs*, Coxwold: The Laurence Sterne Trust.

Mugglestone, Lynda (2003), *'Talking Proper': The Rise of Accent as Social Symbol* (2nd edn), Oxford: Clarendon Press.

— (2005), *Lost for Words: The Hidden History of the Oxford English Dictionary*, New Haven/London: Yale University Press.

— (2006), 'English in the nineteenth century', in Mugglestone (ed.), 275–304.

— (ed.) (2006), *The Oxford History of English*, Oxford: Oxford University Press.

Mullan, John (2001), 'Queeney's English', *The Guardian*, reviews (1 September2001),http://books.guardian.co.uk/reviews/generalfiction/0,,544849,00. html.

Murray, James A. H. (1888), 'Preface to volume 1', *A New English Dictionary*, Oxford: Clarendon Press.

Murray, K. M. Elisabeth (1977), *Caught in the Web of Words: James A. H. Murray and the* Oxford English Dictionary, New Haven/London: Yale University Press.

Navest, Karlijn (2008), '"Borrowing a few passages": Lady Ellenor Fenn and her use of sources', in Tieken-Boon van Ostade (ed.), 223–43.

Nevalainen, Terttu (1999), 'Early Modern English lexis and semantics', in *CHEL* III: 332–458.

— (2004), 'Letter writing: Introduction', in Nevalainen and Tanskanen (eds), 181–91.

— (2006), *An Introduction to Early Modern English*, Edinburgh: Edinburgh University Press.

Nevalainen, Terttu and Helena Raumolin-Brunberg (2003), *Historical Sociolinguistics*, London: Longman.

Nevalainen, Terttu and Sanna-Kaisa Tanskanen (eds) (2004), *Letter Writing*, special issue of *Journal of Historical Pragmatics*, 5/2.

Nevalainen, Terttu and Ingrid Tieken-Boon van Ostade (2006), 'Standardisation', in Richard Hogg and David Denison (eds), *A History of the English Language*, Cambridge: Cambridge University Press, 271–311.

Nokes, David (1995), *John Gay: A Profession of Friendship*, Oxford: Oxford University Press.

— (1997), *Jane Austen: A Life*, New York: Farrar, Strauss and Giroux.

Oldireva Gustafsson, Larisa (2002), 'Variation in usage and grammars: The past participle forms of *write* in English 1680–1790', *Historical Sociolinguistics and Sociohistorical Linguistics*, 2, http://www.hum2.leidenuniv.nl/hsl_shl/index. html (go to: Contents, Articles)

— (2006), 'The passive in nineteenth-century scientific writing', in Kytö, Rydén and Smitterberg (eds), 110–35.

Osselton, N. E. (1963), 'Formal and informal spelling in the 18th century: *Errour, honor*, and related words', *English Studies*, 44: 267–75.

— [1984] (1998), 'Informal spelling systems in Early Modern English: 1500–1800', in Rydén, Tieken-Boon van Ostade and Kytö (eds), 33–45.

— [1985] (1998), 'Spelling-book rules and the capitalization of nouns in the seventeenth and eighteenth centuries', in Rydén, Tieken-Boon van Ostade and Kytö (eds), 447–60.

— (1993), review of *The Oxford English Dictionary*, 2nd edn, *International Journal of Lexicography*, 6/2: 124–31.

Oxford Dictionary for Writers and Editors (1981), Oxford: Clarendon Press.

Percy, Carol (1994), 'Paradigms for their sex? Women's grammars in late eighteenth-century England', in W. Ayres-Bennett (ed.), *La Grammaire des Dames/ Women and Grammar: Histoire, Epistémologie, Langage*, 17: 121–41.

— (1996), 'In the margins: Dr Hawkesworth's editorial emendations to the language of Captain Cook's *Voyages*', *English Studies*, 77: 549–78.

— (2008), 'Mid-century grammars and their reception in the *Monthly Review* and the *Critical Review*', in Tieken-Boon van Ostade (ed.), 125–42.

Pérez-Guerra, Javier Pérez-Guerra, Dolores González-Álvarez, Jorge L. Bueno-Alonso and Esperanza Rama-Martínez (eds) (2007), *'Of Varying Language and Opposing Creed': New Insights into Late Modern English*, Bern: Peter Lang.

Phillipps, K. C. (1970), *Jane Austen's English*, London: Andre Deutsch.

— (1978), *The Language of Thackeray*, London: Andre Deutsch.

— (1984), *Language and Class in Victorian England*, Oxford/London: Blackwell and Andre Deutsch.

Picard, Liza (2000), *Dr. Johnson's London*, London: Phoenix Press.

— (2006), *Victorian London: The Life of a City, 1840–1870*, London: Phoenix Press.

Ponsonby, Arthur (1923), *English Diaries: A Review of English Diaries from the Sixteenth to the Twentieth Century with an Introduction on Diary Writing*, London: Methuen.

Pottle, Frederick A. (1950), *Boswell's London Journal, 1762–1763*, New York: McGraw-Hill.

— (1966), *James Boswell: The Earlier Years, 1740–1769*, London: Heinemann.

Pratt, Lynda and David Denison (2000), 'The language of the Southey–Coleridge Circle', *Language Sciences*, 22: 401–22.

Quennell, Peter (1972), *Samuel Johnson: His Friends and Enemies*, London: Weidenfeld & Nicholson.

Quirk, Randolph, Sidney Greenbaum, Geoffrey Leech and Jan Svartvik (1985), *A Comprehensive Grammar of the English Language*, London: Longman.

Raftery, Deirdre (1997), *Women and Learning in English Writing, 1600–1900*, Dublin: Four Courts Press.

Rissanen, Matti (1999), 'Syntax', in *CHEL* III: 187–331.

Romaine, Suzanne (1998), 'Introduction', in *CHEL* IV: 1–56.

Ross, Josephine and Henrietta Webb (2006), *Jane Austen's Guide to Good Manners*, London: Bloomsbury Publishing.

Rudanko, Juhani (2006), 'The *in -ing* construction in British English, 1800–2000', in Kytö, Rydén and Smitterberg (eds), 229–41.

Rydén, Mats [1984] (1998), 'The study of eighteenth-century English syntax', in Rydén, Tieken-Boon van Ostade and Kytö (eds), 221–33.

Rydén, Mats and Sverker Brorström (1987), *The Be/Have Variation with Intransitives in English*, Stockholm: Almqvist & Wiksell International.

Rydén, Mats, Ingrid Tieken-Boon van Ostade and Merja Kytö (eds) (1998), *A Reader in Early Modern English*, Frankfurt am Main: Peter Lang.

Sairio, Anni (2005), '"Sam of Streatham Park": A linguistic study of Dr. Johnson's membership in the Thrale family', *European Journal of English Studies*, 9/1: 21–35.

— (2006), 'Progressives in the letters of Elizabeth Montagu and her circle in 1738–1778', in Dalton-Puffer, Ritt, Schendl and Kastovsky (eds), 167–89.

— (2008), 'Bluestocking letters and the influence of eighteenth-century grammars', in Dossena and Tieken-Boon van Ostade (eds), 137–62.

Salmon, Vivian (1999), 'Orthography and punctuation', in *CHEL* III: 13–55.

Schäfer, Jürgen (1980), *Documentation in the O.E.D.: Shakespeare and Nash as Test Cases*, Oxford: Clarendon Press.

Schlauch, Maragret (1959), *The English Language in Modern Times (since 1400)*, Warsaw: Państwowe Wydawnictwo Naukowe.

Scragg, D. G. (1974), *A History of English Spelling*, Manchester: Manchester University Press.

Sledd, James and Gwin J. Kolb (1955), *Dr. Johnson's Dictionary: Essays in the Biography of a Book*, Chicago: University of Chicago Press.

Smit, Ute, Stefan Dollinger, Julia Hüttner, Ursula Lutzky and Gunther Kaltenböck (eds) (2007), *Tracing English through Time: Explorations in Language Variation*, Vienna: Braumüller.

Smitterberg, Erik (2006), 'Partitive Constructions in Nineteenth-Century English', in Kytö, Rydén and Smitterberg (eds), 2421–71.

Stein, Dieter and Ingrid Tieken-Boon van Ostade (eds) (1994), *Towards a Standard English 1600–1800*, Berlin/New York: Mouton de Gruyter.

Tieken-Boon van Ostade, Ingrid (1985), '"I will be drowned and no man shall save me": The conventional rules for *shall* and *will* in eighteenth-century English grammars', *English Studies*, 66: 123–42.

— (1986), 'Negative *do* in eighteenth-century English', *Dutch Quarterly Review*, 16/4: 296–312.

— (1987), *The Auxiliary Do in Eighteenth-Century English: A Sociohistorical Linguistic Approach*, Dordrecht: Foris.

— (1990), 'Betsy Sheridan: Fettered by grammatical rules?', *Leuvense Bijdragen* 79: 79–90.

— (1991a), 'Dr. Johnson and the auxiliary *do*', *Folia Linguistica Historica* X/1: 145–62.

— (1991b), 'Samuel Richardson's role as linguistic innovator: A sociolinguistic analysis', in Ingrid Tieken-Boon van Ostade and John Frankis (eds), *Language, Usage and Description*, Amsterdam/Atlanta, GA: Rodopi, 47–57.

— (1992), 'John Kirkby and the practice of speaking and writing English: Identification of a manuscript', *Leeds Studies in English*, 23: 157–79.

— (1994), 'Standard and non-standard pronominal usage in English, with special reference to the eighteenth century', in Stein and Tieken-Boon van Ostade (eds), 217–42.

— (1996a), 'Two hundred years of Lindley Murray: An introduction', in Tieken-Boon van Ostade (ed.), 9–25.

— (1996b), 'Social network theory and eighteenth-century English: The case of Boswell', in Derek Britton (ed.), *English Historical Linguistics 1994*, Amsterdam/Philadelphia: John Benjamins, 327–37.

— (1996c), 'Lindley Murray and the concept of plagiarism', in Tieken-Boon van Ostade (ed.), 81–96.

— (1998), 'Standardization of English spelling: The eighteenth-century printers' contribution', in Jacek Fisiak and Marcin Krygier (eds), *Advances in English Historical Linguistics*, Berlin: Mouton de Gruyter, 457–70.

— (1999), 'Of formulas and friends: Expressions of politeness in John Gay's letters', in Guy A. J. Tops, Betty Devriendt and Steven Geukens (eds), *Thinking English Grammar: To Honour Xavier Dekeyser, Professor Emeritus*, Leuven/Paris: Peeters, 99–112.

— (2000a), 'A little learning a dangerous thing? Learning and gender as expressed in Sarah Fielding's letters to James Harris', in Susan Fitzmaurice (ed.), *Rhetoric, Language and Literature: New Perspectives on English in the Eighteenth Century*, special issue of *Language Sciences* 22: 339–58.

— (2000b), 'Sociohistorical linguistics and the observer's paradox', in Kastovsky and Mettinger (eds), 441–61.

— (2002), '"*You was*" and eighteenth-century normative grammar', in *Of Dyuersite & Chaunge of Langage: Essays Presented to Manfred Görlach on the Occasion of his 65th Birthday*, Katja Lenz and Ruth Möhlig (eds), Heidelberg: C. Winter, 88–102.

— (2003), 'Lowth's language', in Dossena and Jones (eds), 241–64.

— (2005), 'Eighteenth-century English letters: In search of the vernacular', *Linguistica e Filologia*, 21: 113–46.

— (2006), 'English at the onset of the normative tradition', in Mugglestone (ed.), 240–73.

— (2008a), 'Grammars, grammarians and grammar writing: An introduction', in Tieken-Boon van Ostade (ed.), 1–14.

— (2008b), 'The codifiers and the history of multiple negation in English, or, Why were 18th-century grammarians so obsessed with double negation?', in Joan C. Beal, Carmela Nocera and Massimo Sturiale (eds), *Perspectives on Prescriptivism*, Bern: Peter Lang, 197–214.

— (2008c), 'Letters as a source for reconstructing social networks: The case of Robert Lowth', in Dossena and Tieken-Boon van Ostade (eds), 51–76.

— (2008d), 'The 1760s: Grammars, grammarians and the booksellers', in Tieken-Boon van Ostade (ed.), 101–24.

— (ed.) (1996), *Two Hundred Years of Lindley Murray*, Münster: Nodus Publikationen.

— (ed.) (2008), *Grammars, Grammarians and Grammar Writing in Eighteenth-Century England*, Berlin/New York: Mouton de Gruyter.

Tieken-Boon van Ostade, Ingrid and Randy Bax (2002), 'Of Dodsley's projects and linguistic influence: The language of Johnson and Lowth', *Historical Sociolinguistics and Sociohistorical Linguistics*, 2, http://www.hum2.leidenuniv.nl/hsl_shl/index.html (go to: Contents, Articles).

Tieken-Boon van Ostade, Ingrid and Fátima María Faya Cerqueiro (2007), 'Saying *please* in Late Modern English', in Pérez-Guerra, González-Álvarez, Bueno-Alonso and Rama-Martínez (eds), 431–44.

Tieken-Boon van Ostade, Ingrid, Terttu Nevalainen and Luisella Caon (eds) (2000), *Social Network Analysis and the History of English*, special issue of *European Journal of English Studies*, 4/3.

Tieken-Boon van Ostade, Ingrid and Wim van der Wurff (eds) (forthcoming), proceedings of the Third Late Modern English Conference, Leiden, August/September 2007, Bern: Peter Lang.

Tierney, James E. (ed.) (1988), *The Correspondence of Robert Dodsley 1733–1764*, Cambridge: Cambridge University Press.

Tillyard, Stella (1994), *Aristocrats: Caroline, Emily, Louisa, and Sarah Lennox 1740–1832*, New York: Farrar, Straus and Giroux.

Traugott, Elizabeth Closs and Suzanne Romaine (1985), 'Some questions for the definition of "style" in socio-historical linguistics', *Folia Linguistica Historica*, VI/1: 7–39.

Troide, Lars E., Stewart J. Cooke et al. (eds) (1988–), *The Early Journals and Letters of Fanny Burney*, Oxford: Clarendon Press.

Truss, Lynne (2003), *Eats Shoots and Leaves: The Zero Tolerance Approach to Punctuation*, London: Profile Books.

Uglow, Jenny (2002), *The Lunar Men: Five Friends whose Curiosity Changed the World*, New York: Farrar, Straus and Giroux.

Uhrström, Wilhelm (1907), *Studies on the Language of Samuel Richardson*, Upsala: Almqvist & Wiksell.

Vickery, Amanda (1998), *The Gentleman's Daughter: Women's Lives in Georgian England*, New Haven/London: Yale University Press.

Vorlat, Emma (1959), 'The sources of Lindley Murray's "The English Grammar"', *Leuvense Bijdragen*, 48: 108–25.

— (2007), 'On the history of English teaching grammars', in Peter Schmitter (ed.), *Sprachtheorien der Neuzeit III/2*, Tübingen: Gunter Narr Verlag, 500–25.

Wardhaugh, Ronald (2006), *An Introduction to Sociolinguistics*, 5th edn, Oxford: Blackwell.

Willinski, John (1994), *Empire of Words: The Reign of the OED*, Princeton, NJ: Princeton University Press.

Wells, J. C. (1982), *Accents of English*, Cambridge: Cambridge University Press.

Wright, Susan (1994), 'The critic and the grammarians: Joseph Addison and the prescriptivists', in Stein and Tieken-Boon van Ostade (eds), 243–84.

Wyld, H. C. (1936), *A History of Modern Colloquial English*, 3rd edn, Oxford: Blackwell.

Yañez-Bouza, Nuria (2008), 'Preposition stranding in the eighteenth century: *Something to talk about*', in Tieken-Boon van Ostade (ed.), 251–77.

Zirker Jr., Malvin R. (1966), 'Richardson's correspondence: The personal letter as private experience', in Anderson, Daghlian and Ehrenpreis (eds), 71–91.

Weblinks

Note: for updated links, see the *Introduction to Late Modern English* homepage at the website of Edinburgh University Press, at
http://www.eupjurnals.com/book/9780748625987?cookieSet=1

Jane Austen's tombstone: http://www.jasa.net.au/images/grave.jpg

According to Beryl: http://www.thrale.com/history/books/book_2.php

Joseph Banks Collection: http://www.sl.nsw.gov.au/banks/

Mrs Beeton's Book of Household Management: http://www.mrsbeeton.com/ (for the original edition, see Google Book Search)

British Parliamentary Papers http://www.bopcris.ac.uk/18c/

Chadwyck Healey Eighteenth-Century Fiction: http//collections.chadwyck.com

Concise History of the British Newspaper since 1620: http://www.bl.uk/collections/britnews.html

Correspondences: http://www.hum2.leidenuniv.nl/hsl_shl/correspondences.htm

Charles Dickens's will: http://www.familyrecords.gov.uk/frc/extra/dickens_will.htm

Eighteenth Century Collections Online Thomson Gale: http://www.gale.com/EighteenthCentury/

Examining the OED, compiled by Charlotte Brewer: http://oed.hertford.ox.ac.uk

Google Book Search: http://books.google.com/

Hannah Glasse, the First Domestic Goddess: http://www.bbc.co.uk/bbcfour/documentaries/features/hannah-glasse.shtml

Thomas Gray's will: http://www.thomasgray.org/cgi-bin/view.cgi?collection=primary&edition=BrJ_1891&page=285

HSL/SHL: Historical Sociolinguistics and Sociohistorical Linguistics: http://www.hum2.leidenuniv.nl/hsl_shl/index.html

Martha Ballard's Diary Online: http://dohistory.org/diary/

Lady Mary Wortley Montagu, 'Selected Prose and Poetry': http://www.uoregon.edu/~rbear/montagu.html

National Register of Archives: http://www.nationalarchives.gov.uk/ (for wills, see http://www.nationalarchives.gov.uk/documentsonline/wills.asp).

The Old Bailey Online: The Proceedings of the Old Bailey: http://www.oldbaileyonline.org/

The Oxford Dictionary of National Biography, online edition: http://www.oxforddnb.com/

The Oxford English Dictionary Online: http://www.oed.com/

Top 1000 Words in UK English: http://www.bckelk.ukfsn.org/words/uk1000.html

Project Gutenberg: http://www.gutenberg.org/wiki/Main_Page

The Spelling Society: http://www.spellingsociety.org/

The Victorian Web: http://www.victorianweb.org/index.html

ZEN (Zurich English Newspaper Corpus): http://es-zen.unizh.ch/

Index

Note: the identification of the people listed has largely been based on the *ODNB*.